P9-BIQ-953

To,

Ken & Janet,

Warm Regards & Best Wishes

From,

Alan Nazareth

Bangalore, India
December 16, 2012

Gandhi's Outstanding Leadership

by

Pascal Alan Nazareth

Sculptor: D.P. Roy Choudhury

Sarvodaya International Trust
Gandhi Centre of Science & Human Values
Bharatiya Vidya Bhavan

© Pascal Alan Nazareth

First Edition : 2006

Second Edition : 2007

Third Edition : 2010

Fourth (Updated & Enlarged) Edition : 2011

ISBN : 81-89220-10-1

Price :
In India : Rs. 350/-
Foreign : US$ 20

Published by
Sarvodaya International Trust,
2, Ware Road, Bangalore 560005
Tel / Fax: 91 80 4125 3517
E-mail: sarvodayatrust@yahoo.com

Typeset and Printed at
W Q Judge Press, Residency Road, Bangalore 560025
E-mail: judgepress@yahoo.co.in

This book is dedicated to my mother

the late Elizabeth Lucy Nazareth,

who, with her *"widow's mite"*,

was the first supporter of

Sarvodaya International Trust.

A Psalm of Life

"Tell me not, in mournful numbers,
Life is but an empty dream!
For the soul is dead that slumbers,
And things are not what they seem.

Life is real! Life is earnest!
And the grave is not its goal;
Dust thou art, to dust returnest,
Was not spoken of the soul...

In the world's broad field of battle,
In the bivouac of Life,
Be not like dumb, driven cattle!
Be a hero in the strife !...

Lives of great men all remind us
We can make our lives sublime,
And, departing, leave behind us
Footprints on the sands of time.

Foot prints that perhaps another,
Sailing o'er life's solemn main,
A forlorn and shipwrecked brother,
Seeing, shall take heart again."

Henry Wadsworth Longfellow

FOREWORD

Socrates has been compared to a *"mountain peak that dazzles in the last rays of the setting sun"* which though *"lost in the mists of time will yet remain in the minds and hearts of men as long as right is might and life is stronger than death"*. Gandhi would, forever, be such a dazzling mountain peak of righteousness. His scholarly grandson Rajmohan Gandhi expresses this thought beautifully *"Strange yet wise, hard with many, hardest with himself and yet twinkling, drawn instinctively to Truth and persevering in love, his life a fuel for lighting up human suffering, obstinate at times and hazardously sure of himself, Gandhi was with all that, India's good boatman, and through the twentieth century a spark for consciences across the world."*

Gandhi's biographer Louis Fischer quotes General Omar Bradley *"We have too many men of science, too few men of God. We have grasped the mystery of the atom and rejected the Sermon on the Mount"* and writes *"Gandhi rejected the atom and grasped the Sermon on the Mount. He was a nuclear infant and an ethical giant. He knew nothing about killing and much about living in the twentieth century"*

In his *' Pilgrimage to Non-Violence'*, Martin Luther King Jr. declared *"If we assume that mankind has a right to survive, then we must find an alternative to war and destruction. In our age of space vehicles and guided ballistic missiles, the choice is either non-violence or non-existence"*

In November 1989, in a spontaneous upsurge against Soviet occupation of their country over a hundred thousand marchers, many of them students, gathered in Wenceslas Square in Prague. They carried flowers, held candles and waved flags. When they were boxed in and charged by the riot police, their leader Vaclav Havel, echoing Gandhi, exhorted them to refrain from violence. They sat down peacefully in the square and all the roads leading into it and sang nursery rhymes for five full days. It worked and gave the Czechs their *"Velvet Revolution"*. Havel hailed it as *" a rebellion of Truth against lies, of purities against impurities, of the human heart against violence"*

The question *"Is Gandhi relevant today?"* can be asked only by those whose souls are enslaved by the thralldom of the world. What breath is to life, Gandhi is to humanity and civilization. In the words of Mary E King, author of *'Gandhi and Martin Luther King Jr. - The Power of Non Violent Action'*: *"Gandhi was ....a pioneer in leading eight militant struggles - against racism, against colonialism, against the caste system, for popular democratic participation, against economic exploitation, against the degradation of women, against religious and ethnic supremacy, and on behalf of nonviolent methods for social and political transformations. Because of the breadth of his concerns, there is, in a sense, a different Gandhi for each reader.....As long as there is strife, hostilities, ethnic cleansing, religious unrest, internal conflicts and threats of military occupation, people will turn to Gandhi. His usefulness will not end unless conflict ceases."*

Writing on *'Freedom and Equality'*, on the Twentieth anniversary of the Universal Declaration of Human Rights, Noble Laureate Professor René-Samuel Cassin, French jurist and President of the European Court of Human Rights concluded his essay with these words: *"If the world, whose progress towards unity is increasingly determined by technology, is to remain a human world, there is nothing more essential than the realization of Article 1 of the Universal Declaration. Conscious of his dignity, man must defend his freedoms without forgetting that, as Mahatma Gandhi so wisely said, these freedoms must be used to further the fulfilment of his duties and it must be added, to treat his fellow men as equals and brothers."*

Mr. Pascal Alan Nazareth has done much in recent times to honour and celebrate that great moral jewel called Mahatma Gandhi. His present book analysing Gandhi's leadership, listing its achievements and wide spectrum impact and cogently presenting its great relevance to leaders and individuals alike in the contemporary situation is yet another notable contribution.

M. N. Venkatachaliah
October 2, 2005

PREFACE

Even a cursory survey of the global scenario in the last ten years reveals that the major problems the world, many nations, corporations and communities suffer today are due to their leaders forsaking the path of Truth, justice and non-violent conflict resolution in pursuit of national, corporate, religious or personal agendas. The consequences have been disastrous. The impeachment of a US President, conviction of an Indian Prime Minister, indictment of the Chilean and Peruvian presidents, expulsion of eleven members of India's Parliament, bankruptcies of Enron, World Com, Marconi, Tyco and Parmalat, wars in Afghanistan and Iraq, and terrorist attacks in Nairobi, Dar es Salaam, Aden, New York, Washington, Moscow, Bali, Istanbul, Tel Aviv, Rabat, New Delhi, Mumbai, London, Sharm al Sheik and Amman. The imperative need for trustworthy leaders of integrity in all walks of life has never been greater than now.

The last two centuries have been the most blood-stained in human history. In the 20th century alone almost a hundred million people have been killed in the two world wars, the atom bomb drops on Hiroshima and Nagasaki, Arab-Israeli, India-Pakistan, Iran-Iraq, Korean, Vietnamese and Afghan wars, the Spanish, Greek, Chinese and Sudanese civil wars; the Armenian genocide, Hitler's gas chambers, Cambodia's "Killing Fields"; Tibetan, Algerian, Angolan, Mozambican and Bangladeshi national liberation struggles, anti-racism struggles in South Africa and Guatemala, ethnic cleansing in the Balkans and innumerable tribal & secessionist conflicts in Africa and other parts of the world. In all these cases violence was met with more violence and bigger, more effective weapons. The "9/11" spectacular terrorist attack on New York's World Trade Centre, has dramatically changed the nature of armed conflict. It has ushered in the era of asymmetric warfare where the enemy is not a foreign state but a few suicidal terrorists, who strike from within rather than from outside the country and cause enormous devastation by using the host country's own assets such as its airplanes and airports. Antiterrorism analysts now consider a terrorist attack with improvised nuclear arms is a distinct possibility. Martin Luther King's words "*the choice is either non-violence or non-existence*" are far truer today than when he spoke them.

The first 20th century leader to successfully confront the cult of violence and the injustices of racism, colonialism, casteism and other such political and social evils, and fashion an effective non violent strategy for doing this, was Mohandas Karamchand Gandhi, revered by millions as the "Mahatma". Innumerable books have been written about his Truth and non violence 'Satyagraha' strategy, his "*fads*", foibles, asceticism and achievements but hardly any about his leadership, its quality and stature, how it was acquired and has impacted on peoples, societies, movements, institutions, academic disciplines and history, and its relevance to the contemporary war, violence and terrorism plagued scenario. This is a modest attempt to assess these aspects of Gandhi's leadership in historical and practical terms.

All quotations in this book are attributed to the authors but not to the books they appear in. These are listed in the bibliography with full details.

This book would not have seen the light of day but for the active encouragement of many scholarly friends. My manifold thanks to all of them, particularly Dr. B.R. Nanda (New Delhi), Mr Narendar Pani, Mrs Shakuntala Narasimhan and Mrs Srividya Mouli (Bangalore), Ambassador (Retd) A. Madhavan (Mysore), Dr. Leticia Shahani (Manila), Mrs Jenny Lampson (Los Angeles) and Mr G.T. Whitman (New York) for their critical assessment of the text and suggestions for its improvement. My special thanks to Burjor and Nina Kothawala (Bangalore) for urging that this book, originally intended for teachers only, be enlarged for a wide readership, to graphic artist Geeta Vadhera (New Delhi) for her valuable inputs regarding the design and layout, to Gandhi Centre of Science and Human Values for graciously agreeing to co-publish this book and to Viji, Mala and Murli of W.Q. Judge Press for uncomplainingly accepting the many amendments and additions I kept making to what they were assured was the finalized text.

I offer my respectful thanks to Justice M.N. Venkatachaliah, distinguished former Chief Justice of India and Founder Chairman, Sarvodaya International Trust, for writing the erudite Foreword.

I am deeply grateful to my dear wife Isobel who has patiently endured my many hours at the computer and often brought my breakfast, lunch and tea to a table next to it.

P. A. Nazareth
January 30th, 2006

PREFACE TO THE 2011 EDITION

Since the first edition of this book was published in 2006 important changes have occurred in the global scenario and provided further vindication of Gandhi's prophetic vision and focus on *"holding firmly to Truth"*. An Afro American is now President of USA and has publicly affirmed *"there is nothing weak-nothing passive-nothing naïve - in the creed and lives of Gandhi and King"*. He has pledged to rid the world of nuclear weapons and signed a new START Treaty with Russian President Medvedev which will reduce their respective nuclear warheads by 30 percent. The "*War on Terror*" is being phased out and American/NATO troops gradually withdrawn from Afghanistan and Iraq. However, despite the twelve year effort to "pacify" these countries, insurgency is still rampant. On August 6th the Taliban brought down a Chinook helicopter killing all the 31 US and 7 Afghan soldiers on board. Clearly, Drone warfare and Hi-tech weapons are no guarantee of success against poorly armed, fearless warriors determined to resist the foreign invader.

Long considered a stable region under well entrenched authoritarian regions three North African countries (Tunis, Egypt & Libya) and five West Asian ones (Yemen, Bahrain, Oman, Jordan and Syria) suddenly erupted with "*peoples power*" uprisings in early 2011 and brought down two long time dictators and two others to the brink. One dynastic ruler is still on his throne because a friendly neighbour, deeply concerned about such uprisings, provided him with timely military support.

In Libya, a nebulous "*people's uprising*" in its oil rich eastern province secured a remarkably prompt UNSC resolution (though with five abstentions including India, which expressed concern at the wide ranging measures being adopted on the basis of *"very little clear information"*) which authorized member states *"to take all necessary measures to protect civilians and civilian populated areas"*. Since then NATO planes have ceaselessly bombed Libya's military installations, sea ports, TV stations and Tripoli suburbs, killing many civilians including its leader's son and three grand children, The UN was set up to eliminate the scourge of war but three of its veto wielding Security Council members resort to it more readily than to dialogue for settlement of international problems. As wars are extremely expensive these and other war addicted countries are now in deep financial and social crisis with riots, looting and strikes plaguing many of their cities

A remarkable non violent struggle by Pakistan's lawyers succeeded in restoring the peremptorily dismissed chief justice and subsequently in getting its military dictator to resign and "*go on pilgrimage*". It now figures in the Peoples Power lexicon as the "Black Coat Revolution". However, Benazir Bhutto's assassination in the throes of an election campaign, the many terrorist attacks thereafter within Pakistan and on Mumbai, and the sensational discovery that Osama bin Laden was living, since 2005, in a secure mansion in Abbotabad has greatly darkened its sombre reputation as *"prime incubator of terrorism"*. Osama was *"brought to justice"*, rather ignobly, by a helicopter borne US SEAL team, who shot him in the presence of his wives even though he was unarmed and offered no resistance.

India's CWG and 2G mega scandals have *"outshone"* all its earlier ones; but unlike in the pat, the minister, two MPs and their accomplices are now lodged as bail denied pre-trial prisoners in a New Delhi jail. Gandhian Anna Hazare's bold initiative to combat corruption has mobilized public opinion nationwide and impelled the government to introduce a long stalled Lok Pal bill in Parliament. However, Hazare considers it "extremely weak" and has vowed to continue his struggle.

Japan's Fukushima Nuclear disaster has raised vital questions and concerns about the safety of nuclear power plants and Julian Assange's "Wikileaks" have exposed the shocking extent to which untruths, hypocrisy and torture are indulged in by even the most *"respectable"* nations.

This updated, enlarged 2011 edition covers these important developments and presents Gandhi's impact on more leaders and spheres of activity. My grateful thanks to all those who have assisted me with valuable inputs particularly Madhav Godbole, Virendra Prakash and Prateep Lahiri for their *'Indian Democracy on Trial'*, *'Hindutva demystified'* and *'Intolerance decoded'* books, Sudeep Chakravarty, for his *'Red Sun : Travels in Naxalite Country'*, Anil Nauriya for his *'The African Element in Gandhi'*, Malabika Pande and Prof. Brinsley Samaroo for information on Gandhi's "Green book" and efforts to end the odious Indenture System, Asha Sharma for her *'An American in Khadi'* biography of Samuel (Satyanand) Stokes Prof Dennis Dalton for informing me of Nathan Stoltzfus's *'Resistance of the Heart'* book, Roberto Catalano for briefing me about Chiara Lubich and the Focolare movement he founded, and Gandhi Serve Foundation Berlin for information on Gandhi inspired song writers and singers.

My manifold thanks also to Chandramouli and Padmaja of W.Q. Judge Press for their meticulous care in the page making and printing of this updated 2011 edition.

P.A. Nazareth

Bangalore
August 14, 2011

CONTENTS

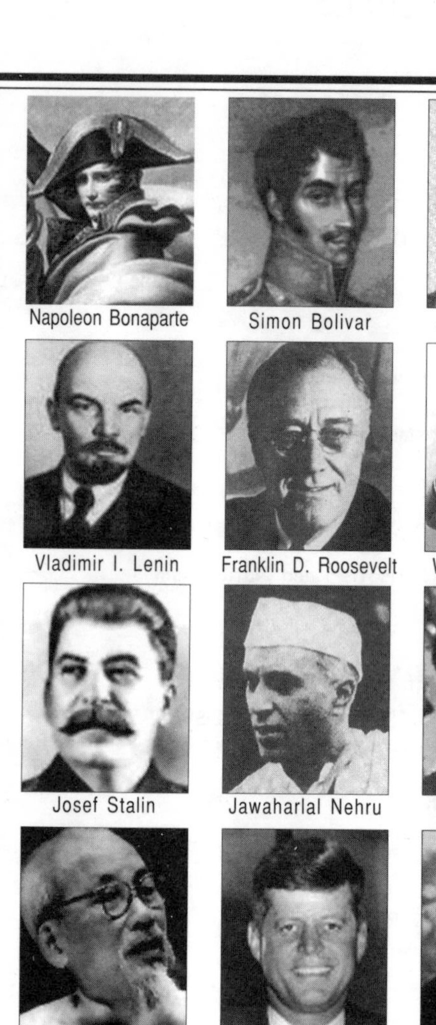

Napoleon Bonaparte | Simon Bolivar | Abraham Linclon | Karl Marx

Vladimir I. Lenin | Franklin D. Roosevelt | Winston Churchill | Adolph Hitler

Josef Stalin | Jawaharlal Nehru | Mao Tse Tung | Albert Einstein

Ho Chi Minh | John Kennedy | Martin Luther King | Indira Gandhi

Ayatollah Khomeini | Margaret Thatcher | Nelson Mandela | Corazon Aquino

Leadership Requirements and Notable Modern Leaders

For Ralph Waldo Emerson "*Great are they who see that the spiritual is stronger than any material force, that thoughts rule the world.*"

John Maxwell, the American leadership guru, gives the following 21 requirements as "*indispensable qualities*" a leader must have to become "*the person others will want to follow* ": Character, charisma, commitment, communication, competence, courage, discernment, focus, generosity, initiative, listening, passion, positive attitude, problem solving, relationships, responsibility, security, self discipline, servanthood, teachability, and vision. As a short definition of leadership he quotes the British Field Marshal Bernard Montgomery. "*Leadership is the capacity and will to rally men and women to a common purpose and the character which inspires confidence.*"

In the above alphabetical listing of leadership requirements Vision comes last. However in any listing of them in order of importance it needs to come first. A leader must know where he wishes to lead his people and how he intends to get them there. Besides he must lead them into a better rather than a worse scenario in which they are placed. For this, besides Vision, he will minimally need Character, Charisma, Compassion, Courage, Dedication, Determination, Communication, Organizational, Managerial and Strategizing Skills, Magnanimity, Self Assurance, Enlightened Patriotism and a Wide Spectrum World View, so as to inspire and lead his people, beyond traditional political, economic, scientific, social, religious or ideological confines and leave a permanent imprint on history. The more enduring and beneficial that imprint, the greater the societal, national, global and intellectual landscape over which it is felt, and the more accurate his/her vision of the future, the more outstanding the leader he/she is.

Surveying modern history, i.e. since the French Revolution which is generally accepted as harbinger of the modern age of nation states, the leaders who stand out as great are Napoleon, Bolivar, Lincoln, Lenin, Kemal Ataturk, Hitler, Churchill, Roosevelt, Stalin, Gandhi, Nehru, Mao Tse Tung, Ho Chi Minh, Gamal Nasser, John Kennedy, Fidel Castro,

Martin Luther King, Indira Gandhi, Ayatollah Khomeini, Anwar Sadat, Margaret Thatcher, Nelson Mandela, Lech Walesa, Vaclav Havel, Corazon Aquino and the 14th Dalai Lama. All of them have led their peoples beyond traditional confines and left an indelible imprint on history, big or small, favourable or unfavourable, local, regional or global.

Leaders who inspire, and command universal respect are those who espoused Right rather than Might, and truth, justice and non-violent conflict resolution rather than hate, violence and war. Lincoln's words *"Let us have faith that right makes might, and in that faith let us to the end, dare to do our duty as we understand it"* are still as powerfully inspiring as they were a hundred and fifty years ago when they were spoken. Napoleon's words, uttered at his remote St. Helena prison are significant. *"Glory is fleeting, obscurity is forever. A new Prometheus, I am chained to a rock to be gnawed by a vulture......There are only two powers in the world - the spirit and the sword. In the long run the sword will always be conquered by the spirit"*. Hitler's words are notable for a contrary reason *"The victor will never be asked if he told the truth"; so also are Churchill's "In war, every Truth has to have an escort of Lies" and Mao's "Power grows out of the barrel of a gun"*.

Nobel Laureate Desmond Tutu in his lecture *"Is there hope for Humanity"* at Indian Institute of Science, Bangalore in December 2005, stated *"Even in hardnosed cynical cultures it is amazing that those we admire, indeed revere, are not the macho, the aggressive, the successful. No, the people we hold almost universally in high regard are Mahatma Gandhi, Martin Luther King Jr, the Dalai Lama, Mother Theresa, Nelson Mandela, and why? Because they are good. We have internal antennae which home in on goodness because we are created for goodness, for love, for gentleness, for compassion, for sharing, We are almost the ultimate paradox, the finite created for the infinite"*.

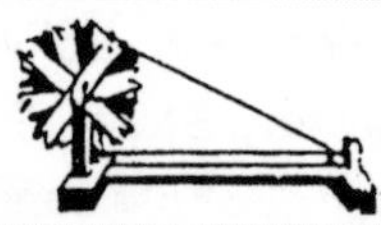

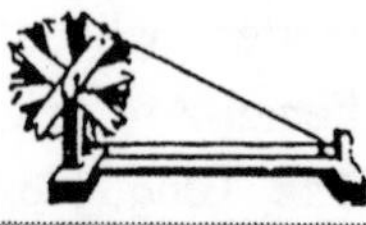

The Most Outstanding Modern Leader

Judging by the magnitude of their respective achievements and the historical and inspirational impact each of them have made, Gandhi emerges the tallest among the listed modern leaders. In a century that has the awesome distinction of being the most violent in history he confronted, non-violently, the largest, most powerful empire and secured freedom for India, which then had a fifth of the world's population, and induced broad spectrum political, economic and social change within it. He subsequently inspired non-violent people's struggles which achieved decolonization worldwide, ended racial oppression in USA and South Africa and terminated dictatorships in Poland, Rumania, Hungary, Czechoslovakia, German Democratic Republic, Estonia, Latvia, Lithuania, Phillipines, Soviet Union, Chile, Serbia, Georgia Ukraine, Uzbekistan, Tunisia and Egypt. His continuing inspiration is seen in the heroic struggles of the Tibetan & Burmese peoples and ecologists, environmentalists social activists and others worldwide. Besides, he has more books written about him and more information centers and societies all over the world to promote his non-violent strategy than any other modern leader. He is also the only one of them to be honoured with a full length opera - '*Satyagraha* ' by Phillip Glass - which though sung in Sanskrit has packed concert halls in leading US and European cities. Richard Attenborough's film '*Gandhi* ' has been seen by many, many, more people than any other film on a modern leader. In the polls taken in 1999 for the '*Man of the Millenium* ' Gandhi came on top in one and within the top three in the others.

The '*Force More Powerful* ' film series, (produced by York Zimmerman Inc and WETA, Washington D.C.) documents successful non-violent struggles in India, USA, South Africa, Denmark, Poland and Chile. The lead line in each of these films is *"Gandhi's discovery of the power of Non-Violence changed the 20th century"*. This can hardly be said of any other modern leader.

About modern leaders Louis Fischer has written "*The big names of recent history : Churchill, Roosevelt, Lloyd George, Stalin, Lenin, Hitler, Woodrow Wilson, the Kaiser, Lincoln, Napoleon, Metternich, Talleyrand etc, had the power of states at their disposal. The only non official figure comparable*

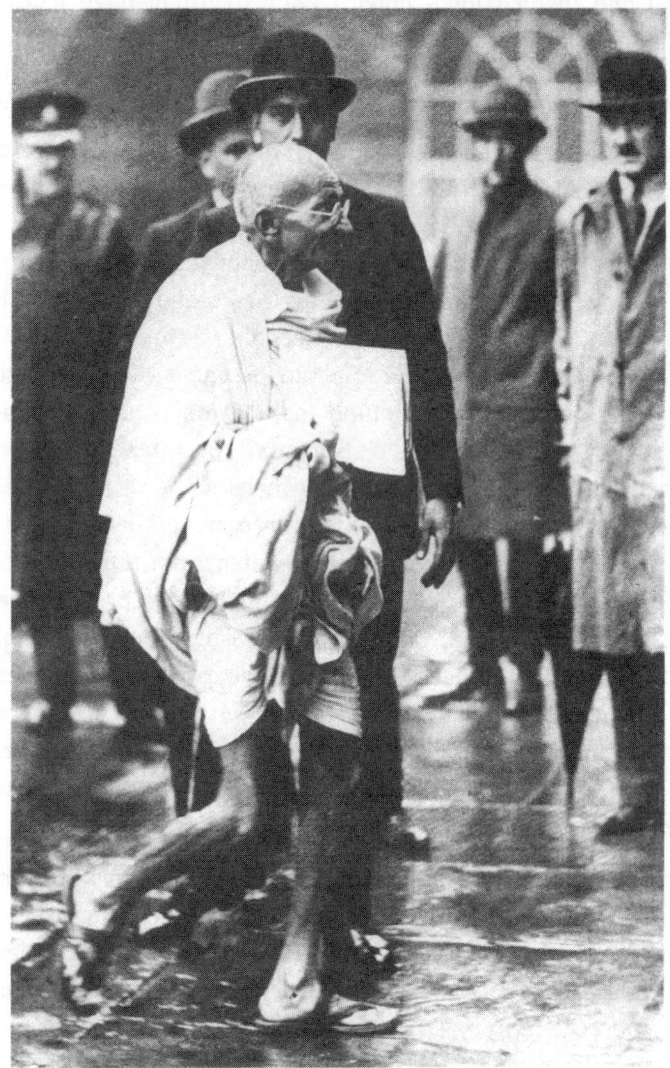

Gandhi arriving at Buckingham Palace

to Gandhi in his effect on men's minds is Karl Marx whose dogma, however, was a prescription for a system of government. One has to go back centuries to find men who appealed so strongly as Gandhi did to the conscience of individuals. They were men of religion, in another era. Gandhi showed that the spirit of Christ and of Buddha and of some Hebrew prophets and Greek sages, could be applied in modern times and to modern politics. He did not preach about God or religion; he was a living sermon. He was a good man in a world where few resist the corroding influence of power, wealth and vanity."

Because we are *"the finite created for the infinite"* the leadership we need, and deserve, has to be rooted in immortal values. In the final analysis good and trustworthy Leadership calls for moral judgements on what is right action because history has amply demonstrated that in the long run Truth alone triumphs. Decisions based solely on technical knowledge do not require leadership. To make right choices leaders need to have deep understanding of the lives and ideas of the world's great moral philosophers and of those who have applied them to solve some of its most difficult problems.

The global scenario has changed enormously in the last six decades. Almost all countries are now independent and rule themselves. Modern technology has shrunk the world. Travel across it that took months and weeks is now completed in hours. Voice, text and pictorial messages are transmitted in split seconds. On the other hand weapons of mass destruction can, and have reduced large cities to ashes in seconds. The economic field is now dominated by the mega firm and multinational corporation whose actions affect millions of lives yet are only minimally controlled by any country's laws. The United Nations was established in 1945 to rid the world of the scourge of war. Yet, a super power still dominates the world like a colossus, puts a *"spin"* on intelligence and engages in *"pre-emptive strikes"* and *"regime change"* at will. The need for a clear concept as to what constitutes enlightened and trustworthy leadership in the contemporary world, and a suitable model for it, is therefore as great as it is urgent.

Assessments of Gandhi's Leadership

"China followed Sun Yat Sen, took up the sword and fell into the arms of Japan. India, weaponless, accepted as her leader one of the strangest figures in history, and gave to the world the unprecedented phenomenon of a revolution led by a saint, and waged without a gun...... He did not mouth the name of Christ, but acted as if he accepted every word of the Sermon on the Mount. Not since St. Francis of Assisi has any life known to history been so marked by gentleness, disinterestedness, simplicity and forgiveness of enemies."

Will Durant

"Gandhi waded into the slough, showed how the slough could be purified and remained personally uncontaminated by his immersion in it. This gives the measure both of Gandhi's own spiritual stature and the magnitude of his service to mankind at a turning point in human history."

Arnold Toynbee

"A leader of his people, unsupported by any outward authority, a victorious fighter who always scorned the use of force, a man of wisdom and humility who has confronted the brutality of Europe with the dignity of the simple human being and has at all times risen superior....... Generations to come, it may be, will scarce believe that such a man as this ever in flesh and blood walked upon this earth."

Albert Einstein

Gandhi was an experimenter in the development of "war without violence'. His work was pioneering and not always adequate, but it represents a major development of historic significance both in ethics and in politics..... Many problems in its further development and application remain. But in words and action Gandhi pointed toward what may be the key to the resolution of the dilemma of how one can behave peacefully and at the same time actively, and effectively oppose oppression and injustice."

Professor Gene Sharp

"Most revolutions create enormous aspirations and never really fulfill them; some betray them utterly. The American Revolution quickly drew boundaries around notions of freedom that were its inspiration, excluding African Americans, native Americans, and to a considerable degree women. The French Revolution produced a frenzy of murderous rage, followed by nearly another century of monarchies. The Russian and Chinese Revolutions created tyranny, oppression and stagnations. Gandhi has been so mythologized since his assassination in 1948, the real man has almost disappeared. But he deserves his position as a resonant symbol of one of the most important phenomena of modern history: the simultaneous assault on colonialism and the oppression of individuals, which has transformed much of the 20th century world."

Prof. Alan Brinkley

"The fragility of modern civilization is exposed by the frighteningly ineffective way in which our world approaches conflict resolution. In international relationships, neither conventional diplomacy nor various uses of military deterrence have improved the thin margin on which the world exists. This somewhat pessimistic reading of history is challenged by one major exception, Mahatma Gandhi's application of policies and techniques of non-violence in India. Gandhi's success both redeems human nature from the inevitability of its historical experience and also suggests the viability of non-violence in modern situations."

Prof. Ralph Bultjens

"Gandhi has a future all over the world....That future should not only be seen in terms of what happens or what might happen in countries and the world. More important is local social transformation and local autonomy. Gandhi's village is known as a municipality in many parts of the world. His panchayat is also known as "local government" and may be a cornerstone in a future world order close to satyagraha and sarvodaya. Electronic people-to-people communication may also bring the world closer to Gandhi's oceanic cirles...... The world is one oikos, one household..... Gandhi has shown the way, and that way is a goal in its own right."

Prof. Johan Galtung

"Physical force is transitory, even as the body is transitory; but the power of the spirit is permanent even as the spirit is everlasting"

Art work by Geeta Vadhera

The Global and Indian Scenarios in which Gandhi Operated

Gene Sharp writes *"Gandhi was the contemporary of Tsar Nicholas, Lenin and Stalin, Kaiser Wilhelm and Adolph Hitler, Woodrow Wilson and Franklin Roosevelt, of the last Emperor of China, Sun Yat Sen, Chiang Kai Shek and Mao Tse Tung. He bridged the span between the time when wars were fought by armies with rifles to the time when they were fought with atom bombs... Racism ran rampant, women, untouchables and many others were denied dignity and opportunities. These were among the social and political evils for which Gandhi sought solutions."*

The challenging scenario within India is well depicted by Martin Green. *"In India, the father figure of revolutionary literature was Bankim Chandra Chatterjee (1838 -94), the Bengali novelist, whose most famous novel 'Anandamath ' became the bible for secret societies and its hero Satyanand, the model for revolutionaries. This novel, which contained the stirring hymn Bande Mataram, acquired the same place among Bengal revolutionaries that Chernyshevsky's 'What then must we do?' had among their Russian counterparts."* He elaborates that among those impacted by this novel was Aurobindo Ghosh. He had studied engineering in Manchester, then went to Cambridge and was selected for the prestigious ICS (Indian Civil Service), but gave it up to join the revolutionaries. Soon thereafter he anonymously wrote *'Bhabhani Mandir'* in which he declared that Mother India, weighed down with poverty, misery and oppression could be made strong and resplendent again only by great sacrifices in her name and worship of the Goddess of Energy. In 1906, a new Bengali weekly called Yugantar was founded, which *"breathed bombs in very line"* and called upon its readers to act like heroes atleast in the way they died if they could not do so in the way they lived. *'Bartaman Rananiti'* (Modern Art of War), published by a friend of Aurobindo in 1907, promoted Bakunin's idea that destruction was another form of creation. A similar but less widespread revolutionary movement developed in Maharashtra out of the Shivaji and Ganapathy festivals initiated by Bal Gangadhar Tilak. Among the revolutionary societies here was the Mitra Mela, to which Savarkar and his brother belonged. It was Tilak who got Savarkar his scholarship to go to London. It was there that he wrote '*Indias War of Independence*' about the 1857 mutiny, and also learnt how to make bombs. He brought back with him a manual on the subject. In conclusion Green writes "*Thus Gandhi and his followers had strong opposition not only from Bengal revolutionaries but also from the Tilak-Savarkar militant nationalists. Many of the revolutionary societies were financed from abroad by a London based Indian named Krishna Varma.*"

Several British officials were assassinated, in India and England, between 1905 - 1915 The most notable among the latter was the assassination of Sir Curzon Wylie in London in 1909. Viceroy Lord Hardinge, narrowly escaped assassination in December 1912. Peter French describes this attack thus "*Two days before Christmas 1912, Hardinge alighted at Delhi Railway station and clambered aboard an enormous elephant. Sitting in an elaborate silver howdah, he advanced slowly down Chandni Chowk, a thoroughfare of great symbolic significance. It had once been the finest boulevard and market of the Moghul empire, only to be turned into a charnel ground in the aftermath of the 1857 revolt, when the victorious British hanged countless Nawabs, rajahs and rebels down the middle of it. Now it had been chosen as the processional route for the Viceroy who had come to inaugurate the construction of Edwin Luytens & Herbert Baker's New Delhi. His Excellency had not got far when his helmet shot into the air, a bang was heard six miles away and the servant holding the State Umbrella was blown to pieces. An unknown Indian had hurled a bomb at the living symbol of imperial power. One of the vice-regal ear drums burst and it was to take many years for all the nails, screws and gramophone needles to work their way out of his body.... The unsuccessful assassin was never caught. This attack was the high point of revolutionary terrorism by Indian nationalists*".

At the 1919 Amritsar Congress when Gandhi spoke about Truth and Non-Violence, Tilak brusquely retorted "*My friend, Truth has no place in politics*". Two decades later, Subhas Chandra Bose, Congress President in 1938, openly disagreed with Gandhi's non-violent strategy, and secretly left India for Germany and Japan. With the latter's collaboration he set up the '*Indian National Army*' with British Indian troops captured by the Japanese in South East Asia, and marched in their train towards India. His slogan was *"Give me blood and I promise you freedom"*. It was an offer of freedom with *"the gun and the boot as against Gandhi's charka and wooden sandals"* states Rajmohan Gandhi pointing out that these challenges were not the only ones he faced. *"The outcastes were nervous about power moving from British to caste Hindu hands. India's princes were suspicious of their subjects and of Congress's intentions. Owners of agricultural lands were fearful of absentee landlords and small cultivators of town based creditors. Communities coveting army or police jobs felt threatened by one another. For protection against rivals each group, communal, caste or class, was inclined to turn to the Raj, thereby strengthening its hegemony even while disliking its alienness and burden.* Gandhi succeeded in getting the Indian National Congress, and the Indian people, to adopt his truth and non-violence strategy only because of his total identification with the poverty stricken Indian people, high moral stature, and the impressive results his Satyagraha campaigns produced 1920 onwards.

"Having flung aside the sword there is nothing except the cup of love which I can offer to those who oppose me".

*"Strength does not come from physical capacity.
It comes from an indomitable will."*

Artwork by K K Hebbar

The Components of Gandhi's Leadership

A. Vision

The prime component of Gandhi's leadership was his elevated vision that humans, the highest manifestation of God's creation, can and would live in harmony and peace, firmly adhering to Truth, Justice, Love and Non-Violence. *"Non-violence is the law of our species as violence is the law of the brute. The spirit lies dormant in the brute and he knows no law but that of physical might. The dignity of man requires obedience to a higher law - that of the spirit.... It is the law of love that rules mankind. Had violence i.e. hate ruled us, we should have become extinct long ago. Mankind has to get out of violence only through non-violence. Hatred can be overcome only by love."*

In his historical perspective he saw dictators and tyrants maintaining their fearful sway only temporarily. All empires built with the sword end up in the dustbin of history; only those built on the spirit with Truth, love and self sacrifice by the great seers and prophets have survived and flourished. Since humans are created *"in the image of God"* and are imbued with the *"Divine Spark"* they have to be led by Truth and love, not by fear and hate. One has to live, and if necessary to die for Truth, but never to hurt or kill anyone.

For Gandhi, Truth (Satya) was as real and omnipotent as God himself. In fact, Truth is God, as Truth is what is and God is the only reality that always IS. "*The world rests upon the bedrock of Satya ... which being what is can never be destroyed. This is the doctrine of Satyagraha in a nutshell*". Truth is the '*Right Path*' and it is '*Right that is Might*' not its opposite. He often quoted the Bhagavad Gita's core philosophical assertion *'Satyanasti paro Dharma'* (There is no greater duty than adherence to Truth).

Truth implies Justice and both are essential requisites for the attainment of peace. *"Peace will come when Truth is pursued, and Truth implies Justice"*. Justice requires that the adversary's views and requirements be given due consideration. "*Three fourths of the miseries and misunderstandings in the world would disappear if we step into the shoes of our adversaries and understand their standpoint*". Justice also requires that the final agreement made be acceptable to all concerned.

Whereas Gandhi was passionately dedicated to Truth even as a youth, particularly after he learnt about Harishchandra's unshakable adherence to it despite innumerable hardships, his deep commitment to non-violence came only in his early thirties after he read Christ's *'Sermon on the Mount'* and *Tolstoy's 'The Kingdom of God is within you'*. The strong non-violence traditions of the Jain community of his native Gujarat had of course mentally prepared him for this. Non-violence thus became his immutable path for realization of Truth. For him it meant complete abstention not only from all physical, mental and emotional injury to others but also cleansing oneself of all hatred and desire for revenge. One had to hate and confront evil but nonetheless love the evil doer because even he is endowed with the Divine spark which love can ignite and induce his conversion . *"Non-violence is based on the assumption that human nature in its essence is one and therefore unfailingly responds to the advances of love... The hardest metal yields to sufficient heat. Even so, the hardest heart must melt before the heat of non-violence and there is no limit to the capacity of non-violence to generate heat."*

For him: *"The objective of all non-violent activity is always a mutually acceptable agreement, never the defeat, much less the humiliation of the opponent "* and *"A non-violent revolution is not a programme for seizure of power. It is a programme for transformation of relationships ending in a peaceful transfer of power."*

Gandhi's vision, though considered utopian by some and arcadian by others, was actually an elevated, wide spectrum, deeply spiritual yet practical one. Like the tall redwood tree, which views the farthermost horizon, yet is fully aware of every environmental nuance around its sumptuous girth and at its deepest root, Gandhi perceived the macro and micro effects of human behaviour in diverse fields. His vision can justifiably therefore be described as "*prophetic*".

B. Courage and Character

Gandhi was not born courageous. In his childhood and youth he was extremely timid. He was greatly afraid of snakes, ghosts, thieves and darkness. It was his devoted maid Rambha who enabled him to overcome these fears by getting him to invoke Lord Ram's name as an effective antidote for all fears. At school he was an active participant in various activities, including sports, and at times even functioned as an umpire. But this self confidence was only among those he was very familiar with.

After his return from London, when he commenced legal practice at Bombay in 1893, he was still so timid that he failed miserably in arguing his first case in court. In his autobiography he writes "*I stood up, but my heart sank into my boots. My head was reeling and I felt as though the whole court was doing likewise. I could think of no question to ask. The judge must have laughed, but I was past seeing anything. I sat down and told the client that I could not conduct the case. I hastened from the court not knowing whether my client won or lost her case. I was ashamed of myself and decided not to take up any more cases until I had courage enough to conduct them. Indeed I did not go to court again until I went to South Africa.*"

The first noticeable change from timidity to boldness came when he was rudely ejected from the office of the British Political agent in Rajkot, Charles Ollivant, in December 1892. Having known him in London, he had gone to intercede on behalf of his brother Laxmidas who had come to the former's adverse notice. He was so outraged by the rude treatment, he received (which he describes as *"the first shock"* and one that *"changed the course"* of his life) that he seriously considered legal action against Ollivant for "*assault*". The eminent barrister Sir Pherozeshah Mehta advised him against it. Ollivant's rebuff made him resolve never again to espouse any improper matter and "*somehow to leave India*". He gladly accepted the invitation that came soon thereafter from Abdullah and Company of Durban, to handle their legal case in South Africa. About the "*first shock*" Copley writes "*Gandhi absorbed a far reaching lesson from this set back in that he subsequently placed a public ethic of incorruptibility above all sectional demands of family, caste and community, a value system with devastating implications for Indian society.*"

His next major transformation came within ten days of his arrival in South Africa. He was on his way from Durban to Johannesberg when he was thrown out of the train at Pietermaritzberg even though he had a valid first class ticket, was well dressed and inconvenienced no one. His crime was being seated in a "*whites only*" compartment and refusing to shift to the "*van*". He was just 24 years old then. His reaction to this humiliation was quite different to that of Ollivant's rebuff and is a good indication of the evolution of his personality and the sprouting of his leadership. In his autobiography he writes *"I began to think of my duty. Should I fight for my rights or go back to India.... It would be cowardice to run back to India without fulfilling my obligation. The hardship to which I was subjected was superficial - only a symptom of the deep disease of colour prejudice. I should try if possible to root out the disease and suffer the hardships in the process. Redress for wrongs I should seek only to the extent that would be necessary for the removal of the colour prejudice."*

Unlike his *"first shock"* when securing an apology from Ollivant was his prime concern, on this occasion it was the "*deep disease of colour prejudice"* and not the affront to his dignity which impelled him to action. Besides, though tempted to leave South Africa he firmly resisted it, because this "*would be cowardice*". Many years later, when questioned by Christian missionary John Mott as to what was the most *"creative experience"* of his life, he replied that it was the Pietermaritzberg episode. *"That changed the course of my life. My active non-violence began from that date and God put me through the test during that very journey"* Whereas both "*shocks*" changed the course of Gandhi's life, the former was a *"fight for self respect"* while the latter was awakening to the great social evil of colour prejudice. However, the enunciation of his doctrine of Satyagraha was still thirteen years away.

The morning after being ejected from the train at Pietermaritzberg he sent a telegram to the General Manager of the Railways. He met local Indians to ascertain the nature and extent of the *"deep disease"* and urged them to join him in resisting it. On arrival in Pretoria - he suffered further humiliations there as also enroute - he convened a meeting of Indians, and proposed the setting up of an association to represent their grievances to the authorities. He offered to place at their disposal *"as much of my time and service as was possible"*. As a result the Natal Indian Congress was set up in 1894. One of its first achievements was to secure a reduction of a proposed Pound 25 a year poll tax on Indians to Pound 3. Another early success was permission for *"properly dressed"* Indians to travel first class on the Railways.

The key to understanding Gandhi's transformation from extreme timidity to fearless leadership is to be found in the evolution of his spiritual makeup. He had been brought up as a devout Vaishnava Hindu and remained a life long devotee of Lord Ram. However, he had not read the Bhagawad Gita until he got to London, where he learnt about it from two Theosophists who had become acquainted with it through Edwin Arnold's *'Song Celestial'*. In his autobiography he writes *"I felt ashamed as I had read the divine poem neither in Sanskrit nor in Gujarati...I began reading the Gita with them. The verses in the second chapter made a deep impression on my mind and still ring in my ears:*

"If one ponders on objects of the sense, there springs attraction
From attraction grows desire, which flames fierce passion
Passion breeds recklessness; then the memory - all betrayed -
Lets noble purpose go and saps the mind,
till purpose, mind and man are all undone"

Subsequently he read and memorized the *Gita* in its Gujarati and Sanskrit versions. It became his *"infallible guide of conduct"*, his *"dictionary of daily reference"* and *"the book par excellence for the knowledge of Truth"* It taught him the vital truths that the soul is immortal, that death is not an end but a new beginning, and that when confronted with untruth and injustice, one's bounden duty was to confront it. His first acquaintance with the Bible and Christ's *'Sermon on the Mount'* was also in London. The latter became a vital input in his adoption of non-violence as the other pillar of his Truth based Satyagraha strategy.

Tolstoy's *'The Kingdom of God is within you'*, which he read in Durban in 1894 *'overwhelmed'* and *"left an abiding impression"* on him. He read Ruskin's *'Unto this Last'* while on a train journey from Johannesburg to Durban in 1904. In his Autobiography he writes that it *"brought about an instantaneous and practical transformation in my life. I believe that I discovered some of my deepest convictions reflected in this great book of Ruskin"*. He was so impacted by it that he translated it into Gujarati and titled it *'Sarvodaya'*, (the welfare of all). This became the beacon of his economic and social programmes.

'*Satyagraha* ' was born soon after the historic September 11, 1906 public meeting at the Empire Theatre in Johannesberg, which Gandhi had convened and at which, according to Louis Fischer, he showed *"awesome, Himalayan self assurance"*. Following the collective vow participants at this meeting took, he offered a prize for an appropriate name for the new non-violent struggle they had decided upon. A cousin, Maganlal Gandhi suggested *"Sadagraha"* (firmness in a good cause). Gandhi amended it to *"Satyagraha"* (firm

The Empire Theatre, Johannesberg
(The building no longer exits)

adherence to Truth). Louis Fischer annotates it thus *"For Gandhi, Satyagraha was "the vindication of Truth not by infliction of suffering on the opponent but on one's self". That requires self control. The weapons of the Satyagrahi are within him. Satyagraha is peaceful. If words fail to convince the adversary perhaps purity, humility and honesty will. The opponent must be "weaned from error by patience and sympathy", weaned not crushed, converted not annihilated...You cannot inject new ideas into a man's head by chopping it off; neither will you infuse a new spirit into his heart by piercing it with a dagger".* For Johan Galtung *"Satyagraha is an exercise of power, not so much through power over others as through power over oneself".*

By the time Satyagraha was born, Gandhi had given up his smart legal office and residence and moved with his family to *'Phoenix Settlement'*, committed all his wealth and professional earnings to a community fund to sustain Satyagrahi families and allowed his insurance policy to lapse as *"God would take care of the family."* He had also taken a vow of sexual abstinence. The solid foundation for his outstanding leadership had now been firmly laid and it was in Apartheid South Africa, *"that God forsaken country where I found my God"*, that this happened.

It was in July 1907 that Gandhi launched his first Satyagraha. It was against the Asian Registration Act, which for South African Indians was the *"Black Act"*. Led by Gandhi they decided to resist it by refusing to register. General Smuts, the Transvaal Colonial Secretary, tricked Gandhi into a compromise whereby Indians would voluntarily register and thereafter the Act would be repealed. When the latter did not happen, Gandhi and his fellow Satyagrahis publicly burned their passes in front of the Haminia Mosque in Johannesberg and were imprisoned for it. On his release he set up 'Tolstoy Farm' outside Johannesberg to accommodate Satyagrahi families.

Henry David Thoreaus' *'Civil Disobedience'* Gandhi read when he was in the Volksrust Prison in October 1908. The book was in the prison library. Gandhi found it a *"masterful treatise"*. He was greatly impacted by Thoreau's comment about his imprisonment *"I did not feel for a moment confined and the walls seemed a great waste of stone and mortar.....As they could not reach me, they had resolved to punish my body"* . However, as he wrote in a letter to Kodanda Rao of the Servants of India Society "*The statement that I derived my idea of Civil Disobedience from the writings of Thoreau is wrong. The resistance to authority in South Africa was well advanced before I read Thoreau's essay. But the movement was then known as passive resistance. As it was incomplete I had coined the word Satyagraha for Gujarati readers*"

In September 1913, in protest against a Transvaal Supreme Court decision that Hindu, Muslim and Parsee marriages would not be recognized as valid, Gandhi led a march of over 2000 Satyagrahis into the Transvaal. Simultaneously Indian indentured workers in the Newcastle coal fields went on strike. With this Smuts capitulated. The 1914 Smuts - Gandhi agreement and the subsequent Indians Relief Act of June 1914 redressed many South African Indian hardships, recognized Hindu, Moslem and Parsi marriages and abolished the hated Pound 3 annual tax on non contractual Indian labourers . Gandhi described it as the *'Magna Carta'* of Indians in South Africa. It was his first major leadership achievement.

In 1918, twenty five years after the Pietermaritzberg episode, he wrote "*We are regarded as a cowardly people*" and recommended Satyagraha as a technique to transform Indians, just as it had transformed him, from extreme timidity to fearlessness. For him non-violence is "*the weapon of the really brave*" and "*He who fears, fails*". As the armour of the non-violent warrior is his unshakable faith in God, he has, nothing to fear not even death for even death can be victory. "*They may torture my body, break my bones, even kill me but then they will have my dead body, not my obedience*"

Among his other notable affirmations on fearlessness are:
"*Fear and Truth are mutually contradictory terms*".
"*Being a slave to fear is the worst form of slavery*"
"*The golden rule is to act fearlessly upon what one believes to be right*"
"*The greatest help you can give me is to banish fear from your hearts*"

"*You do not know what a coward I was when I was young. I am not quite a coward today. Multiply my example and you will have one whole nation shaking off its cowardice.*"

C : Compassion, Dedication and Determination:

Gandhi's compassion is clearly seen in his constant focus on the oppressed and impoverished. He identified himself and empathized with them, dressed like them and after 1917 even lived like them in a mud hut, though brought up in comparitive luxury in his youth and held a British legal degree. *"I shall work for an India in which the poorest shall feel that it is their country, in whose making they have an effective voice"* he affirmed.

In his long letter to the Viceroy Lord Irwin prior to the Salt March he wrote *"Why do I regard the British rule as a curse? Because it has impoverished the dumb millions by a system of progressive exploitation and by a ruinous, expensive military and civil administration which the country cannot afford".* References to the *"impoverished dumb millions"* were numerous and frequent in his speeches and writings. His emphasis on Khadi was primarily for their benefit. *"Khadi means employment for the poor and freedom for India. Britain holds India because it is a fine market for Lancashire...."*

His compassion is also testified by the *"talisman"* he gave to India's new leaders. *"Whenever you are in doubt, try the following expedient. Recall the face of the poorest and the most helpless man whom you have seen and ask yourself whether the step you contemplate is going to be of any use to him. Will he be able to gain anything by it? Will it restore to him control over his own life and destiny? In other words will it lead to self rule for the hungry and spiritually starved millions of our countrymen?"*

Sculpture by B.V. Talim

However, the best testimony of his compassion is his walking barefoot on his visit to Noahkali in August 1947. When his grand niece Manu protested he replied *"We do not go to our temples, mosques or churches with shoes on... We now tread on that holy ground where people have lost their loved ones... How can I wear chappals there?"*.

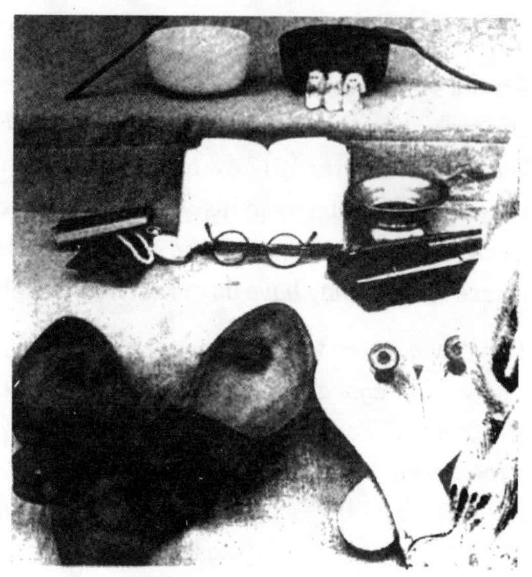

Gandhi's possessions

Gandhi's dedication, particularly to India's unity and prevention of its partition is testified by his fourteen meetings with Jinnah in September 1944 during which he even offered him the Prime Minister's office but to no avail. He humbled himself to go to Jinnah's residence at 10 Mount Pleasant Road, Mumbai for all these meetings even though his national and international stature was much higher than Jinnah's.

When Gandhi was assassinated in January 1948 his only earthly possessions were two sets of wrap around cotton cloths, a wrist watch, his spectacles, three sacred books, two wooden food bowls and spoons, two pairs of wooden sandals and a walking stick! This is dedication and self abnegation par excellence.

The firmness of Gandhi's determination is seen in his promptly calling off his February 1922 Satyagraha when incidents of violence occurred. In calling it off he declared *"I had called on the people to launch upon civil disobedience before they had qualified themselves for it and this mistake seemed to me of Himalayan magnitude"*.

Commenting on this Vincent Sheean wrote *"No act of his life was more bewildering to the Indian masses than Gandhi's abandonment of Satyagraha at this moment. It took a long time for Indians in general, Hindus as well as Moslems, to understand that the frail little man meant what he said, that he had a will of iron, and that no power on earth could induce him to pursue an action if he felt that it violated his principles."*

His determination is also seen in his historic *"fast unto death"* in September 1932 over the British grant of a separate electorate for *"untouchables"*. He saw this as a nefarious device to split the Hindu fold and perpetuate untouchability. He gave up the fast only when Dr. B.R.Ambedkar, the untouchable leader, agreed he would accept Gandhi's assurances of equitable treatment for his community and not avail of the separate electorate. The Poona Pact of September 25, 1932, embodied these assurances and is a good indication of Gandhi's *"victory for both sides"* approach. In return for giving up the separate electorate, Ambedkar secured an increase of *"untouchable"* reserved seats from 71 the British had offered, to 149! About the Poona Pact Rajmohan Gandhi writes *"From behind bars, a prisoner had jolted a nation's customs and imposed his will on an empire... The world seemed to marvel and a writer in the Boston Globe said that 'the debt Gandhi undertakes to settle is the debt of the human conscience to other human consciences."*

Gandhi's compassion, dedication and determination are all embodied in his visit to Calcutta to stem the communal killings there rather than be in New Delhi to participate in the Independence Day celebrations on August 15th, 1947. *"The interior voice tells me to go on fighting against the whole world, even though I am alone."* His favourite hymn during all such periods of crisis was Tagore's *'Ekla Chalo Re'*, which in English translation reads as under:

"If no one listens to your call, walk alone
If in fear, they cower mutely facing the wall,
O hapless one, open your mind and speak out alone"

James K. Mathews commends Gandhi's determination thus *"In great part his secret of leadership was in his strength of purpose. He was ever and ever restating it so that it might be clear to himself and to his associates."*

D. Communication Skills

Gandhi's communication skills were initially honed by his letter writing to South African and British authorities and newspapers. In 1904 he started his first newpaper 'Indian Opinion' in South Africa and subsequently in India 'Young India' and 'Harijan' (both in English) and Navjeevan (in Gujarati). In all these he wrote extensively on various current issues so as to keep all concerned, including his opponents, well informed of his ideas, programmes and plans.

His remarkable booklet '*Hind Swaraj* ', a manifesto for India's independence, was written in just ten days between November 13 -22, 1909 on board the ship '*Kildoman Castle*' while returning to South Africa after a fruitless lobbying mission to London. It was written entirely on the ship's stationery and according to some sources *"when the right hand got tired he continued with the left;"* writing 40 of the 275 manuscript pages thus. It was as if Divine revelation was impelling him to write as it was being imparted to him. Antony Parel avers *"Hind Swaraj is the seed from which the tree of Gandhian thought has grown to its full stature.... For those who wish to study his thought more methodically it remains the norm by which to assess the theoretical significance of his other writings, including the autobiography.... It has been compared to such diverse works as Rousseau's Social Contract and the Spiritual Exercises of St. Ignatius Loyola"*. However, his *Autobiography* sub titled '*The Story of my Experiments with Truth*', published in 1927, is the most communicative of all his writings and frankly reveals details of his upbringing, youthful foibles, early marriage, strong sexual drive and efforts to sublimate it, and the spiritual and literary influences that shaped the evolution of his personality.

His other means of communication were his Satyagrahas, Padayatras, fasts and prayer meetings. Of these his Chamaparan, Kheda, Bardoli and '*Quit India* ' Satyagrahas, Transvaal & Dandi padayatras and 1932 and 1947 fasts were the most impactful.

His historic Salt padayatra (march) and his publicly breaking the salt law was a communications masterpiece. British Journalist Webb Miller's on-

Gandhi on the Salt March

site report on it was carried in over 1000 newspapers worldwide. The New York Times editorialized that whereas Britian had lost America on tea, it was losing India on salt ! TIME magazine put him on the front cover of its January 4, 1931 issue as its '*Man of the Year* '.

Each of his fasts kept all of India as also the British on tenterhooks. About his 1932 fast Fischer wrote "*The day before the fast started, twelve temples in Allahabad were made accessible to Harijans for the first time....Every subsequent day until September 26th and then every day from September 27th to October 2nd, Gandhi's birthday, which was Anti-Untouchability week, scores of holy places lowered the bars against Harijans....Gandhi's fast touched Hindu India's heart. Gandhi had an artist's genius for reaching the heart strings of the inner man...Gandhi's fasts were means of communication. The news of the fast was printed in all papers. Those who read told those who did not read. The cities knew and the peasants marketing in the cities knew and they carried the report to the villages...*"

After his August 1947 Calcutta fast succeeded in ending the communal riots there Lord Mountbatten wrote to compliment him. "*In the Punjab we have 55,000 soldiers and large scale rioting on our hands. In Bengal our forces consist of one man and there is no rioting. May I be allowed to pay my tribute to the one man boundary force".* The historian E.W.R. Lumby wrote *"His triumph was complete and the peace that he brought was destined to endure....He had in fact worked a miracle, perhaps the greatest of modern times."*

His prayer meetings were generally held in his ashrams, but sometimes also in public places. On the latter occasions they were attended by thousands. His February 3rd, 1946 prayer meeting in Calcutta is estimated to have attracted over half a million people. As each of his prayer meetings would be followed by comments on topical issues they carried his message to millions of people in India and abroad.

Nehru described Gandhi's impact thus: *"His voice was somehow different from the others. It was quiet and low and yet it could be heard above the shouting of the multitude; it was soft and gentle and yet there seemed to be steel hidden away somewhere in it... We did not quite know what to make of it but we were thrilled."*

In his 1995 Gandhi Peace Foundation Lecture the eminent columnist Nikhil Chakravarthy focused on the importance Gandhi placed on the written word and how his weeklies '*Indian Opinion* ', '*Young India* ' and '*Harijan* ' came out regularly (the *Harijan* came out in 12 editions and 9 different languages) despite all his other activities and imprisonments. He averred *"As a communicator Gandhiji was aware of the need to take into account the level of awareness of his target reader or listener.... By the correct standards of a communicator, Gandhi chose the form of struggle, the target and even the language of every campaign in keeping with the level of consciousness of the common people".*

Gandhi's communication skills transformed India's freedom struggle from one waged by a small, elite, urban group into a mass movement in which millions of Indians, from every strata of society, enthusiastically participated. It was the largest, *"Peoples Power"* struggle in history.

E. Organizational Skills and Charisma.

Gandhi's organizational skills are best seen in the manner in which he restructured the Indian National Congress between 1915 and 1930. When he joined, it had many weaknesses. Its proceedings were conducted in English even though less than 1% of India's then population of 250 million spoke it. It was predominantly Hindu, Brahmin and high caste. Its membership was largely from the big cities of Calcutta, Bombay and Madras. It lacked effective executive machinery.

His first move was to set up an ashram at Kochrab village in Gujarat. With this his operational base was firmly planted in rural India and close to the peasants. When cholera struck this area some months later, the ashram was moved to Sabarmathi village, close to Ahmedabad. Both these ashrams, like his Phoenix Settlement and Tolstoy Farm in South Africa, were centers for training in community living and non-violence as *"Training is as necessary for civil disobedience as for armed revolt"*.

He next dethroned English by insisting Indian languages be used for work at provincial levels. At the first Gujarat political meeting in November 1917 he ruled that all speeches should be in Gujarati. Everyone including Jinnah conformed, only Tilak spoke in Marathi. However none spoke in English.

He then brought in leaders from *"new areas"* like Gujarat, United Provinces (so called because it combined North West Frontier Province and Oudh with Allahabad as capital) and Bihar. Among these were Vallabhai Patel, Mahadev Desai, Rajendra Prasad, Vinobha Bhave, Jay Prakash Narayan, J.B.Kriplani, C. Rajagopalchari and most importantly Motilal and Jawaharlal Nehru. A few years later came the remarkable Khan Abdul Gaffar Khan.

Commenting on these leaders joining the Congress, Antony Copley writes *"Gandhi's moral influence on these followers was astonishing. They were all men who might have pursued successful professional or administrative careers. Most striking may be was the conversion of Motilal Nehru, a highly westernized lawyer, who proved ready to throw over the habits of a life time, join his son Jawaharlal in the wearing of Khadi and accept Gandhi's policy of non-cooperation."* About Motilal Nehru succumbing to Gandhi's charisma, Martin Green writes *"Motilal drove to the law courts with liveried servants behind a fine pair of horses and lived in a house called Anand*

Bhavan, equipped with modern English comforts including wines and cigars.... When Motilal followed Jawaharlal into Gandhi's camp, everything in his life style had to change - cars, clothes, food, drink - from Englishness to Indianness, from modernity to tradition, from splendour to simplicity. The Anand Bhavan bonfire of foreign cloth must have been one of the biggest and most sacrificial."

Gandhi's great achievement in inducing these men, and subsequently many other such people from India and abroad, to join him is ample proof of his incredible charisma.

The 1919 Rowlatt Act, which gave the govt. powers of arbitrary arrest and detention without trial, provided Gandhi with a good opening to launch his first Nationwide Satyagraha in India and extend the Congress membership base. A Satyagraha Sabha Association was set up in Bombay on February 24, 1919. It was decided to firmly resist this "*Black Act*" and court arrest. By mid March over 800 people had enrolled as satyagrahis for this resistance and pledged their willingness to undergo imprisonment and any other hardships this might entail. On April 7th, Gandhi launched his '*Satyagraha*' by open sale of his '*Hind Swaraj*' and other banned literature. When he was arrested riots broke out in Ahmedabad and other places. On April 13, occurred the brutal massacre of 379 men, women and children at Amritsar's Jallianwala Bagh. The inspiring leadership Gandhi provided in its aftermath propelled him to national prominence and respect. Nehru describes his impact thus "*This programme (Satyagraha) was a totally different thing from what the Congress had so far been doing; indeed it was quite a novel thing for the world, for the Satyagraha in South Africa had been very limited in its scope.... The old and experienced Congress leaders hesitated and were filled with doubt. But there was no doubting the temper of the average Congressman or the man in the street or the masses. Gandhi carried them off their feet, almost hypnotized them.*"

At the 1920 Nagpur Congress session, Gandhi's proposal to create a 15 member Working Committee was approved. It was to be elected by an All India Congress Committee of 350, which in turn would be elected by provincial committees elected by district and taluk committees. With this organizational structure the Congress could for the first time justifiably claim to be an all India political organization. Separately other national bodies such as the All India Spinners Association and the All India Village Industries Association were also set up.

During his struggle against racial oppression in South Africa many of Gandhi's staunch supporters were Muslims. In the Congress there were only a few of them. He therefore decided to remedy this and attended the 1917 Muslim League session in Calcutta. At this time there was much concern about the fate of Ottoman Turkey and particularly about its Emperor Caliph's continued control of Islam's Holy places. There was threatening talk of *"Direct action"*. In 1919, the Indian Khilafat Committee approached Gandhi for his advice and assistance. He saw this as a good opportunity to woo the Muslims. He agreed to support the Khilafat agitation and managed to secure the approval, though reluctant, of the Congress. For about 18 months from October 1920 to March 1922 Gandhi led the combined struggle for Swaraj and the revision of the Treaty of Sevres imposed by Britain and France on Turkey. During this period there was close unity between Hindus and Moslems. B.R.Nanda indicates Gandhi's principal aims in supporting the Khilafat movement were: *"to prevent it from turning violent and to draw the Muslim community into the orbit of the national movement".* He adds that Gandhi achieved *"a great measure of success in his first aim but not in the second. The 'grand alliance' between the Congress and the Khilafat Organizations did not mature into a permanent Hindu- Muslim accord."* However, Gandhi's decision to support the Khilafat agitation is clear proof of his keen desire to secure Hindu-Muslim unity. Had the '*grand alliance*' endured, it would have prevented the partition of India as Jinnah would not have had a separatist Muslim constituency to mobilize and lead.

The non cooperation and civil disobedience movements of the 1920s and the Champaran, Kheda and Bardoli satyagrahas transformed the Congress from the essentially elite, urban debating society it had been until 1915, into a well structured, disciplined and mass based national political party and freedom movement by 1925. Its leadership came from all parts of the country including small towns. Its basic objective had also been transformed from securing dominion status to achieving *"Swaraj"* (independence). All this was primarily Gandhi's contribution. Patrick French writes *"Gandhi diverted Congress away from its upper class Brahmin base and from the use of English, a language understood by only a tiny minority of the population....If 1919 was the year of the boycott of British made goods, 1920 marked the moment of quiet revolution. Shops, schools and colleges were boycotted and bonfires were made of imported foreign cloth. Jail going became a symbol of pride rather than of shame. Within a remarkably short time Gandhi had become the undisputed King of Congress, having generated a mass popular following and sidelined traditional politicians."*

F. Strategizing Skills

Good leadership also requires excellent strategizing skills. Gandhi proved a genius at it. By combining Truth, non-violence and self suffering he fashioned his innovative Satyagraha strategy. It was first used in 1907 to oppose the *"Black Act"* (Asian Registration Act) in South Africa but its initial conceptualization has been traced to 1906. It literally means '*firmly adhering to Truth*' but is generally taken to mean '*Truth Force*', '*Soul Force*' or '*Love Force*'. It is not Christ like passive resistance but active non-violent resistance to evil and injustice. *"Passive resistance has been regarded as a weapon of the weak. That is why the name "Satyagraha' was coined in South Africa to distinguish the movement there from passive resistance.... Non-Violence is not a weapon of the weak. It is a weapon of the strongest and the bravest"* he affirmed, and added:

"This force (satyagraha) is to violence and therefore to all tyranny and injustice, what light is to darkness. In politics, its use is based upon the immutable maxim, that government of the people is possible only so long as they consent either consciously or unconsciously to be governed."

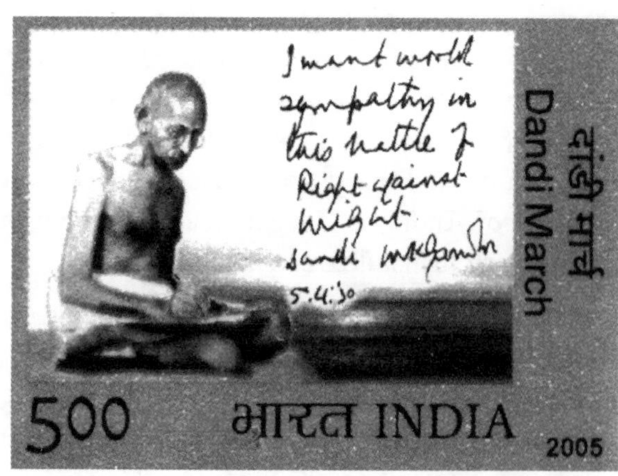

Courtesy: Indian Post and Telegraph Department

Erik Erikson, Krishanlal Sridharani and Richard Gregg have described Satyagraha as *"militant non-violence"*, *"war without violence"* and *"moral jiujitsu"* respectively. About Gandhi's militancy Mark Jugensmeyer has written

"Gandhi was a fighter. Whatever else one might say about him - that he was a saint, a clever politician, or a "seditious fakir" as Winston Churchill once put it - Gandhi certainly knew how to fight. In fact his approach to conflict resolution is one of Mohandas Gandhi's enduring legacies."

In fashioning his Satyagraha strategy Gandhi disclaimed originating any new philosophy and affirmed he had *"simply tried in my own way to apply the eternal principles of Truth and Non-Violence to our daily life and problems ......I have nothing new to teach the world. Truth and non-violence are as old as the hills"*. However Rahgavan Iyer and Antony Copley have argued that Satyagraha was in fact a significant theoretical contribution. *"Gandhi's claim that ahimsa lay at the heart of Satya was interesting and by itself unorthodox; the ancient Vedic texts, the sacred writings of early Hinduism, make no such claims for ahimsa and the concept only percolated into Hinduism through the rival faiths of Jainism and Buddhism. Gandhi was effectively arguing in a highly innovative and heretical way"* As animal sacrifices were widely prevalent in Hinduism until the advent of Jainism and Buddhism and it was the former that proscribed them and made ahimsa *"paramo dharma"* (the highest duty) Copley's assertion seems valid.

Gandhi's choice of the Charka as the prime weapon of India's national struggle is a good example of his strategizing skill. Until then, spinning was primarily a female activity and very few men, if any, had ever been involved in it. In his autobiography Gandhi reveals *" I do not remember to have seen a handloom or a spinning wheel when in 1909 I described it in Hind Swaraj as the panacea for the pauperism of India....Even in 1915 when I returned to India from South Africa I had not actually seen a spinning wheel"*. By conceptualizing it as the panacea for India's economic distress and making its use mandatory for everyone in the national struggle, he undermined Britain's economic dominance of India, brought equality between women and men in spinning activity and between them and the untouchable, who previously was engaged only in scavenging and other despised work. *"The spinning wheel is the solace of the untouchable whom we have hitherto so sinfully despised"*. Hand spun, hand woven clothes and caps became the standard garb of Indian nationalists and foreign clothes ended up in bonfires. India's weaving industries revived and the sale of British textiles in India declined considerably. Export of British textiles to India dropped from 90.6 million pounds in 1924 to 83.9 MP in 1928 to 52.9 MP in 1930. The Secretary of State for India acknowledged in the House of Commons that whereas the Great Depression had resulted in a 25% drop in British textile exports to India, their further 18% fall was due *"directly to the boycott program carried on by the Indian National Congress."* During the October 1930 - April 1931 period, when this boycott was at its height, said decline reached 84% ! Fischer commends Gandhi's Charka strategy thus : *"Gandhi was trying to bridge brain and brawn, to unite city and town, to link rich and poor. To help the underdog you must understand him and to understand him you must at least sometimes work as he does. Spinning was an act of love, another channel of communication. It was also a method of organization. "Any single district that can be fully organized for Khaddar is, if it is also trained for suffering, ready for civil disobedience" he said"*.

The Salt March is specially notable for its strategizing aspect. Judith Brown extols it as *"a superbly ingenious choice"*. Salt, a daily requisite for even the poorest individual, was abundant in the seas along India's long coast line. Yet Indians were barred from making it. Only the colonial govt. could produce and sell it. Besides, a tax levied on it annually collected Rs.60 million. Gandhi's march to Dandi with 78 of his well trained disciples was carefully planned to pass through areas well prepared for Satyagraha over several months. Hundreds joined the march enroute. By the time they reached Dandi the marchers were in the thousands. With all of them joining Gandhi in making salt, and millions of others doing likewise in coastal towns and villages all over India, it was mass defiance of an unjust British law, and *"insurrection without arms"* as Fischer describes it.

For Frances Harper : *" Gandhi's most important contribution to the theory of non-violence was his insistence that the resisters must keep the initiative at all times. While the opponent must be given ample opportunity to consider the proposals, he must not be allowed to ignore them. Gandhi fully understood that half the battle, indeed often the most difficult part of it, is to convince the opponent that he must deal with the resisters"*.

For Copley *"The confrontation and eventual agreement between Viceroy Irwin and Gandhi is a high point in the history of Gandhian Satyagraha"*.

Rajmohan Gandhi quotes George Woodcock thus *"In his superb sense of timing, in his quick intuitive grasp of the balance of forces, in his instinct for effective symbolic action and in his grasp of the strategy of struggle, Gandhi was one of the most able politicians of his time."*

G. Management Skills

The prime management elements in Gandhi's satyagrahas, padayatras, fasts, prayer meetings and negotiations with political rivals and the British rulers were transparency, methodical and humane approach, and insistence on ethical means to achieve the desired objectives.

His completely transparent approach emanated from his dedication to Truth. He affirmed:

"Secrecy aims at building a wall of protection around you. Ahimsa disdains all such protection. It functions in the open in the face of odds, the heaviest conceivable. We have to organize for action a vast people that have been crushed under the heel of unspeakable tyranny for centuries. They cannot be organized by other than open, truthful means."

In all Gandhi's satyagraha and padayatra campaigns a basic set of rules was followed : clearly identify the issue on which the struggle would be launched, highlight its "*Truth*" to the opponent and request negotiations, keep the opponent and newsmedia fully informed of the campaign's objectives and plans; instruct, inspire, train and lead the non-violent warriors, fund raise and economize maximally so as to sustain the campaign as long as necessary and make suitable arrangements for the care of those who would be injured or arrested, as well as for their families. When the opponent finally agrees to negotiate make a mutually acceptable agreement and adhere to it faithfully. *"The objective of all non-violent struggle is to arrive at a mutually acceptable agreement and never the defeat, much less the humiliation of the opponent."*

The best example of his transparent approach is his letter to Viceroy Lord Irwin before undertaking his Salt Satyagraha. In it, after listing the manifold injustices meted out to the Indian people, he wrote : *"If you cannot see your way to deal with these evils, and my letter makes no appeal to your heart, on the eleventh of this month, I shall proceed with such co-workers of the ashram as I can take, to disregard the provisions of the Salt Tax. I regard this tax to be the most iniquitous of all from the poor man's stand point... This letter is not in any way intended as a threat but is a simple and sacred duty, peremptory on a civil resister."*

His methodical approach is best seen in the Champaran satyagraha. undertaken in April 1917 on the pleading of an unknown, illiterate indigo peasant. It was his first major leadership test in India and established the efficacy of his satyagraha strategy.

Having decided to go to Champaran, he went there by way of Muzzafarpur so as to get accurate information about indigo cultivation from Prof. J.B. Kripalani of the Arts College there. He then proceeded to Champran and called on the Secretary of the British landlords association. His request for information on the landlords' levies on the peasants was rebuffed. He then requested a call on the Tirhut Divisional Commissioner, who refused to meet him and ordered him leave that area immediately. Gandhi disobeyed this order and proceeded to Motihari, capital of Champaran Dt. At the railway station, where a vast multitude awaited him, he was ordered to leave that district. He received the order and inscribed thereon he was disobeying it. The next day he was summoned to appear in court, whereupon, he telegraphed Rajendra Prasad at Patna to come to Motihari with some Indian lawyers. He also sent a telegram to the Viceroy.

When Gandhi appeared in court thousands of peasants had gathered around it. In the court were Indian lawyers and journalists. Gandhi pleaded guilty and was ordered released on bail until sentence was pronounced. He refused to pay the bail. The magistrate saw no option but to waive it. Some days later, the Lt. Governor of Bihar ordered that this case be dropped.

Gandhi then undertook a wide ranging public enquiry into the peasants grievances. Rajendra Prasad and his lawyer friends assisted in this. Almost ten thousand depositions were taken and relevant documents painstakingly collected. Thereafter he called on Lt. Governor Sir Edward Gait and induced him to set up an Enquiry Commission. This comprised govt. officials, landlords and Gandhi representing the peasants. The evidence he presented was so incriminating the landlords had little option but to agree to compensate the peasants. Not wanting to humiliate and embitter them, Gandhi demanded only 50% of the amounts unjustly exacted from the peasants, but finally settled for only 25%. Subsequent events justified his generous approach. A few years later the landlords transferred their estates to the peasants and left India.

Soon after securing the amicable settlement from the landlords, he got down to organizing educational, health and sanitation facilities for the peasants. His wife Kasturba, son Devadas and secretaries Mahadev Desai and Narahari Parikh came to Champaran and took turns in managing these facilities during the initial period.

Originally planned as a seven day visit, his stay at Champaran ultimately lasted seven months. With his subsequent visits there, it took almost a whole year of his life. It is clear proof that even in dealing with local issues he had the bigger picture in mind viz India's liberation not only from the British but from all oppression - of poverty, unemployment, illiteracy, illhealth, uncleanliness and fear. Unlike the militant nationalists who directed their fire solely at the victimizers, Gandhi focused also on the victims and sought to enable them to boldly stand up against all oppression whether political, economic or social.

For Gandhi, the means adopted were as important as the end itself. "*The means may be likened to a seed, the end to a tree. There is the same inviolable connection between the means and the end as there is between the seed and the tree... A Satyagrahi's first concern is not the effect of his action. It must always be its propriety. He must have faith enough in his cause and his means, and know that success will be achieved in the end.* " Adoption of vile and violent means only results in more of the same, vitiates the desired objectives and brutalizes human nature. In this respect he was quite different from most modern leaders for whom revolution, pragmatism and effective firepower have been the prefered means to achieve their ends.

Aldous Huxley concurs with Gandhi about the "*inviolable connection between the means and the end*". He writes "*The end cannot justify the means for the simple and obvious reason that the means employed determine the nature of the ends produced*". He gives instances from the French Revolution, where the demagogic and brutal means adopted by its leaders recoiled on them, destroyed the republic, gestated military dictatorship and then an emperor who embroiled France in twenty years of continuous wars which killed over three million people.

Commenting on Gandhi's view on means and ends Copley names Marx, Lenin, Mao Tse Tung and Gandhi as the four most influential social and political thinkers of the twentieth century and adds "*Yet Gandhi is very much the odd man out in such company: it would be more accurate to see him as their antagonist than as a fellow thinker......Theirs (Marx, Lenin, Mao) was an unscrupulous, ruthless, Machiavellian acceptance that the ends justify the means; a tolerance of the brutishness and violence of power politics. Gandhi possessed an acute moral awareness that means would colour the ends and that only just, non-violent means would lead to a just and harmonious society. It is that optimism and that endlessly argued idea which probably make Gandhi so attractive and so relevant a figure to the world of today."*

By empathizing with the masses, praying, working and living with them, selecting simple issues like cotton and salt which they understood Gandhi managed to inspire and enthuse them; convince them that Truth, non-violence and the spinning wheel were effective weapons for India's political, economic and social emancipation, that a mere 100,000 Englishmen in India could not rule its 350 million people if the latter refused their cooperation and were willing to suffer the consequences; that all Indians, men and women, rich and poor, high caste, low caste and untouchable, had a vital role to play in the liberation of India and all subject peoples. Concurrently, he also managed to train, plan, fund raise, finance, lead and effectively control vast groups of people with disparate interests and backgrounds. Millions responded to his call; they spun cotton, they burnt foreign cloth, they submitted to beatings and imprisonment and stolidly refrained from violence. This was the most amazing transformation of a sub continent, long gripped with lethargy, fear and despair, into a landmass throbbing with vigour and patriotic fervour, with varied ethnic, religious, cultural and social groups brought together, imbued with common purpose, all ready to die for the cause but never to kill. It certainly was the greatest management achievement of the twentieth century. Suzanne and Lloyd Rudolph wrote *"Gandhi evoked in himself and those who "heard" him, responses that transcended the routine of ordinary life, producing extraordinary events and effects on character, which metaphorically can be described as "magical".*

H. Magnanimity.

Gandhi's magnanimity is best seen in his forgiveness of those who hated, reviled and attacked him. On four occasions he was physically attacked - in Durban in January 1897, in Johannesberg in January 1908, in Pune in June 1933 and in New Delhi on January 22, 1948 (when a bomb exploded at his prayer meeting). In every case he forgave his attackers and insisted they should not be prosecuted. His statement after the arrest of the Pathans involved in the Johannesberg attack, was typical ; "*They should be released. They thought they were doing right and I have no desire to prosecute them*".

Among his greatest political revilers were Ambedkar, Churchill and Jinnah. The first mentioned castigated him as "*the most dishonest politician in Indian history...with pernicious saintly idiosyncracies*" ; the second contemptuously described him a "*a half naked and seditious fakir*" and "*an old humbug*". Yet Gandhi spoke of them thus :

"*I have the highest regard for Dr. Ambedkar. He has every right to be bitter. That he does not break our heads is an act of self restraint on his part..... The same thing happened to me in my early days in South Africa where I was hounded out by the Europeans wherever I went. It is quite natural for him to vent his wrath*".

"*Mr. Churchill is a great man. He belongs to the blue blood of England. The Marlborough family is very famous in British history. He took the helm when Great Britain was in great danger.... No doubt he saved the British Empire from a great danger at that time.....(However) Mr Churchill has been too hasty in his sweeping generalization. India's population is several millions. Of these only a few have taken the path of barbarism.*"

Meeting the press after the breakdown of his 14 long sessions of talks with Jinnah in September 1944 he said "*We have parted as friends. These days have not been wasted. I am convinced that Mr. Jinnah is a good man. I hope we shall meet again. I am a man of prayer and I shall pray for understanding*".

I. Self Assurance

Gandhi, like Abraham Lincoln, was well endowed with self assurance, composure and humour. It enabled them to remain unruffled even when false accusations and ridicule were hurled at them. When a political opponent accused Lincoln of being *"two faced"* he smilingly responded *"If I was two faced would I be wearing this one?"*.

When the young Sarojini Naidu went to meet Gandhi in London (in 1915, when he was enroute to India from South Africa) she found him seated on the floor, on a black prison blanket, having his dinner of crushed tomatoes and olive oil from a wooden bowl with battered tins of peanuts and biscuits around him. She burst out laughing and exclaimed he looked more like Mickey Mouse than the great Indian hero of South Africa. He laughed too and responded *"You must be Sarojini Naidu. Who else would be so irreverent? Come in and share my meal."* This short simple piquant remark captivated her. She declined to share his "abominable mess" of a meal, but became and remained, his dedicated disciple until his assassination forty three years later, and her own death a year thereafter. It was she who coined the reverent phrase *"Father of the Nation"*.

The "irreverent" Sarojini Naidu with the "Father of the Nation"

After the Round Table Conference in 1931, when Gandhi was received by King George V, he curtly asked *"Why did you boycott my son?"* (referring to the Gandhi instigated boycott of the 1921 Prince of Wales' India visit). Gandhi promptly responded *"Not of your son, Your Majesty, but of the official representative of the British Crown".* When leaving Buckingham Palace, journalists expressed consternation at his calling on the King dressed the way he was. He nonchalantly replied *"His Majesty was dressed enough for both of us!"* Subsequently, accosted by a group of youngsters near Kingsley Hall where he was staying with *"Hey, Gandhi where's your trousers"*, he laughed heartily and replied *"You people wear plus-fours, mine are minus fours!"*

Pearl Buck commends his humour thus *"Gandhi was not only a saint; he was a humorist. The two are not often in combination, but when they are the creature is invincible".*

Gandhi was a great favourite of leading European and American cartoonists for almost four decades. These cartoons amused him as much as they did most others.

J. Enlightened Views on Religion, Patriotism and Nationalism

Gandhi's fundamental contribution in the field of religion was to give primacy to Truth and rationality rather than conformity to traditional practices. In fact he made Truth the basis of all morality by declaring : "*I reject any religious doctrine that does not appeal to reason and is in conflict with morality*".

Though a deeply devout Hindu, Gandhi's basic approach to religion was '*sarvadharma samabhav*' (equal respect for all religions). For him all religions had equal status and were different paths to the same goal of achieving union with the Divine. His religion was that "*which transcends Hinduism, which changes one's very nature, binds one indissolubly to the truth within and ever purifies. It is the permanent element in human nature which leaves the soul restless until it has found itself*". He affirmed "*For me different religions are beautiful flowers from the same garden or branches of the same majestic tree*". At his prayer meetings there were readings from all the holy books. His favorite hymn began with the line "*He alone is a true devotee of God who understands the pains and sufferings of others*".

"The essence of all religions is the same, only their approaches are different"

For him "*The hands that serve are holier than the lips that pray*". His religion essentially was a deeply spiritualized humanism.

He affirmed "*Independent India as conceived by me will have all Indians belonging to different religions, living in perfect friendship.......God did not create men with the badge of superiority or inferiority; no scripture which labels a human being an inferior or untouchable because of his or her birth can command our allegiance. It is denial of God and Truth which is God*".

In 1931 he wrote in Young India "*It has been said that Swaraj will be the rule of the majority community i.e. the Hindus....If this were to be true, I for one would refuse to call it Swaraj and would fight it with all the strength at my command, For to me Hind Swaraj is the rule of all the people and the rule of justice.*"

On January 23, 1948, just a week before his assassination he declared "*It would spell the ruin of both the Hindu religion and the majority community if the latter, in the intoxication of power, entertains the belief that it can crush the minority community and establish a purely Hindu Rashtra*".

Lauding this enlightened approach Fischer wrote "*Mahatma Gandhi, a supremely devout Hindu, was incapable of discriminating against anyone on account of religion, race, caste, colour or anything. His contribution to the equality of untouchables and to the education of a new generation which was Indian instead of Hindu or Moslem or Parsee or Christian has world significance.*"

Gandhi's great respect for the Koran is revealed in his following affirmations:

"*I have read the Koran more than once. My religion enables me, obliges me, to imbibe all that is good in all the great religions of the earth. I have come to the conclusion that the teaching of the Koran is essentially in favour of non-violence. It holds that non-violence is better than violence. Non-violence is enjoined as a duty, violence is permitted only where necessary.*"

"*Islam's distinctive contribution to India's national culture is unadulterated belief in the oneness of God and a practical application of the truth of the brotherhood of man for those within its fold. In Hinduism the spirit of brotherhood has become too much philosophized. Similarly, though philosophical Hinduism has no other God but God, it cannot be denied that practical Hinduism is not so emphatically uncompromising on this as Islam*".

C. F. Andrews has written about Gandhi's *"profound admiration"* for Prophet Muhammad, and for his son-in-law Ali. *"The bare simplicity with which they lived, their chivalrous devotion to the poor, their intense belief in God's overruling majesty - all these things have had a great effect upon him, for there is a Puritan strain in Mahatma Gandhi to which such things as these most forcibly appeal"*.

Gandhi's reverence for Christ is embodied in his following statements : *" What does Jesus mean to me? To me, he was one of the greatest teachers humanity has ever had."*

" Jesus was the most active resister known perhaps to history. His was non-violence par excellence".

" Jesus expressed as no other could, the spirit and will of God. It is in this sense that I see him and recognize him as the Son of God. And because the life of Jesus has the significance and the transcendence to which I have alluded, I believe that he belongs not solely to Christianity but to the entire world, to all races and people. It matters little under what flag, name or doctrine they may work, profess a faith or worship a God inherited from their ancestors".

On his way home after the 1931 Round Table Conference in London he stopped in Lausanne (to meet Romain Rolland), and in Rome where he visited St. Peters and the Sistine Chapel. Seeing a painting of the crucified Christ in the chapel, he commented *" What would not I have given to be able to bow my head before the living image of Christ crucified. I saw there at once that nations like individuals could only be made through the agony of the cross and in no other way. Joy comes not out of infliction of pain on others but out of pain voluntarily borne by oneself."*

Louis Fischer has written that when he arrived at Sewagram Ashram in May 1942 he noticed there was *" only one decoration on the mud walls of his hut: a black and white print of Jesus Christ with the inscription 'He is our peace'"*. When asked about it, Gandhi replied *" I am a Christian and a Hindu and a Moslem and a Jew.... Looking at all religions with an equal eye, we would not only not hesitate, but would think it our duty to blend into our faith every acceptable feature of other faiths"*.

C.F. Andrews, who describes Gandhi's Satyagraha as *'Corporate moral resistance'* has affirmed *"perhaps it would be true to say that since the days of the early Christian Church, no such effective acts of passive resistance have been organized as those which Mahatma Gandhi inspired."*

It was because of Gandhi's great respect for all religions that he opposed proselytization. As this generally involves propagating that one's religion is better than others, it often stirs social strife, particularly if material inducements are also offered. In *Young India* (23/4/1931) he wrote "*Faith is not imparted like secular subjects. It is given through the language of the heart. If a man has a living faith in him it spreads its aroma like the rose in scent. Because of its invisibility, the extent of its influence is far wider than that of its visible beauty. I am then not against conversion. But I am against the modern methods of it. Conversion nowadays has become a matter of business like any other. I remember having read a missionary report saying how much it cost per head to convert and then presenting a budget for "the next harvest"..... Conversion in the sense of self purification, self realization is the crying need of the times."*

When his eldest son Harilal converted to Islam in 1936 Gandhi commented "*If his acceptance was from the heart and free from any worldly considerations I should have no quarrel but I have the gravest doubt about this .... I do not mind whether he is known as Abdullah or Harilal, if by adopting one name for the other, he becomes a true devotee of God, which is what both the names mean*".

Gandhi's patriotism and nationalism were equally enlightened and in accord with the ancient Indian maxim '*Udara charita nam tu vasudaiva Kudumbakam*' (for the broad minded all mankind is one family). He did not regard India as a nation in the narrow sense; it was a civilization with special spiritual qualities and a duty to serve humanity. He wrote "*I live for India's freedom and would die for it. But my patriotism is not exclusive. It is calculated to benefit all in the true sense of the word. Through the deliverance of India, I seek to deliver the so called weaker races of the world.... For me, patriotism is the same as humanity. It is not exclusive. I am patriotic because I am human and humane. I will not hurt England or Germany to serve India*".

"*My nationalism includes the love of all nations of the earth irrespective of creed .... It is not nationalism that is evil; it is the narrowness, selfishness, exclusiveness which is the bane of modern nations which is evil. Each one wants to profit at the expense and on the ruin of the other. Indian nationalism has, I hope, struck a different path to find full self expression for the benefit and service of humanity at large*".

K. Broad Spectrum World View :

Though fully engaged in India's freedom struggle Gandhi never lost sight of the world and its travails. His world view was all inclusive and broad spectrum. Having studied in England he was well acquainted with its politics, culture and people. He had many friends there particularly among vegetarians, Theosophists and Liberals. In South Africa, where he spent 21 years, he experienced the most virulent British & Boer racism. Among his early supporters there were two Jews and a British clergyman. It was through the former he first became aware of feudal oppression in Russia. After he read Tolstoy's '*The Kingdom of God is within you*' he became more aware of the deplorable conditions of the Russian peasantry. In 1905, he wrote in '*Indian Opinion*': "*The power of the Viceroy is in no way less than that of the Tsar. The difference is that the British are more efficient and less crude in their brutal oppression. As a result the Russians, in desperation, become anarchists and terrorists.*"

After Gandhi's return to India his confrontation with the British Empire was far more challenging than it had been in South Africa. It required nearly all his time and energy. Yet he did not lose sight of the world.

About the 1917 Russian Revolution he declared in a speech at Madras "*I am yet ignorant of what exactly Bolshevism is. I do not know whether it is for the good of Russia in the long run. But I know that in so far as it is based on violence and denial of God, it repels me*".

About the 1920 Treaty of Sevres he wrote (in a letter dated May 25, 1920 to C.F. Andrews) "*The position created by the Peace Treaty is simply intolerable. The Arabians have lost what independence they had under the Sultan because they were more than a match for him. And now if the King of Hejaz and Amir Feisal can help it, Arabia and Mesopotamia will be drained dry for both these men will be puppets in the hands of British officers whose one aim would be to make as much money as possible for British Capitalists.*" A few days later, in Young India (June 30, 1920) he referred to "*British interest in the oil of Mosul*".

When Major-General Oliver (Lee) Stack, Governor General of Sudan was assassinated in November 1924 and the British imposed extremely harsh political and economic penalties on Egypt Gandhi wrote "*Egypt fares no better than we do. A mad Egyptian kills a British officer - certainly a detestable crime. The punishment is not only a detestable crime, but it is an outrage upon humanity. Egypt has nearly lost all it got. A whole nation has been mercilessly punished for the crime of one man. It may be that the murder had the sympathy of the Egyptians. Would that justify terrorism by a power well able to protect its interests without it?"* (Young India, December 26, 1924, CW, Vol 25, p 488)

About Spain and China he wrote "*The fate of Republican Spain is hanging in the balance. So is that of China. If in the end they lose, it will not be because their cause is not just...... I suggest that, if it is brave, as it is, to die as a man fighting against all odds, it is braver still to refuse to fight and yet to refuse to yield to the usurper*".

When, some months after the Japanese invasion of China a delegation from the former country called on him and urged Japan-India friendship he sternly told them "*You have left the West far behind in diplomacy, in cheap manufactures, in armed warfare, in exploitation. How then can there be friendship between you and us so long as you see nothing wrong in exploitation*" (Harijan, 24-12-1938).

After the 1938 Munich agreement, in which England and France conceded German take over of Czechoslovakia, he averred with prophetic foresight "*England and France quailed before the combined violence of Germany and Italy The agreement that has been signed is a peace that is no peace. The war is only postponed* ".

He lauded the heroic Polish resistance to Nazi invasion thus "*The Poles knew they would be crushed to atoms and yet they resisted the German hordes. That is why I call it almost non-violence*".

In early 1942, with Japan's military threat against India looming large, Gandhi wrote a letter to President Roosevelt which inter alia stated:

"*Dear Friend,*

I twice missed coming to your great country. I have the privilege of having numerous friends there, both known and unknown to me. Many of my countrymen have received and are still receiving higher education in America. I know too that several have taken shelter there. I have profited greatly by the writings of Thoreau and Emerson. I say this to tell you how much I am connected with your country........ My personal position is clear. I hate all war. If therefore I could persuade my countrymen, they would make a most effective contribution. Under foreign rule however we can make no effective contribution in this war, except as helots..... I have suggested that if the Allies think it necessary, they may keep their troops in India, at their own expense, not for keeping internal order, but for preventing Japanese aggression and defending China. So far as India is concerned she must become free even as America and Britain are. It is on behalf of this proposal that I write this to enlist your active sympathy".

The tragedy of Germany's Jews touched him deeply. In his paper '*Harijan*', he wrote on November 11 & 26, 1938: "*My sympathies are all with the Jews. I have known them intimately in South Africa. Through these friends I came to know of their age-long persecution. They have been the untouchables of Christianity. ..... The German persecution of the Jews seems to have no parallel in history. The tyrants of old never went so mad as Hitler seems to have done. If there ever could be a justifiable war in the name of and for humanity, war against Germany to prevent the wanton persecution of a whole race would be completely justified. But I do not believe in any war....... The Jews of Germany can offer Satyagraha under infinitely better auspices than the Indians of South Africa. The Jews are a compact, homogenous community in Germany. They are far more gifted than the Indians of South Africa and they have organized world opinion behind them. I am convinced that if someone with courage and vision can arise among them to lead them in non-violent action, the winter of their despair can be turned into the summer of hope.....*"

His great sympathy for the Jews notwithstanding, he did not approve of a separate state for them on Palestinian land. "*My sympathy does not blind me to the requirements to Justice. It is wrong and inhuman to impose the Jews on the Arabs. What is going on in Palestine today cannot be justified by any moral code of conduct. The mandates have no sanction but that of the last war. The nobler course would be to insist on a just treatment of the Jews wherever they were born and bred. The Jews born and bred in France are French precisely in the same sense as the Christians born in France are French. Every country is their home, including Palestine, not by aggression but by loving service...*"

The Jewish Philospher Martin Buber disagreed with Gandhi that the condition of Indians in South Africa and of Jews in Germany was similar and that non violent resistance would succeed against Hitler. In a long, remarkably respectful letter, written from Jerusalem on February 24, 1939, he affirmed "*No 'Satyagraha' of the power of the truth could withstand a diabolic universal steamroller*". About the right of Arabs and Jews to the "*land of*

Israel" he wrote "*Our settlers do not come here as do the colonists from the Occident, with natives to do their work for them; they themselves set their shoulders to the plough, and spend their strength and their blood to make the land fruitful. But it is not only for ourselves that we desire its fertility. The Jewish peasants have begun to teach their brothers, the Arab peasants, to cultivate the land more intensively....together with them, we want to cultivate the land - to "serve" it, as the Hebrew has it. The more fertile this soil becomes, the more space there will be for us and for them. We have no desire to dispossess them; we want to live with them. We do not want to rule; we want to serve....You once said, Mahatma, that politics enmeshes us nowadays like a serpent's coils ; You said you desired, to wrestle with the serpent. Here is the serpent in the fullness of its power! Jews and Arabs both have a claim to this land; these claims are reconcilable as long as they are restricted to the measure that life allots .... that is, if they are translated into the language of needs of living people and their children. But they are turned through the serpent's influence into claims of principle and politics, and are represented with all the ruthlessness that politics instills.... The serpent conquers not only the spirit but also life. Who would wrestle with it?* "

These clever arguments did not alter Gandhi's views; nor did this happen after the meeting with Immanuel Olsvanger, a representative of the Jewish Agency, which his close friend Herman Kallenbach had arranged. Simone Panter- Brick, in her book, '*Gandhi and the Middle East*' has written about this meeting.

In July 1939, May & June 1940 and December 1941 Gandhi wrote letters to Hitler in which he addressed him as "*friend*", praised his devotion to his fatherland and stated "*nor do we believe that you are the monster described by your opponents*". He appealed to him to "*prevent a war which may reduce humanity to the savage state*". He however added that there "*was no room for doubt that many of your acts are monstrous and unbecoming of human dignity*". Commenting on these letters Arthur Herman has written "*Gandhi had the gift to see the goodness in all human beings, even in Hitler, Churchill had the gift to see the evil because he recognized that quality in himself. The man who denounced Hitler as dictator and murderer was also the one who ordered the firebombing of German cities. He was the prime minister who would order doctors to let Gandhi die in prison and allow millions of Indians to die of famine in 1943 rather than risk diverting the war effort".*

On the eve of the San Francisco Conference which created the United Nations, Gandhi issued a statement which inter alia stated : "*I reiterate my conviction that there will be no peace for the allies or the world unless they shed their belief in the efficacy of war and its accompanying terrible deception and fraud. Peace must be just. In order to be that it must neither be punitive nor vindictive. Germany and Japan should not be humiliated. The fruits of peace must be equally shared. Exploitation and domination of one nation over another can have no place in a world striving to put an end to all wars. Strong nations should be the servants of the weak not their masters or exploiters; Future peace, security and ordered progress of the world should be the responsibility of a world federation that would ensure the freedom of its constituent parts.*"

In March 1947, addressing the Asian Relations Conference's closing session at New Delhi he stated : "*It will be a sorry thing if we go away from this conference without a firm determination that Asia shall live and live as free as every Western nation.... If you want to give a message to the West it must be the message of love and the message of truth*".

Gandhi with Asian Relations Conference Participants

Gandhi's Leadership Achievements

A. Mobilization and Rejuvenation of the Indian People

The eminent psychologist Eric Erikson who analysed one of Gandhi's early 'Satyagrahas - the 1918 Ahmedabad mill workers strike - wrote in his book '*Gandhi's Truth* ', "*When I began this book, I did not expect to rediscover psychoanalysis in terms of truth, self suffering and non-violence; but now that I have done so I see better what I hope the reader has come to see with me, namely that I felt attracted to the Ahmedabad event, because I sensed an affinity between Gandhi's truth and the insights of modern psychology*". Erickson went on to compare the Freudian technique for renewing growth in neurotic individuals with that developed by Gandhi to restore hope to a downtrodden and dejected people. Whether or not Gandhi consciously employed a Freudian technique, the remarkable fact is that he did succeed in restoring hope to India's 350 million poverty stricken, dispirited people and to mobilize them effectively in the non-violent national struggle for independence. As early as 1912, having witnessed Gandhi's non-violent struggle in South Africa, senior Indian nationalist Gopal Krishna Gokhale had declared "*Gandhi has in him the marvelous spiritual power to turn ordinary men around him into heroes and martyrs*".

A particularly notable success in the mobilization of the Indian people for the non-violent freedom struggle was with the warlike Pathans. Their outstanding (6'6") leader Khan Abdul Ghaffar Khan, who came to be called the "*Frontier Gandhi*" and latterly has even been extolled as a "*Moslem St. Francis*" recounted Gandhi's influence on him thus "*As a young boy, I had violent tendencies; the hot blood of the Pathans was in my veins. But in jail, I had nothing to do except read the Koran. I read about the Prophet Mohammed in Mecca, about his patience, his suffering, his dedication. I had read it all before as a child, but now I read it in the light of what I was hearing all around me about Gandhiji's struggle against the British Raj....When I finally met Gandhiji, I learned all about his ideas of non-violence and his Constructive Program. They changed my life forever.*"

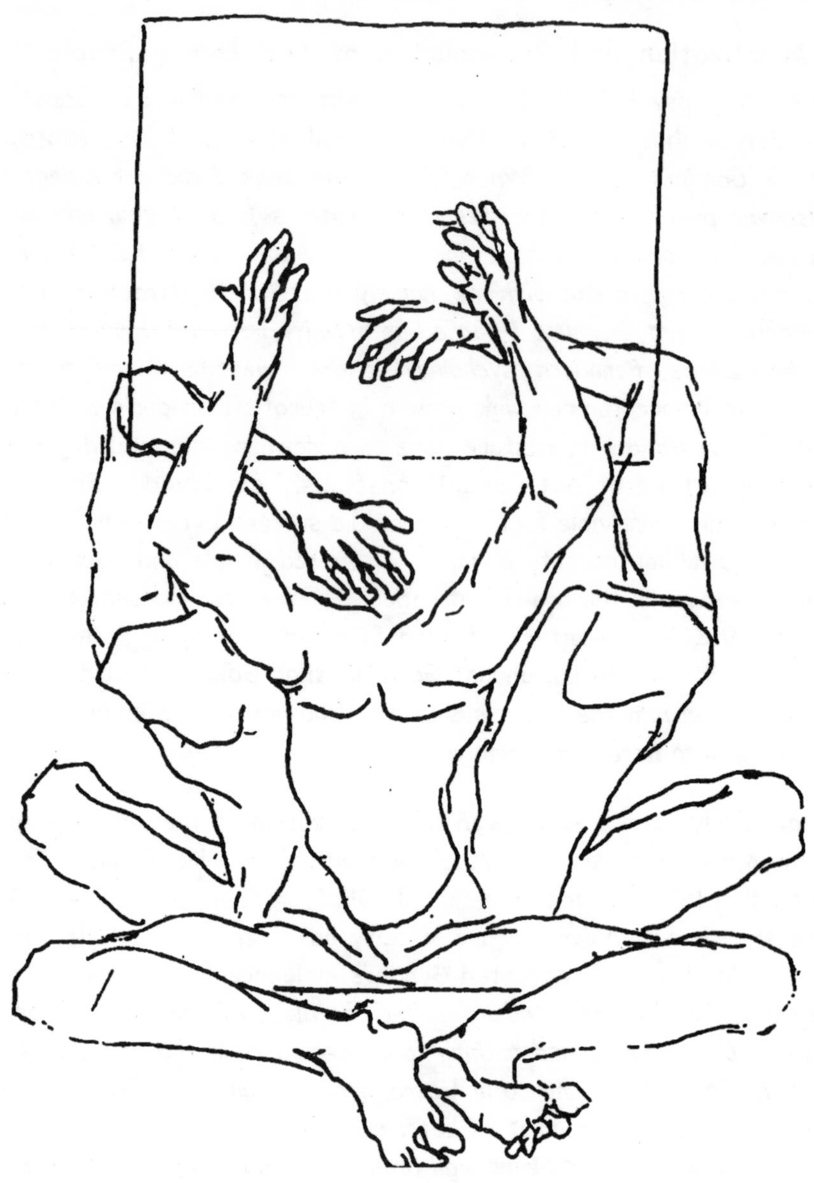

"An eye for an eye only ends up making the whole world blind"

Art work by Shamshad Hussain

Gandhi with "Frontier Gandhi"

Ghaffar Khan succeeded in organizing a 100,000 strong Pathan army of non-violent warriors, the '*Khudai Khidmatgars*' to wage the freedom struggle in the North West Frontier Province. Inspired by him, Pathan women also participated in this struggle confronting British troops with Korans clasped to their chests.

The anthem Ghaffar Khan composed for his Khudai Kidmatgars was as under :

We are the army of God by death or wealth unmoved
We march, our leader and we, ready to die.
We serve and we love, our people and our cause,
Freedom is our goal, our lives the price we pay.

President Ronald Reagan is not considered the brightest of US Presidents, yet he made a very perceptive remark about leadership. He said "*Great leaders do not do great things themselves; they inspire their people to do great things.*" Gandhi certainly met this criterion.

B. Non-violent Liberation of India from Colonial Subjugation.

At the end of World War I, when Gandhi came into the Indian political arena, England was at the height of its power. The German, Austrian and Ottoman Empires had been defeated and destroyed. India shone brightly as *"the brightest jewel in the British Crown"* . The British empire extended all the way from Fiji in the east to Vancouver in the West. Even in November 1942 Churchill firmly refused to countenance India's independence stating he had *"not become the King's First Minister in order to preside over the liquidation of the British Empire"*. Yet, within five years India was free and Britain left India, not as a despised colonial power but as a friend! Independent India requested its last Viceroy Lord Mountbatten to be its first Governor General. Soon thereafter it decided to join the Commonwealth as an equal partner. Gandhi's affirmation that *"a non-violent revolution is not a programme for 'seizure of power' but one of transformation of relationships ending in a peaceful transfer of power"* was amply vindicated.

Patrick French, the severest critic of Gandhi's fads and foibles, acknowledges that *"he was a political and social leader of unparalled skill and determination, without whom India would not have won independence from British rule in 1947. He was the fulcrum of the freedom movement"*.

Arnold Toynbee commended Gandhi for being *"as much a benefactor of Britain as of his own country. He made it impossible for us to go on ruling India, but at the same time he made it possible for us to abdicate without rancour and without dishonour."*

Gandhi with Lord & Lady Mountbatten

C. Establishment of a strong, all inclusive political party and introduction of dignified negotiations and transparency in the political realm.

Claude Markovits writes "*Gandhi's most durable political legacy in India was the creation of a great, multi-class political party which was dominant till the early 1990s. From the late 1930s that party ceased to represent truly Gandhian ideals, but Gandhi....never openly disavowed it, making it possible for his lieutenants to use his charisma to establish their own political legitimacy..... Prior to him, negotiation with the colonizer was seen either as sheer bargaining or as a demonstration of weakness, the sign of deep inferiority complex. He imposed the idea that Indians could negotiate on equal footing with the colonial government and make concessions without necessarily being considered cowards.......In the management of the movements he directed Gandhi introduced principles of transparency unknown before. All expenses had to be justified and a balance sheet kept on a daily basis. Gandhi brought open economic calculation, a consideration of cost - benefit into the political realm.*"

Gandhi at the 1931 Round Table Conference at London

D. Elimination of "Untouchability"

Gandhi's steadfast pursuit of Truth made him perceive quite early the indignity and oppression of the caste system for those below its lowest level, namely the outcastes who were generally known as the *"untouchables"* but were also referred to as ati-shudras, panchamas and pariahs. These unfortunate people, who for centuries had to live outside the village limits, perform the most despised menial tasks and live on carrion, he renamed *"Harijans"* (children of God) and made their emancipation an integral element in the national struggle for independence. He explained the rationale for their new name thus " *'Harijan' means 'a man of God'. All the religions of the world describe God preeminently as the Friend of the friendless, the Help of the helpless and the Protector of the weak.......In India who can be more friendless, helpless and weaker than those classified as untouchables"*

Speaking at the Suppressed Classes Conference in Ahmedabad in 1920 he stated " *What crimes, for which we condemn the Government as Satanic, have not we been guilty of towards our untouchable brethren?.... We make them crawl on their bellies; we have made them rub their noses on the ground; with eyes red with rage we push them out of railway compartments.... We have become "pariahs of the Empire" because we have created "pariahs" in our midst. The slave owner is always more hurt than the slaves... If I have to be reborn, I should be reborn an untouchable, so that I may share their sorrows, sufferings and the affronts leveled at them in order that I may endeavour to free myself and them from that miserable condition."*

In Young India (May 25th, 1921) he wrote "*Swaraj or independence is meaningless if we continue to keep a fifth of India under perpetual subjection. Inhuman ourselves, we may not plead before the throne for deliverance from the inhumanity of others*". Subsequently he wrote *"If it was proved to me that untouchability is an essential part of Hinduism, I would declare myself an open rebel against it."*

Gandhi regarded untouchability as an atrocious perversion of Hinduism and worked strenuously to eradicate it. When he set up his first Ashram in India, just outside Ahmedabad, he named it *Harijan Ashram* and admitted a Harijan family to it. Their daughter Lakshmi he adopted as his own. Revulsed by this, some high caste Hindus terminated their financial support for the Ashram. This did not deter him.

In 1924 he traveled all the way to Vykom in Travancore state to launch satyagraha there against denial of usage of public roads adjacent to the temple to "*untouchables*". He exhorted the satyagrahis thus : "*We are endeavouring to rid Hinduism of its greatest blot. The prejudice we have to fight against is an age long one. This struggle is but a small skirmish in the big battle. We expect that our efforts will result in amelioration of the general condition of the untouchables in every direction* " This long drawn out satyagraha was only partially successful but it impacted beneficially on high caste Hindus elsewhere and emboldened "*untouchables*" to undertake similar action in other temple towns.

In 1932 he undertook a "*fast unto death*" against the British Communal Award which granted a separate electorate for untouchables which he felt would split the Hindu fold and perpetuate untouchability. The fast was also intended to convince high caste Hindus about the "*sin of untouchability*". Soon after this fast ended and the Poona Pact, (wherein the untouchable leader and eminent lawyer Dr. B.R. Ambedkar agreed that his community would not avail of the separate electorate) was signed, he set up the Harijan Sevak Samaj, launched the '*Harijan* ' weekly, and devoted the next nine months to an extensive anti-untouchability campaign tour of India.

On the eve of Independence when Nehru was forming his interim cabinet, Gandhi urged him to include Dr B.R. Ambedkar in it. When Nehru demurred on grounds that he was not a Congress Party member and had been maligning it, he gently reminded him that power was coming "*to India, not to Congress*". Ambedkar thus became Law Minister and Chairman of the Constitution Drafting Committee. This gave him ample opportunity to put his stamp on the draft constitution and include many safeguards in it for disadvantaged social groups. Most importantly, untouchability in all its forms was to be banned. However, it was the overwhelming majority of the Congress party in the Constituent Assembly and Gandhi's great moral influence on it that ensured all these measures were adopted.

Dr. Ambedkar with some Constitution Drafting Committee Members

Dhananjay Keer, who describes Ambedkar as the *"modern Manu"* writes *"An untouchable who was kicked out from carts and segregated in schools in his boyhood, insulted as a professor and ousted from hostels, hotels, saloons and temples and cursed as a British stooge...became now the first Law Minister of a free nation and the chief architect of its constitution. It was a great achievement and a wonder in the history of India"*

Those formerly known as *"untouchables"* and subsequently as *"Harijans"* and *"dalits"*, have emerged as an important political group, with a nation wide party of their own since the early 1980s. A dalit woman, Ms. Mayawati, twice Chief Minister of Uttar Pradesh, India's largest state in coalition governments during the 1998 - 2003 period, is now Chief Minister of that state with her own party majority. A brilliant dalit, Mr. K.R. Narayan, secured a London School of Economics degree, became India's Ambassador to Turkey, China and USA and subsequently Minister for Science and Technology, Vice President of India and President of India (1997-2002). Gandhi would have been delighted over this, but perhaps only partially so. Asked by a journalist in December 1947 *"Who will be President of the Indian Republic? Should we not have Jawaharlal Nehru ?"* he replied *" If I have my way, the first President of the Indian Republic will be a chaste and brave Bhangi girl. If an English girl of seventeen could become the British Queen and later even Empress of India, there is no reason why a Bhangi girl of robust love of her people and unimpeachable integrity of character should not become the first President......"*

Sadly, Gandhi's assassination within six months of India's independence and the shift of focus thereafter from his village based *"Constructive Programme"* to urban and industrial development, have left many dalits in the rural areas in their age old deplorable state, even though a large number of them have risen to high official and political positions. In some areas their condition has actually worsened as their efforts to ameliorate themselves through education and political participation have engendered anger and violence not only from upper castes but also from castes just one or two levels above them. As one sociologist put it with reference to Tamilnadu *"Formerly Dalits were excluded and suppressed. Now they are included and oppressed"*. India's economic Liberalization and privatization since 1991 has also affected them adversely since private firms are refusing to grant the employment quota reservations which dalits have had in public sector firms.

E. Emancipation of Indian women

Traditionally, the role of Indian women was strictly confined to the family and home. Organizations like the Women's Indian Association and National Council for Indian Women, founded in the early 1900s, did exist but consisted only of aristocratic women like the Maharanis of Baroda and Bhopal. They maintained close connections with the British and focused mainly on *"charities"*. Ordinary Indian women were almost totally absent from the public domain.

Quite early in his national struggle Gandhi declared *"As long as women do not come to public life and purify it, we are not likely to attain Swaraj. Even if we did, I would have no use for that Swaraj in which women have not made their full contribution"*. He called on Indian women to join the struggle. They responded to his call. Initially they came as volunteers at Congress sessions but by the time of his non cooperation, anti foreign cloth and salt satyagrahas, thousands were active participants. The poetess Sarojini Naidu became one of his deputies. At his gentle urging women donated their jewellery, marched in processions, picketed liquor and foreign cloth shops, sold khadi at street corners and

Mahatma Gandhi brought a new dimension into our lives. When he spoke of non-violence, he meant not merely the avoidance of violent action but cleansing our hearts of hatred and bitterness. He unveiled the spiritual political power of illiterate & humble have-nots and pointed out that the only programmes worth pursuing were those which could be translated into action. He said that every decision & programme should be judged from the viewpoint of the poorest & the weakest.

Indira Gandhi

Prime Minister Mrs. Indira Gandhi
Courtesy : Professor Ralph Bultjens

provided sanctuary in their homes to *"satyagrahis"*. About his jewellery collections Fischer has written *"Gandhi was an incurable and irresistible fund raiser. He found special relish in stripping women of their jewellery"* and quoted Gandhi : *"I want to create in them a distaste for much ornamentation, and a desire to part with their jewellery for the sake of the poor"*.

When the 1942 *'Quit India '* Movement was launched and Gandhi and other leaders were arrested and taken away from the Gowalia public meeting in Bombay, a brave young woman named Aruna Asaf Ali unfurled the Indian flag at that venue. Another brave woman Usha Mehta, along with three other such women, set up and operated a secret *"Congress Radio from somewhere in India"*. Through Gandhi's non-violent national movement, Indian women for the first time combined their roles as wives and mothers with their new roles of *"non-violent warriors"*.

When Independence came women were accorded full legal equality with men. In the first Union Cabinet the health minister was Rajkumari Amrit Kaur, a princess of Kapurthala, who in 1915 had given up royal comforts to become Gandhi's disciple. Mrs Vijaya Lakshmi Pandit was India's first Ambassador to the Soviet Union and subsequently to the US & Mexico. In 1953 she was elected President of the UN General Assembly. Within fifteen years thereafter, Indira Gandhi became Prime Minister of India and continued in that high office for 16 years with only an intervening two year break. Since then, numerous Indian women have risen to high positions in politics, diplomacy, business, banking, industry, biotechnology, newsmedia and other professions including aviation. Since July 25, 2007 the President of India and since June 3, 2009 the Speaker of the Lok Sabha (Lower House of Parliament) are women. After the 2011 state elections the number of women chief ministers has doubled from 2 to 4, the new ones being in West Bengal and Tamilnadu. Since independence India has had 14 women Chief Ministers including these four.

As importantly, women's empowerment and self help groups have sprouted in various parts of India, including the rural areas. The most notable of these is SEWA (Self Employed Women's Association), based in Ahmedabad. It was established in April, 1972 by Mrs. Ela Bhat, a lawyer and Gandhi inspired social activist, who was deeply concerned by the ruthless exploitation of rural women who came to the cities in search of work. SEWA strives to obtain for these women, initially "headloaders" and cart-pullars in Ahmedabad's cloth market, (who were mostly illiterate harijan women) fair wages, satisfactory working conditions, legal protection and welfare measures. In 1989 it had 25,917 members, all of whom were in Gujarat. In 2008, its members all over India, were 9,66,139 and now were not only manual urban workers but also included rural hawkers & vendors and a wide variety of home based workers. Vivek Pinto writes"*What is particularly Gandhian about the heroic struggle of these women is that they have resorted to 'direct action' - engaging with and writing to employers and the police - and formed themselves into cooperatives, emphasizing non-violence, self reliance and development of financial and managerial self sufficiency.*"

These impressive gains in the status and empowerment of Indian women are a direct outcome of Gandhi's non-violent national movement and his insistence on women's participation in it. In most European countries, as also in the US, women secured the right to vote only after many years of arduous struggle, and only after 1918. However, much ground still remains to be covered as Indian women have not even achieved 30% equality with men in political and other fields. In 1941 Gandhi had written "*Though Satyagraha has brought India's women out from their darkness as nothing else could have in such an incredibly short space of time, Congressmen have not yet felt the need to see that women become equal partners in the fight for Swaraj. They have not realized that woman must be the true helpmate of man in the mission of service*". Unfortunately, this mindset still seems to prevail among most of India's male politicians.

"Woman is the companion of man, gifted with equal mental capacities. She has the right to participate in the minutest detail in the activities of man."

- Art work by Rekha Rao

F. Abolition of the Indenture System

A significant but little known achievement of Gandhi was the abolition of the odious indenture system whereby poor, unemployed Indians were transported to far flung British colonies as cheap labour.

It was in South Africa that Gandhi first witnessed the deplorable conditions in which indentured Indians lived and worked. Besides, they had no franchise,could not walk on public footpaths, could not be out of doors after 9 PM without a permit and had to pay a three Pound poll tax. It was in order to ameliorate these conditions that his visit to South Africa, initially expected to last only a few weeks, ultimately lasted 22 years. During this period he mobilized the Indians in that country, founded the Natal Indian Congress (1894), Phoenix and Tolstoy farms (1903 & 1910), '*Indian Opinion*' newspaper (1903) and fashioned his potent Satyagraha strategy (1906) with which he secured substantial reforms from the Natal (1907) and Transvaal (1914) governments in favour of the Indians in these states.

In 1896, when in India, he publicized the travails of Indians in South Africa through speeches and a "*Green pamphlet*" he had written (called green because of the colour of its cover!). A Reuters report about this reached South Africa and caused an uproar. When Gandhi disembarked in Durban with his family, on December 28th, 1896 he was so viciously attacked by a white mob that he might well have been killed had not the kind hearted wife of the local police superintendent rescued him.

In 1901, he visited Mauritius to study the circumstances of Indian labourers there. In 1912, when Indians in Fiji requested his assistance in solving their problems he induced Manilal Doctor to go there and stop over in Mauritius on his return.

During this period he corresponded with Gopal Krishna Gokhale and Dadabhai Naoroji. Both of them appreciated and supported his efforts on behalf of overseas Indians. It is mainly because of this that the anti-indenture campaign became an issue for the Indian National Congress (INC). Until then because of rosy Colonial Office reports (e.g those of Comins (1893) and Sanderson(1910)) about indentured Indians in other British colonies, that many educated Indians, including INC members, had considered this "*immigration*" a beneficial "*safety valve*" for India, It is only in and after 1913 that Anti-indenture resolutions began to be adopted. That passed at the 1915 INC called for its early abolition as it was "*a form of slavery which socially and politically debases the labourers and is seriously detrimental to the economic and moral interests of the country*".

Soon after Gandhi returned to India in 1915 he induced Charlie Andrews to go to Fiji and report on the condition of Indentured Indians there. Andrews went accompanied by a colleague named William Pearson. Their report was highly critical. Published by the League for Abolishment of Indentured Labour it provided excellent ammunition for anti-indenture campaigners who now took their campaign into the recruitment areas and urged the people to expel the "*Arkatiyas*" (recruiters) from their villages.

At the January 1917 Calcutta INC it was resolved that "*nothing short of complete abolition of indentured labour, whether described as such or otherwise, can effectively meet the evils which have been admitted by all concerned to have done irreparable harm to the labourers*". Gandhi declared civil disobedience would be launched unless said abolition was made. On March 20th 1917, Viceroy Lord Hardinge announced that all further recruitment of indentured labour would end. However, in July that year the Colonial Office announced a new scheme. Titled the "*Islington Scheme of Assisted Emigration*", it claimed to be devoid of all odious features of the indenture system. Nonetheless Gandhi strongly opposed it and held it was "*a new system of indentureship......not in the interests of the labourer but those of the colonial employer*". The INC endorsed this view. In January 1919, the Viceroy recommended against its introductoion and it was dropped.

Brinsley Samaroo in his scholarly paper "*The Mahatma's Caribbean concerns* has written "*Within the spaces of his peaceful war against an empire over which the sun never set, Gandhi found time for temporarily lost generations of labourers toiling on plantations of Natal, Mauritius, Fiji and the Caribbean. By example, advice and agitation on their behalf, he gave voice to these people.....He created new hope among them and was therefore instrumental in the diaspora's reconstruction after the deconstruction caused by their transportation from India and the rigours of plantation life. Diaspora Indians therefore made him their own Mahatama.*"

It is pertinent to recall here that during the 1837 - 1917 period when the indenture system operated, 1,194,957 Indians were transported to 14 far flung British colonies with the largest numbers sent to Mauritius (453,063), British Guyana (238,909), Natal (152,184) and Fiji (60,965).

G. Ending Indian feudalism

Before Independence, India was a highly feudal land of princes, colonial administrators and paupers. The princes lived in regal splendour, competing with each other in lavish entertainment of British officialdom, which actively encouraged this and indulged in much pomp and pageantry in London as well as India. Patrick French writes. "*King George V's coronation in 1911 was a spectacular propaganda coup, with myriad Indian princes and imperial prime ministers filling Westminster Abbey for the seven hour ceremony.....This was the age of high imperialism when brute force was to an extent forsaken in favour of pomp as a means of asserting authority. A giant Durbar was subsequently held in Delhi which was attended by all the Indian princes*".

Gita Mehta highlights the incredibly profligate life styles of Indian princes with a princely dog "*marriage*" as an example. "*The marriage of the two dogs Roshanara, veiled and covered in gems, to Bobby in red silk pyjamas (to make sure he does not violate the bride before the wedding!) was conducted with all the ceremony that would have accompanied the marriage of a royal princess. A court minister solemnly read out a list of the wealth Roshanara was bringing to the marriage including a golden palanquin....At the end of the ceremony, the visiting rulers circled the dogs with gold coins and their aides placed gifts in a large basket. The strains of Mendelsohn's Wedding March were faintly audible...An enormous rectangular table for two hundred guests dominated the banquet hall for the nuptial dinner. In the center of the rectangle dancing girls sang and danced for the dogs.*"

British Officials with Indian Princes

Maharaja of Benares

Gandhi's first confrontation with this pomp and spendour came in 1916 at the inauguration of Benares Hindu University. Viceroy Lord Hardinge and many Indian princes were present:, He boldly spoke thus: "*His Highness the Maharaja of Benares spoke about the poverty of India. Other speakers too laid great stress upon it. But what did we witness in this great pandal. An exhibition of jewellery which made a splendid feast for the eyes of even the greatest jeweller from Paris. I compare these richly bedecked noblemen with the millions of the poor and say to them, there is no salvation for India unless you strip yourselves of this jewellery and hold it in trust for your countrymen in India*".

A March 29, 1939 news report in International Herald Tribune about the marriage of the Maharaja of Indore to Marguerite Lawler, an American woman, indicated his annual income as US$ 70 million with only 1.5 million people as his subjects.

The Princes were not only flamboyant but also highly autocratic. Nehru wrote about them thus "*The Indian states represent today probably the extremest type of autocracy existing in the world.....It is really astonishing how these feudal old world enclaves have carried on with so little change right into the middle of the twentieth century.*" He quoted the Maharaja of Bikaner's arrogant boast that the Indian rulers "*through centuries of heredity can claim to have inherited the instincts of rule and a certain measure of statesmanship...*"

Under Gandhi's instructions the Congress party maintained a discreet non interference policy in the affairs of the Princely states until the late 1930s (so as not to drive them closer into the arms of the British). However, Gandhi's focus on "*the millions of the poor*" gestated widespread revulsion against the princely life styles. Some rulers like the Maharajas of Baroda and Mysore were stirred by Gandhi's message and supported him. Many others however foresaw that the Gandhi led freedom struggle would mean the end of their feudal regimes and opposed it. Examples of this were the Jamsaheb of Nawanagar who declared" *Why should I not support the Muslim League. Mr. Jinnah is willing to tolerate our existence, but Mr. Nehru wants the extinction of the Princes"*, and the Maharaja of Travancore whose Dewan announced on 13 June 1947 that Travancore would "*set itself up as an independent and sovereign state"*. However this group of princes discovered to their chagrin that the freedom upsurge in British India had also aroused their subjects many of whom strongly supported it. At this point Gandhi declared "*The princes must recognize the paramountcy of the people as they recognized the paramountcy of the British Government. Then they can freely carry on"*. Vallabhai Patel, Home Minister in the Interim Government, made the same point but more emphatically and sternly. This left the Princes little option but to make virtue of necessity and gracefully signify their accession to India or Pakistan. Before August 15, 1947 all princely states within the territory of India (excluding Hyderabad) or having a common frontier with it (excluding Kashmir) acceded to it. The distinct possibility of India's balkanization because of the sovereignty dreams of recalcitrant princes was thus averted. In reciprocation for their accession to India, they were compensated with privy purses, diplomatic appointments and governorships for almost thirty years.

Gita Mehta makes a good accounting of what India lost through Partition and gained through accession of the princely states."*The British Empire's partition awards lost India an area of 364,737 square miles and a population of 82 million. After the integration of the Indian kingdoms, India acquired approximately 500,000 square miles of territory and 87 million new citizens.*"About this accession of the Princely states Vallabhai Patel averred "*The capacity for mischief and trouble on the part of the rulers....is far greater than could be imagined. Let us place ourselves in their position and then assess the value of their sacrifice."*

Indian feudalism was also entrenched in the Zamindari system, a carry over from the Moghul era. It became very oppressive after the British '*Permanent Settlement* ' of 1793. 60% of all farmers in Bengal, United Provinces and Bihar owned less than 8% of the land. Zamindars also known as Taluqdars, owned most of the rest. They generally were absentee landlords living in great comfort in the cities. Nehru indicates that besides the high rents for which "*receipts were hardly ever given*", taluqdars *"often make their tenants pay for every special expenditure - a marriage in the family, cost of the son's education in foreign countries, a party to the Governor or other high official, a purchase of a car or elephant."*

As early as 1937 the Congress had resolved that the Zamindari system must end. However, Gandhi had stated that *"what one would love to see is proper, impartial and satisfactory understanding between the zamindars, big and small, the ryots and the government, so that when the law is passed, it may not be a dead letter nor need force to be used against the zamindars or the ryots. Would that all changes, some of which must be radical, take place throughout India without bloodshed and without force."*

In 1951 the Zamindari system was abolished and all its lands, except those zamindars or their families personally cultivated were taken over and transferred to those that tilled them. The zamindars were paid non justiciable compensation. The early abolition of the Zamindari system was a major achievement but further progress of land reform for transferring land from large to small farmers and more so to landless labourers, has been slow and patchy. Nobel laureate Amartya Sen has averred *"My own state of West Bengal is an exception in this and has received a great deal of benefit precisely from the success of land reforms there, including a reasonably high rate of agricultural economic growth".*

The bloodless ending of feudal and autocratic life styles and the zamindari system, and the smooth integration, except for two of them, of the numerous princely states into the Indian Union, is another significant outcome of Gandhi's non-violent national struggle focused on the poor and exploited peasant. It contrasts sharply with the

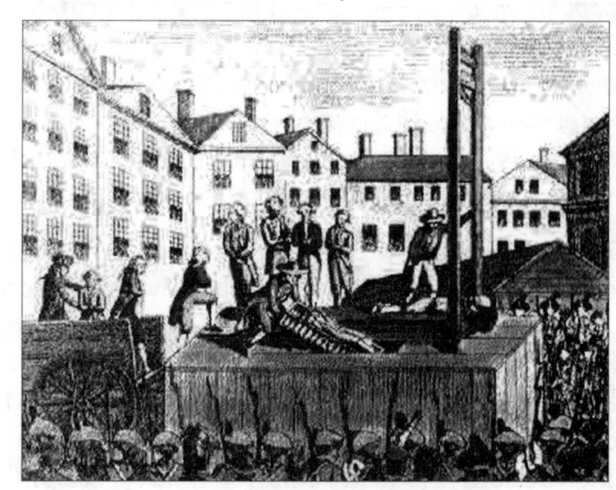

The French Guillotine

considerable bloodshed in the American, French, Italian, German, Russian Chinese and Ethiopian Revolutions and Civil Wars before independence and national unification were achieved, and feudalism and slavery ended.

H. Revival of India's rural industries

Gandhi's choice of the 'Charka' as the prime physical weapon of his non-violent national struggle and his insistence that all participants in it, spin cotton and wear only hand spun, hand woven clothes initially revived the weaving and allied industries. Subsequently, there was a revival in the whole spectrum of cottage and village industries. Gandhi's disciple, Kamaladevi Chattopadhyaya contributed the most in bringing this about. It was she who founded the Indian Crafts Council to lobby for the welfare of craftsmen and for the revival of their crafts. For her, *"craftsmanship grew from the village community, its joys and burdens, the change of the seasons, the memories filled with song and verse legends, myths and local romances from the core and substance of their daily existence."* In 1952 she was appointed Chairperson of the All-India Handicrafts Board and in that capacity brought handicrafts into the ambit of the national economy. She set up design centers to upgrade them and motivated the Central and State Governments to open Handicrafts Emporia in all major cities.

Separately, the Khadi and Village Industries Commission has also rendered yeoman service in reviving, supporting, upgrading and marketing the products of Khadi and village industries. Of late it has succeeded in persuading some of India's leading designers to utilize Khadi in their fashion and furnishing creations.

Today, India's handicraft industries, located predominantly in rural areas, are providing employment to over 30 million families of spinners, weavers, embroiderers, leather, marble & metal workers, wood, bone & stone carvers, carpet and rug makers etc. India's annual exports of these items earns it over US$ 1 billion. Gandhi's maxims *"production by the masses, not mass production"* and *"The cure for unemployment is provision of employment and not a dole "* have been well vindicated.

Village embroiderers

I. Harmonization of Capital Labour Relations

Some critics have accused Gandhi of focusing only on peasants and landless labour and neglecting industrial workers. This is unfair and untrue. He had great concern for these workers and deplored the fact that "*The working classes have all these centuries been relegated to a lower status. They have been shudras and the word has been interpreted to mean an inferior status.*"

He averred "*I want no differentiation between the sons of a weaver, an agricuturist and a school master.... No labour will be considered too low or too high. .... I have been saying for years labour is far superior to capital. Without labour gold, silver and copper are a useless burden. It is labour which extracts precious ore from the bowels of the earth. Labour is priceless, not gold. I want marriage between capital and labour. They can work wonders in cooperation. But that can happen only when labour is intelligent enough to cooperate with itself and then offer cooperation with capital on terms of honourable equality.*"

The Triumph of Labour

Sculptor : D P Choudhury

The practical and successful application of Gandhi's ideas on capital-labour relations is seen in the aftermath of the 1918 Ahmadabad Textile workers strike. The workers had struck work demanding a 50% wage increase on grounds of increased cost of living. Their employer was unwilling to offer more than 20%. He, Ambalal Sarabhai, was Gandhi's principal supporter, while his sister Ansuya was the leading protagonist of the workers. Gandhi urged a 35% increase and went on a fast until it was granted. Soon thereafter the Textile Labour Association which was a federation of seven unions of Ahmedabad textile mills was set up. It was a capital-labour organization and as Copley has written "*reflected Gandhi's deep commitment to class reconciliation and arbitration of disputes. Strikes were to be a last resort and it was committed to the Gandhian ideal of non-violence*". The objectives of the Communist Workers and Peasants party were quite the opposite.

Erik Erikson, avers the ATWS "*Event*" has a "*central position in Gandhi's life, in the history of Indian labour and in that of militant non violence ....The gains were institutionalized in an industry wide board of Arbitrators, among whom were Gandhiji and Mangaldas Girardhas. The Ahmedabad Textile Labour Association which was founded is given first rank in most non-political treatises dealing with the labour movement in India*". He points out that its membership which was 14,000 in 1925 had risen to 100,000 in 1959, and quotes a February 1967 Statesman news report as follows. "*A textile worker in Ahmedabad today is the highest paid among his colleagues elsewhere in the country. He was getting 20% less wages than that prevailing in Bombay in 1920 when Textile Labour Association came into being. But today his is 10% more. This, the TLA leaders claim, is entirely attributable to the long spell of industrial peace in Ahmedabad, which in turn is the result of its general adherence to the principle of arbitration in settling labour disputes. In this respect TLA can certainly claim to be the pace-setter.*"

   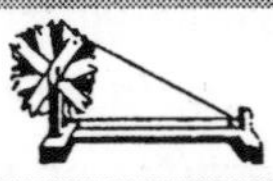 

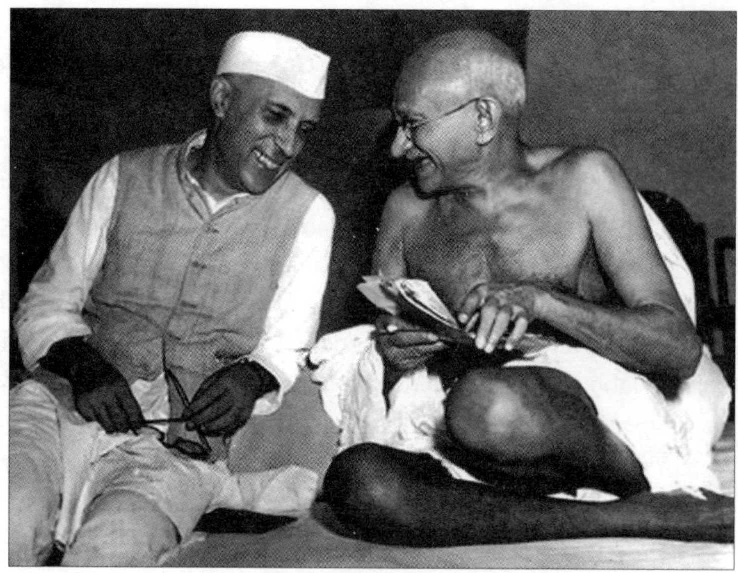

Nehru with his mentor

J. Conceptualization of India's foreign policy

India's non aligned foreign policy, which was fashioned in embryonic form during the freedom struggle, was essentially the Gandhian approach of striving for freedom and justice for subjugated peoples and engaging in non-violent conflict resolution for safeguarding peace. Its prime elements were antiracism, anti fascism, anti-imperialism decolonization, international cooperation and peace, in keeping with Gandhi's assertions "*Through the deliverance of India, I seek to deliver the so called weaker races of the world*" and "*There is no limit to extending our services to our neighbours across state frontiers. God never made frontiers.*"

Jawaharlal Nehru, India's first Prime Minister was also its Foreign Minister during his entire term in office, and the architect of its foreign policy. B.R. Nanda has written "*He had been deeply influenced by a quarter century's experience in the struggle for freedom led by Gandhi. He interpreted this struggle as part of the resurgence of Asia. The fact that a predominantly non-violent movement had made it possible to liquidate imperialism in India seemed to prove that physical force was not necessarily the arbiter of the destiny of nations. Thanks to Gandhi and the grass roots experience of Indian politics, Nehru was also conscious of the inadequacy of both Western capitalism and Soviet Communism for India."*

Even prior to India's independence, as Head of the Interim Government, Nehru had spoken thus in a September 7, 1946 radio broadcast. "*We propose as far as possible, to keep away from the power politics of groups, aligned against one another, which have led in the past to world war and which may again lead to disasters on an even vaster scale. We believe that peace and freedom are indivisible and the denial of freedom anywhere must endanger freedom elsewhere and lead to conflict and war. We are particularly interested in the emancipation of colonial and dependent countries and peoples and in the recognition, in theory and practice, of equal opportunities for all races."* Soon thereafter he convened the Asian Relations Conference at New Delhi. It opened on 23 March 1947. At it he stated *"For too long we of Asia have been petitioners in Western Courts and Chancelleries. That story must now belong to the past. We propose to stand on our own feet and to cooperate with all others who are prepared to cooperate with us. We do not intend to be play things of others"*. All these ideas strongly echoed those of Gandhi and were embodied in the '*Panch Sheel*' principles formulated by Nehru in 1954. They became the core of India's foreign policy and comprised non interference in each other's internal affairs, goodwill towards all, non involvement in military alliances, judging each issue on its merits, negotiated solutions to international problems and support for the United Nations. Until the collapse of the Soviet Union in 1991 this was the foreign policy of over 120 newly independent countries, among whom India had an influential leadership position.

Copley writes *"Gandhian style resistance to apartheid was part of the wider struggle against colonialism and neo-colonialism. With India being the first colonial society to acquire independence, it was inevitable that Gandhi's method should be keenly studied within the Third World and, as Nehru became increasingly important in international affairs as the moving spirit behind the Non Aligned Movement, India's example became all the more influential."*

Regarding India's decision to join the British Commonwealth S.R. Mehrotra has averred that it came as *"a surprise to many people in India and abroad, more so because this decision was taken by a government headed by Jawaharlal Nehru who, since the late 1920s,had been a bitter opponent of the idea of Dominion status and an ardent advocate of complete Independence for his country .....He regarded Britain as the arch-priest of imperialism"*. Fischer has pointed out that while in London for the 1931 Round Table Conference, Gandhi was asked after a talk at the Raleigh Club. *"How far would you cut India off from the Empire?"* He replied *"From the Empire entirely; from the British nation not at all... The Emperorship must go and I should love to be an equal partner with Britain sharing her joys and sorrows, and an equal partner with the Dominions. But it must be a partnership on equal terms....England and India should be bound by the silken cord of love"* Fischer adds *"In these statements, Gandhi described precisely and with remarkable prevision, the status which Independent India voluntarily assumed in the Commonwealth in 1948. More, the protagonists of that move used the very same argument - and almost the exact words - which Gandhi had used in London seventeen years earlier"*. Speaking to the Indian Constituent Assembly Nehru stated that India joining the Commonwealth *"would have met with the approval of Gandhiji"* .

Prof. Nicholas Manserg in *'The Commonwealth Experience'* has stated that *"Nehru reinterpreted the idea of the Commonwealth to fit his own philosophy of international relations. It was a bridge between East and West, between various continents, races and cultures, a grouping of friendly nations, across the frozen configuration of international relations ...It was an example to the world of Gandhian principles applied to relations between nations."*

Addressing the UN General Assembly on November 3rd, 1948 Nehru inter alia stated *"I am not afraid of the future. I have no fear in my mind even though India, from a military point of view, is of no great consequence. I am not afraid of the bigness of great powers, their armies, their fleets and their atom bombs. That is the lesson which my master taught me. We stood as an unarmed people against a great country and a powerful empire. We were supported and strengthened because throughout all this period we decided not to submit to evil.... I do not know if it is possible to apply this to the problems which face the world to day...but I think if we banish fear, if we have confidence, even though we may take risks of trust rather of violent language, violent actions and in the end war... those risks are worth taking."*

Even as late as January 1962 Nehru was affirming Gandhi's imprint on India's foreign policy. Faced with Western criticism of India's military take over of Goa, he declared:" *Its nonsense to say that we have lost face, moral or otherwise. At the same time I will admit that there has been something lost in terms of our philosophy of finding peaceful solutions to all such problems. The military approach - that is any kind of warlike action - is alien to our culture and tradition. In fact we want the use of force outlawed. .... The means employed are as vital for us as the ends they serve. This is what Gandhi taught us; and really this was the dilemma that held us back from any military action in Goa for 14 long years."*

Gandhi with Tagore, May 1925

Gandhi with Romain Rolland, December 1931

Gandhi's Impact On:

a) Renowned Intellectuals

Count Leo Tolstoy: Gandhi became acquainted with Tolstoy in 1894 through his book '*The Kingdom of God is within you*', which deeply impressed him. Subsequently he read other of his books as also his '*Letter to a Hindoo*', addressed to Tarakanath Das, editor of a militant magazine called 'Free Hindustan', published in Vancouver. He translated that letter into Gujarati and described Tolstoy as "*one of the clearest thinkers in the Western World*". In October 1909, from London, he wrote respectfully to Tolstoy informing him of his non-violent struggle against racial oppression in South Africa. In his reply Tolstoy wrote "*I have just received your most interesting letter, which has given me much pleasure. God help our dear brothers and co-workers in the Transvaal. The same struggle of the soft against the harsh, of meekness and love against pride and violence, in making itself felt every year more and more among us*". To Gandhi's second letter, written from Johannesberg in early April 1910, and enclosing his recently written book '*Hind Swaraj or Indian Home Rule*' Tolstoy replied : "*I have received your letter and your book 'Indian Home Rule'. I read your book with great interest because I think that the question you treat in it - passive resistance - is a question of the greatest importance not only for India but for whole humanity.....I am not quite well at present and therefore abstain from writing to you all what I have to say about your book and all your work which I appreciate very much but I will do it as soon as I will feel better.*" He signed the letter as "*your friend and brother L. Tolstoy*" Tolstoy died on November 7, 1910.

Albert Einstein, the most renowned scientist of the twentieth century wrote a letter, in German, to Gandhi in 1931. Its English translation is : *Potsdam, 27 September 1931.*

Respected Mr. Gandhi !
I use the presence of your friend in our home to send you these lines. You have shown through your works, that it is possible to succeed without violence even with those who have not discarded the method of violence. We may hope that your example will spread beyond the borders of your country, and will help to establish an international authority, respected by all, that will take decisions and replace war conflicts.
With sincere admiration, Yours

A. Einstein.

I hope that I will be able to meet you face to face some day.

Gandhi replied as under

LONDON, October 18, 1931

DEAR FRIEND

I was delighted to have your beautiful letter sent through Sundaram. It is a great consolation to me that the work I am doing finds favour in your sight. I do indeed wish that we could meet face to face and that too in India at my Ashram. Yours sincerely,

M. K. GANDHI

b). Nobel Laureates

Rabindranath Tagore, awarded the Nobel Prize for Literature in 1913, **was** initially quite critical of Gandhi's non cooperation movement as a "*negative and isolationist approach*". However, later he was won over completely and wrote "*He stopped at the threshold of the huts of the thousands of dispossessed, dressed like one of their own. He spoke to them in their own language. Here was living truth at last and not only quotations from books....At Gandhi's call India has blossomed forth to new greatness, just as once before in earlier times when Buddha proclaimed the Truth of compassion and fellow feeling, among all living creatures*". It was he who first addressed Gandhi as the "*Mahatma*".

When Gandhi commenced his "fast unto death" on...... in protest against the grant of a separate electorate for untouchables, Tagore addressed his Shantiniketan School inmates thus "*A shadow is darkening today over India like a shadow cast by an eclipsed sun...Mahatmaji, who through his life of dedication has made India his own in Truth, has commenced his vow of extreme self sacrifice... The penance which Mahatmaji has taken upon himself is not a ritual but a message to all in India and to the world. Let us try to understand the meaning of his message.*"

Romain Rolland: This 1915 Nobel Laureate for Literature,first heard of Gandhi from Tagore and C.F. Andrews and thereafter read his writings and speeches. He was deeply inspired by Gandhi's spirituality and his non-violent struggle for India's emancipation from colonialism and its own social evils. In 1924 he wrote a biography which he titled '*Mahatma Gandhi - The Man Who Became One with the Universal Being*'. In it he affirmed "*The apostle of India is the apostle of the world ..... The battle that the Mahatma began fighting four years ago is our battle. All his struggles are hallowed by religious serenity*". This book was translated into French and German and became a best seller in both these countries. When hardly anyone in Europe could comprehend the meaning and potency of '*Satyagraha*', Rolland became, in his own words, "*one of the first in the West to discover and spread the Word of the Mahatma.*"

Rolland's first letter to Gandhi was written in October 1925 to introduce Ms Madaleine Slade, "*a dear friend of my sister and myself, whom I look upon as a spiritual daughter and I am delighted is coming to put herself under your direction*". Thereafter there was regular correspondence between them, directly and through Ms Slade. However, the first time they actually met each other was in early December 1931 on Gandhi's return journey from the London Round Table Conference. Gandhi made a five day stop over in Switzerland, spending three of them with Rolland at his home in Villeneuve on Lake Leman, and then visiting Laussane and Geneva to address meetings there. Their correspondence continued unbroken until Rolland's death on December 30, 1944. In the statement Gandhi issued on this sad event he stated "*He lived for truth and non violence. He responded to all suffering. He revolted against the wanton human butchery called war.*"

George Bernard Shaw, when he came to call on Gandhi in London in 1931, was already a renowned playwright, Nobel Laureate and staunch anti-war activist. In his typical wit and "*modesty*" he greeted Gandhi with "*Mahatma Minor has come to call on Mahatma Major!*" In a letter he later wrote to Nancy Astor, he affirmed "*Gandhi is not a crook; he is a saint . . . under the covenant of grace.*"

Gandhi too thought highly of Shaw. "*I think he is a very good man ...... the Arch Jester of Europe, he has a Puck-like spirit and a generous ever young heart,*" Later, after reading Shaw's '*The Black Girl in Search of God* he remarked: "*In everything of his that I have read there has been a religious centre.*"

Gandhi and Shaw thought alike on many issues particularly vegetarianism, education,dignity of labour, simple living, war and parliamentary democracy. Among Shaw's well known and witty quotes on these issues are :

"*Animals are my friends... and I don't eat my friends*"

"*A fool's brain digests philosophy into folly, science into superstition, and art into pedantry. Hence University education.*"

"*A day's work is a day's work, neither more nor less, and the man who does it needs a day's sustenance, a night's repose and due leisure, whether he be painter or ploughman.*"

"*It is said that every people has the Government it deserves. It is more to the point that every Government has the electorate it deserves; for the orators of the front bench can edify or debauch an ignorant electorate at will. Thus our democracy moves in a vicious circle of reciprocal worthiness and unworthiness.*"

"*My way of joking is to tell the truth. It's the funniest joke in the world.*"

In 1981, 53 Nobel Laureates issued a manifesto calling upon world leaders, national governments and international organizations to formulate a comprehensive programme to combat the '*Global Holocaust*' of hunger and under development. It contained the following sentences "*Although the powerful of this earth bear the greatest responsibility, they are not alone. If the helpless take their fate into their own hands, if increasing numbers refuse to obey any law other than the fundamental human right, which is the right to life, if the weak organize themselves and use non-violent actions exemplified by Gandhi, it is certain that an end could be put to this catastrophe in our time.*"

His Holiness the Dalai Lama, in his Nobel Prize acceptance speech in December 1989, spoke thus: "*I accept the prize with profound gratitude on behalf of the oppressed everywhere, and all those who struggle for freedom and work for world peace. I accept it as a tribute to the man who founded* *the modern tradition of non-violent action for change - Mahatma Gandhi - whose life taught and inspired me. And of course, I accept it on behalf of the six million Tibetan people, my brave countrymen and women inside Tibet, who have suffered and continue to suffer so much...."*

Other Nobel Laureates who have publicly acknowledged Gandhi's influence on them are **Albert Luthuli**, **Desmond Tutu** and **Nelson Mandela** of South Africa, **Adolfo Perez Esquivel** of Argentina, **Oscar Arias Sancez** of Costa Rica **Lech Walesa** of Poland, **Rene Cassin** of France, **Shimon Peres** of Israel, **Mairead Corrigan** and **Betty Williams** of Ireland, **Mother Theresa** and **Amartya Sen of India**, **Aung San Su Kyi** of Myanmar (whom Alan Clements has described as "**Burma's Gandhi**"), **Wangarai Maathai** of Kenya who has evolved a network of 600 communities across her own and 20 other African countries, which has planted of over 30 million trees) and **Presidents Jimmy Carter and Barack Obama** of USA.

In accepting his Nobel Prize President Obama, in the unenviable position of a commander in chief of armed forces simultaneously at war in two countries, stated "*As someone who stands here as a direct consequence of Dr. Martin Luther King's life's work, I am living testimony to the moral force of non-violence. I know there is nothing weak -nothing passive - nothing naïve - in the creed and lives of Gandhi and King. But as a head of state sworn to protect and defend my nation, I cannot be guided by their examples alone. I face the world as it is, and cannot stand idle in the face of threats to the American people.*"

The Dalai Lama

Desmond Tutu

Mother Theresa

Wangarai Maathai

c). Exceptional Individuals

Foreign

Henry Polak, a British Jew, was sub editor of the Transvaal Gazette when Gandhi first met him in 1904. He subsequently studied law and became an articled clerk in Gandhi's Johannesberg office. It was he who lent Gandhi Ruskin's '*Unto This Last*' and later supported him by appearing in court on behalf of Indian satyagrahis. In 1909 he visited India to brief Gokhale and others about Gandhi's South African struggle. In 1913 he actively participated in Gandhi's Satyagraha and was imprisoned. His wife Millie Polak's book '*Mr Gandhi : The Man*' is an early biographical sketch of him.

Joseph J. Doke was a Baptist Minister of Johannesberg whom Gandhi first met in 1907, when he was severely beaten by a group of Pathans for registering himself despite his earlier calls not to do so. Doke took him to his home and ensured he got all the requisite medical care during the ten days he stayed in his home. A close friendship developed between them. Whenever Gandhi was imprisoned or traveled abroad Doke edited his 'Indian Opinion'. In his biography of Gandhi he wrote "*Our Indian friend lives on a higher plane than most men do. ....Those who do not know him think there is some unworthy motive behind...to account for such profound unworldliness. But those who know him well are ashamed of themselves in his presence....He is one of those outstanding characters with whom to walk is a liberal education, to whom to know is to love.*"

Hermann Kallenbach, an extremely wealthy German Jewish architect of Johannesberg, was the one who donated the land (1,100 aces), on which Gandhi set up Tolstoy Farm in 1910 to house families of imprisoned satyagrahis and engage in community farming. It was a mutual interest in Buddhism which first brought him and Gandhi together. But subsequently Kallenbach gave up his beautiful hilltop house with a commanding view of Johannesberg and came to live with Gandhi at Tolstoy farm. Giving up the luxurious live he had been used to, he heroically accepted every deprivation, chore and dietary restriction on the farm as also incarcerations in Transvaal prisons with Gandhi. Fischer writes "*If anybody can be called Gandhi's second in command of the Sarvodaya movement (in South Africa) it was Kallenbach.*" In 1914, when Gandhi sailed for England enroute to India Kallenbach accompanied him. Unfortunately WWI broke out soon thereafter

Gandhi in London with Rev Charles Andrews (extreme left), Madeleine Slade (second from right) and others

and Kallenbach was interned in England for the duration of the war. After the war he returned to Johannesberg and stayed in regular touch with Gandhi. He also made two visits to India to spend time with him. Gandhi described him as "*a man of strong feelings, wide sympathies and child like simplicity.*"

Charles Freer Andrews, ("*Charlie*" to Gandhi), son of an ardent imperialist Tory for whose children "*Deeds that won the Empire*" was compulsory reading, joined the priesthood and in early 1904 arrived in India to teach at St. Stephen's College, New Delhi. From its vice principal Sushil Kumar Rudra he learnt of India's national struggle and quite unlike other British clergy for whom "*faith in God ran parallel to faith in the Raj*" acquired much sympathy for India and Indians.

Among Charlie's early Indian friends were Tagore and Gokhale. In 1913 Gokhale requested him to go to South Africa to assist Gandhi. He landed in Durban on January 1st 1914. On meeting Gandhi he respectfully touched his feet. This shocked South African whites. A Durban newspaper editor fumed this was "*unfortunate, most unfortunate*". However, this did not deter Charlie, whose respect for Gandhi, having witnessed his heroic efforts there, grew enormously and blossomed into a life long friendship. In South Africa he saw for the first time the most virulent form of racialism and was outraged by it. He described Gandhi as a "*moral genius*" and a "*commanding spiritual personality*". Satyagraha he extolled as "*corporate moral resistance*".

Charlie accompanied Gandhi to London in 1931 and arranged meetings for him with leading British intellectuals. This provided Gandhi excellent opportunity to convince them that he was not a "*humbug*" and "*an impossible fanatic*". These meetings also helped redeem Charlie's reputation as "*God's own fool*". Earlier than any other Englishman he perceived that India was astir and needed to be treated with dignity and justice. About him Gandhi wrote " *I have not known a better man or a better Christian.*"

Madeleine Slade, daughter of a British Admiral, first heard of Gandhi from Romain Rolland who referred to him as "*another Christ* ". Thereafter she read his book on Gandhi and felt impelled to go to India and work with him. Her parents, who moved in London's top social circles, were greatly embarrassed that their daughter had "*joined the entourage of the arch - rebel of the British Empire*".

On her arrival at Gandhi's Ashram in November 1925, he told her "*You shall be my daughter*". He named her "*Mira behn*". She was only 23 years old then and stayed with him always thereafter except during his jail terms. Sometimes she too was imprisoned. She accompanied him to London in 1931 and three years later undertook a visit to USA to promote India's cause there. She subsequently functioned as Gandhi's emissary to the Viceroy and other senior officials and resided in India for 11 years after Gandhi's assassination. After her final return to England she wrote an autobiography titled '*The Spirit's pilgrimage*'. It was a moving yet objective tribute to Gandhi.

Charlie Chaplin called on Gandhi when he was in London for the 1931 Round Table Conference. Time Magazine (October 5th, 1931) reported this meeting thus: "*Mahatma Gandhi even talked to Charlie Chaplin—at the cinemactor's request. When told by his Indian friend Mrs. Sarojini Naidu "the famous Mr. Chaplin wants to see you," Gandhi seemed puzzled and asked: "What is he famous for? Who is this Mr. Chaplin?" The famed Cinemactor had been stopping the week-end with pugnacious Winston Churchill, M.P., public foe of Indian Independence. Mr. Churchill has called Mr. Gandhi "a half-naked, seditious fakir!". Mr. Chaplin, possibly primed by Mr. Churchill, fired the following question at Mr. Gandhi soon after he was introduced : "Why do you champion such a crude device as the hand spinning* *wheel? Inventions are the inheritance of mankind and should be allowed to relieve the burdens of mankind. I am diametrically opposed to the abolition of machinery!" Spinner Gandhi answered "The hand wheel and the hand loom are necessary to provide occupation for India's millions. Modern machinery installed in India would leave our people too much leisure. Also we would produce more than we need and thus enforce idleness upon some other part of the world as a result of our overproduction." Abruptly St. Gandhi jerked out his dollar watch, announced that it was 7 p.m. — time to pray. Mr. Chaplin was moved to kneel and he scarcely wobbled during the long Hindu prayer. Departing after some further talk with the Mahatma, he gasped to reporters: "Gandhi is a tremendous personality, tremendous! He is a great international figure! More, he is A GREAT DRAMATIC FIGURE !"*

Lanza del Vasto, poet, artist, and nonviolent activist, was of aristocratic birth. He learnt of Gandhi through Romain Rolland's biography and went to India in December 1936 to meet and work with him. Gandhi named him Shantidas, "*Servant of Peace.*" After spending six months with Gandhi he visited holy places on the Ganges, as also Jerusalem and Bethlehem, before returning to Paris. In 1943 he wrote a book titled '*Return to the Source*'. Subsequently he wrote '*Warriors of Peace: Writings on the Technique of Nonviolence*' and '*Make Straight the Way of the Lord: An Anthology of the Philosophical Writings*'

In 1948 he founded '*Community of the Ark*' (COA) in an effort to establish a '*Gandhian Order in the West*'. The first community, set up in a small rented farm in southwest France, was unsuccessful as many who came to it were unable to adjust to community life.

In 1954, Lanza went back to India to participate in Vinoba Bhave's "*Bhoodan*" (Land Gift) movement and learn more about nonviolent social change. On his return, he re-established the CAO at Haut-Languedoc, a deserted village, near Lodève in the Borie Noble. This time, anyone wanting to become a full member—a "*Companion*"—had to undergo a three-year trial period and be approved unanimously by other Companions. By 1979, this Community had spread to three neighbouring villages and among its "*companions*" and "*visitor residents*" were nationals of most west European countries. Also, whereas initially they were mainly intellectuals and aristocrats, they were now from diverse backgrounds and small Communities had sprung up in some Latin American countries, and Quebec in Canada.

The "*Companions*" live by the principle of "*bread labor,*" (which Gandhi, Ruskin and Tolstoy had urged) and see it as the key to a "*nonviolent economy*" which exploits neither people nor nature. They use simple tools as these can be produced locally and generate employment. They produce handspun wool for garments, and promote carpentry, stonecutting, blacksmithy, pottery, and printing. Each object produced is artistically decorated so as to give creative satisfaction to the worker. Only Candles are used for indoor lighting, and vegetables are stored in cellars without refrigeration. Echoing Gandhi, Lanza declared "*We are accused of going against the times. We are doing that deliberately and with all our strength........The machine enslaves, the hand sets free.*"

Next to bread labour, the *Companions* place highest importance on spiritual life as peace can only be achieved when individuals gain inner peace. The adherents of all religions are welcome. Recordings of CAO music have twice won international awards.

The *Companions* in France also launched a series of Gandhi style nonviolent campaigns the most notable of which were the first-ever occupation of a nuclear power facility and a successful campaign to block expansion of an army base on the nearby Larzac plateau. These campaigns became models for later European nuclear disarmament campaigns which in turn inspired America's anti-nuclear struggle at Seabrook, New Hampshire.

Danilo Dolci, sociologist, social activist and poet achieved fame with his successful non violent struggle against the Mafia in Sicily and came to be known as the "*Gandhi of Sicily*". His life as a social activist began in 1952 when he decided to head for "*the poorest place I had ever known*" — the squalid fishing village of Trappeto about 30 km west of Palermo in Sicily. A village without electricity, running water or sewers and impoverished, illiterate, unemployed people ignored both by State and Church. Dolci began by setting up an orphanage for the five orphans he adopted. Later he organized landless peasants into co-operatives and went on hunger strikes to force the local and national authorities to pay attention to this poverty stricken area. In November 1955 he fasted for a week in Partinico to promote the building of a dam over the Iato River that could provide irrigation for the entire valley.

Dolci soon became aware of the Mafia's stranglehold on this region. He therefore launched a crusade to expose its support for the region's politicians and appeared before the Antimafia Commission in Rome to give proof of this. In 1967, he publicly accused three powerful Christian Democrat leaders of Mafia links. He was jailed for libel. Dolci hit back by setting up a private radio station and broadcasting these allegations His determination and courage to confront the Mafia and those linked with it, made him known and admired all over Italy.

Dolci's many books focussed on the poor, neglected people of Sicily and voiced their deep frustrations and anger. If the world now knows about the dark, secretive, ruthless world of the Sicilian Mafia, it is largely due to him. He had studied architecture in his youth but his renown came as an architect of social change.

Samuel Evans Stokes alias Satyanand Stokes (16 August 1882 - 14 May 1946) was the son of a well to do Philadelphia businessman who had pioneered elevators in America. At age twenty-two he came to India (in 1904) to work at a leper colony at Subathu, in the Simla Hills run by Dr Marcus Carleton. He did this against his parents wishes. He had not completed his education, nor acquired any professional skill. He even rejected the opportunity to work at the *Stokes and Parish Machine Company* set up by his father.

In India, in order to bridge the gulf between himself and the people, he attempted giving up everything he possessed to live a life of poverty and renunciation. A deeply religious Quaker he became like a Christian sanyasi. In 1912, he married a local Christian woman named Agnes. Subsequently (in 1932) he converted to Hinduism assumed the name "*Satyanand*". His wife changed her name to "*Priya Devi*".

To ameliorate the condition of the local people he started a school and campaigned for the end of '*begar*' - a system wherein the illiterate locals were forced to work under unfair and inhuman conditions - and succeeded in getting the authorities to abolish it. When Gandhi learnt about it, he wrote in 'Young India: *"No Indian is giving such battle to the government as Mr Stokes. He has veritably become the guide, philosopher and friend of the hill men."*

In 1916, he introduced the *American Delicious* variety of apple, a new strain developed by the Stark brothers of Louisiana, USA, in the Simla Hills and distributed its seeds to local farmers. Apple orchards soon sprang up all over that and neighbouring areas and transformed them economically.

The Jallianwala Bagh massacre shocked and revulsed him and he became a strong supporter of the Indian national movement. He wrote a booklet titled '*Awakening India* ' for which Gandhi wrote the Foreword.

In his 1921 booklet titled '*National Self-Realisation* ', he wrote: *"Our immediate object is to make the government of this land representative of the will of the people. Ultimately, complete Swaraj is the only goal for India."*

Later the same year he wrote to Gandhi : *"I have become more and more convinced that the movement which you have initiated calls us to the deepest and noblest in our nature. It is that old call to victory by the path of utter self-renunciation, to purification by the path of self-sacrifice."*

He was the only non-Indian to sign the Congress manifesto in 1921 which inter-alia called upon Indians to quit government service., Soon thereafter, when on his way to attend a Punjab Provincial Congress Committee meeting, he was arrested on a charge of sedition and sentenced to six months imprisonment. He spent this period in Lahore jail, which made him the unique American who even suffered imprisonment for India's freedom. About his imprisonment the Mahatma wrote: *"That he should feel like an Indian, share his sorrows and throw himself into the struggle, has proved too much for the government. To leave him free to criticize it was intolerable; his white skin has proved no protection for him..."*

Stokes was also the only American to become an All India Congress Committee (AICC) member. Along with Lala Lajpat Rai, he represented Punjab. He continued his dedicated crusade for India's freedom right upto his death in May 1946, just fifteen months before India achieved independence.

His grand-daughter Asha Sharma has written an engrossing biography of him, which has been published in India as '*An American in Khadi* 'and in the US as '*An American in Gandhi's India*'. His Holiness the Dalai Lama has written the Foreword to the latter.

Laurence ("Laurie") Wilfred Baker, an award-winning British architect, joined the Quakers at an early age and was sent to China in 1937 to work with the Friends Ambulance Unit there. After four years, on his way back to England, he had an unexpected three month stay in Bombay because of the delayed arrival of his ship. His Quaker friends took him to meet Gandhi. In his autobiography he wrote " *I had the thrill, and the blessing, of talking with Gandhiji about the lives of people in India and China and explaining to him how my Chinese cloth shoes were made and then to have 'Quit India' shouted after me as I returned through the streets to the house where I was staying..... I talked with him about my urge to return to work in India even though the British were being called upon to quit. He encouraged me to return to India."*

Laurie Baker returned in 1945 and initially worked for sixteen years at Pithorgarh in Uttarakhand, building leprosy hospitals. Thereafter he moved to Peerumed to work with Kerala tribals, and in 1970 to Trivandrum, the state capital. In 1984, he set up there the Centre of Science and Technology for Rural Development (COSTFORD) for promoting low cost housing. He died on April 1, 2007 at age 90.

It was at Pithorgarh that he first observed the methods and practices of indigenous architecture which used mud walls, cow dung, laterite, bamboo etc and concluded that these materials had distinct merits of their own and generally better suited for Indian conditions. The characteristic architectural style that came to be associated with his name always retained a site's natural character and integrated it seamlessly into cost-effective, energy-efficient, uniquely space utilized, simple yet beautiful buildings. His style has been lauded both as "*sustainable*" and "*organic*" architecture. He himself has been hailed as "the conscience keeper of Indian architecture".. Unfortunately Gandhi did not live to see any of his buildings, which would undoubtedly have gladdened him.

Laurie Baker averred "*I believe that Gandhiji is the only leader who has talked consistently with common-sense about the building needs of our*

(Left) Centre for Development Studies. Thiruvananthapuram. One of Laurie Baker's first buildings.
(Right) The Indian Coffee House in Thiruvanthapuram

country. One of the things he said that has influenced my thinking more than anything else was that the ideal house in the ideal village will be built with materials which are all found within a five-mile radius of it. What clearer explanation is there of what appropriate building technology means. I confess that as a young architect, born, brought up, educated and qualified in the West, I thought at first Gandhiji' ideal was a bit 'far-fetched' .... But now, in my seventies and with forty years of building behind me, I have come to the conclusion that he was right, literally, word for word. If only I had not been so proud and sure of my learning and my training as an architect, I could have seen wonderful examples of Gandhiji's wisdom all round me throughout the entire period I lived in Pithoragarh district."

Ahangamage Tudor Ariyaratne, who founded the Sarvodaya Shramadana Movement (SSM) in Sri Lanka in 1958, is deeply imbued with Buddha's teachings as also those of Gandhi and Vinobha Bhave. His SSM contains three strands: "*Gandhian ideals, Buddhist philosophy, and ecumenical spirituality.*" He has stated "*We in Sarvodaya follow Gandhiji's integrated approach to development, peace and education. They are all interconnected - Satyagraha, Swadeshi, Aparigraha or non-possession, trusteeship, non-exploitation, appropriate use of machinery, and basic education. So are Lord Buddha's teachings of Dependent Arising, the Four Noble Truths and the Noble Eight Fold Path*". He has successfully combined Gandhi's secular principles of political, economic and social development with the Buddhist ideals of selflessness and compassion and redefined '*Sarvodaya*' (the welfare of all) as "*the Awakening of All - from an individual Human Personality to Humanity as a whole*". He affirms "*This awakening has spiritual, moral, cultural, social, economic and political dimensions. Whatever we do in one of these sectors influences all other sectors.*"

His movement, like Gandhi's, places the village at the center of social change as "*The village represents the heart of the nation and the source of its spiritual and moral vision.*" His call has been for a non-violent spiritual revolution to transform the social order, replace structural violence within it, and create a no poverty, no affluence society. He has stated "*When we work towards the welfare of all, the means we use have to be based on Truth, Non-violence and Selflessness in conformity with Awakening of All.*"

The SSM effort begins with a discussion in a village as to what its needs are and how they can be met. It then proceeds to set up a village council, build a school and health clinic, create employment so that the village economy becomes self-sustaining. In addition, it organizes public meditations in which adherents of all faiths in that and neighbouring villages meditate together and become united in a common spirituality. Ariyaratne has personally led hundreds of these meditations, throughout Sri Lanka. On 29th August 1999 nearly 200,000 people, all dressed in white, came to the three hour meditation he held at the Vihara Maha Devi Park in Central Colombo. He has regularly urged Buddhist monks to be active in village life and the laity to reject consumerism and lead simple lives. He emphasizes dedicating oneself to the service of others as "*I cannot awaken myself unless I help awaken others.*"

SSM is now serving in 15,000 of Sri Lanka's 38,000 villages, reaching four million of Sri Lanka's twenty million people. Four thousand villages are registered as legally independent Sarvodaya Shramadana Societies and are participating in programs of the Sarvodaya Economic Enterprise Services (SEEDS) division. There are 5,000 pre-schools with 8,000 pre-school teachers. A Shanthi Sena (Peace Brigade) with members aged 15 to 30, numbers over 100,000 volunteers in 9,000 units. Sarvodaya has 34 district centers, including eight in Tamil areas of the northern and eastern provinces, and 345 divisional units. There are 12 development education institutes. A full-time staff of 600 supports the work of 19 units devoted to the achievement of six empowerment goals: spiritual, social, economic, technological, and legal. SSM's relief and welfare work in the aftermath of the 2004 Tsunami has been widely acknowledged as substantial.

Among the many awards Ariyaratne has received are the Ramon Magsaysay Award for Community Leadership in 1969, the Niwano Peace Prize in 1992 and the Gandhi Peace Prize in 1996 and Sri Lankabhimanya, the highest National Honour of Sri Lanka in 2007.

INDIAN

Abul Kalam Muhiyuddin Ahmed, generally known as **Maulana Azad** (as he was a renowned Islamic scholar and *Azad* was his pen name), first came to notice as a journalist boldly attacking the "*Raj*" in his *Al-Hilal* journal, published from Calcutta. When this was banned in 1914 he started *Al-Balag*, which also was banned some years later. During this period he was closely associated with Aurobindo, S.S.Chakravarthy and other militant nationalists. Subsequently,he got deeply involved in the Khilafat Movement and met Mahatma Gandhi. This transformed him and he became an ardent supporter of non violent resistance and joined the Congress Party. He began to spin, and make his own clothes. He urged fellow Muslims to join the national struggle. Since Gandhi shared his deep interest in Islam a close friendship developed between them.

In 1920, he along with Dr. Mukhtar Ahmad Ansari, and Hakim Ajmal Khan founded the Jamia Millia Islamia, initially at Aligarh but subsequently moved to Delhi, as an Islamic nationalist institution of higher learning. Gandhi blessed the effort and undertook fund raising for it.

In 1923 Maulana Azad was elected President of the Congress Party, the youngest person to occupy that post.

When Gandhi embarked on the Salt March to Dandi in 1930, Azad organized and led the subsequent satyagraha at the Dharasana salt works. He was imprisoned along with hundreds of others but released soon after the Gandhi-Irwin Pact was signed . When the 1937 elections were held he did not contest but undertook to fund raise, recruit volunteers and organize election rallies across India. He firmly resisted Jinnah's claim that he was the sole representative of Indian Muslims and deplored his vituperation of Congress rule as "*Hindu Raj*," and its resignation from provincial governments in 1939 as a "*Day of Deliverance*" for Muslims.

Azad was elected Congress President at its 1940 Ramgarh session. In his presidential address he lambasted religious separatism in the following memorable words, "*Islam has now as great a claim on the soil of India as Hinduism. If Hinduism has been the religion of the people here for several thousands of years Islam also has been their religion for a thousand years. Just as a Hindu can say with pride that he is an Indian and follows Hinduism, so also we can say with equal pride that we are Indians and follow Islam. I shall enlarge this orbit still further. The Indian Christian is equally entitled to say with pride that he is an Indian and is following a religion of India, namely Christianity.*" Subsequently when Jinnah taunted him as a Congress "*Showboy*" his rejoinder was "*I am proud of being an Indian. I am part of the indivisible unity that is Indian nationality. I am indispensable to this noble edifice and without me this splendid structure is incomplete. I am an essential element, which has gone to build India. I can never surrender this claim.*"

Following the 1942 '*Quit India*' movement Azad along with all other Congress leaders was imprisoned. On their release, when he learnt of Gandhi's talks with Jinnah, in a rare instance of public disagreement with the Mahatma, he criticized the move as "*ill-advised*". He foresaw that these talks would heighten Jinnah's stature, strengthen his claim to be sole representative of the Muslims, and his obduracy. His great respect and friendship for Gandhi however remained undiminished. On January 18, 1948, when Gandhi decided to break his fast, it was from his hands that he accepted a glass of orange juice.

On the issue of partition, Azad like Gandhi and unlike Nehru and Patel after 1946, steadfastly opposed it. He affirmed "*It seems that the scheme of Pakistan is a symbol of defeatism and has been built up on the analogy of the Jewish demand for a national home. It is a confession that Indian Muslims cannot hold their own in India as a whole and would be content to withdraw to a corner specially reserved for them.... As a Muslim, I for one am not prepared for a moment to give up my right to treat the whole of India as my domain and share in the shaping of its political and economic life. To me it seems a sure sign of cowardice to give up what is my patrimony and content myself with a mere fragment of it."*

After Independence he served as Minister of Education and laid the foundations for India's primary, secondary and higher education and scientific research. His other seminal contribution was setting up the Indian Council for Cultural Relations which today has a global presence with over 40 Indian Cultural Centres in Asian, African, Caribbean and some western countries.

Vinoba Bhave, the disciple who was most like Gandhi, first met him in 1916 and joined his Sabarmati Ashram a year later on completion of his Sanskrit studies. Before meeting Gandhi he was mentally debating whether to become a religious hermit or join the militant nationalists in their fight against the British. On joining Gandhi's Ashram he declared he had found there "*the peace of the Himalayas united with the revolutionary fervor of Bengal*". He worked closely with Gandhi right up to the latter's assassination in January 1948.

After Gandhi's death he decided that since India had achieved its goal of *Swaraj* its new goal should be *Sarvodaya,* the "*welfare of all.*" Since Gandhi had urged poverty eradication, rural development, Harijan welfare and non violent social change he decided in 1951 to embark on this effort and chose the Telengana district of Andhra Pradesh for doing so. He could not have picked a more difficult spot. This district was in the throes of a Communist organized rural insurgency that was determined to break the stranglehold of the landlords by driving them out or killing them, and distributing their land to the landless. It controlled large tracts of this district and the Indian army had been sent to confront them. Each side was killing villagers they suspected of supporting the other side. Vinoba wished to end this violence and find a solution to the root causes of this conflict. So, refusing police escort, he and a small group of supporters set off on foot. On the third day, he stopped at the village of **Pochampalli**, a Communist stronghold, and set himself up in the courtyard of a Muslim mosque. People from all sections of the village came to see him. Among them were 40 landless Harijan families. They confessed their support for the Communists, because only they would give them land. They asked whether he could persuade the government to do so. He replied, "*What use is government help until we can help ourselves?*" Late that afternoon, after his prayer meeting which drew very many people from that and neighbouring villages he asked "*Brothers, is there anyone among you who can help these Harijan friends?*" A prominent landowner stood up and said. "*I am ready to give one hundred acres.*" It seemed like a miracle. Equally astounding was the Harijan response. They needed only 80 acres and would accept no more! Vinoba saw God's hand in all this and announced he would walk through the entire region to collect other such gifts for the landless. This was the genesis of the Bhoodan movement. He went from village to village telling the landlords "*I am your fifth son. Give me my share of land*". In almost every case they obliged. Why? Partly because to them Vinoba was a saint, the Mahatma's reincarnation and obliging him would earn them spiritual benefit. But partly, also out of fear of being killed or dispossessed by the Communists unless they obliged. As a result, 12, 201 acres were collected in the first in 51 days. By 1958 over 3 million acres had been collected in various parts of the country. It was an impressive achievement,

Vinoba had hoped that through his Bhoodan movement he could bring about a radical nonviolent transformation of Indian society. For him the root cause of poverty and oppression was possessiveness and greed. If people could be persuaded to overcome these traits, social inequalities and exploitation would be eliminated. As he put it, "*All revolutions are spiritual at the source. All my activities have the sole purpose of achieving a union of hearts. ....We do not aim at doing mere acts of kindness, but at creating a Kingdom of Kindness.* " His usual greeting was "*Jai jagat! (Victory to the world)*". His world view, like Gandhi's encompassed all of creation.

Though the Bhoodan movement can only be termed a limited success as much of the donated land turned out to be unproductive, it had the indirect benefit of inspiring *Sampattidan, Buddhidan* and *Shramdan*, (donation of wealth, knowledge and labour respectively) which many public spirited people, professional groups and NRIs have adopted ever since.

Dr. M.C. Modi, is the best example of Buddhidan. Having heard a speech by Gandhi in 1942 at Beelagi near Bijapur his home town, he decided to dedicate his life to provide free eye care to the poor. By the time he died at age 90 in November 2005 he had conducted 595,019 eye operations. In the process he visited 46,120 villages and examined 12,118,630 patients, One day in 1976 he performed 833 cataract operations and entered the Guinness Book of Records, which lists him as the "*most dedicated doctor*" for performing the highest number of eye surgeries. He was honoured with India's Padma Sri and Padma Bhushan Awards in 1956 and 1968 respectively.

Dr. Bindeshwar Pathak, a Brahmin engineer, was inspired on Gandhi's birth centenary in 1969 to dedicate himself to the emancipation of India's scavengers. He designed a simple (sulabh) "*gravity toilet*" connected to a septic pit and since 1972 has set up innumerable Sulabh Souchalayas all over India thus emancipating almost 50,000 scavenger families from their despised traditional occupation. In this process he has also brought much relief to millions of slum dwellers and homeless people without access to toilets and bathrooms. He has won many national and international awards for his work including the Padma Bhushan in 1991, St. Francis of Assissi Award in 1992 and Stockholm Water Prize in August 2009. His widely reported achievement was getting 10 former scavenger women walk a designer ramp at the UN in New York in July 2008. This special event was named, '*Mission Sanitation- Cultural Saga for a Cause*'. These women sashayed down the ramp with well known models wearing their creations. Speaking on the occasion one of them named Lakshmi Nanda stated "*It was thrilling. We walked along with famous models who were wearing saris, lehengas and gowns - all of which were what we had created with the help of designer Abdul Haldar*" adding "*Initially people hesitated to buy our things, but slowly things have started changing. Now not only do people buy our things, but also invite us to their homes. Our children go to school with the other kids... it's a life we have all long yearned for.*"

S.K. George is the most notable among Gandhi's Indian Christian disciples. As a youth he had joined Bishop's College Calcutta to study theology and become a pastor of the Anglican Church. However, he was "*gripped*" by the message of Gandhi and boldly declared "*Gandhi today is giving a practical demonstration of the applicability of the teachings of Jesus the Master, to modern problems. That was a sorely needed demonstration. The Christian Church despite all its adoration of Jesus, its exaltation of him to the throne of Divinity, has all along relegated his teachings as impracticable idealism.*" He called upon his fellow Indian Christians to join the national struggle. The head of the Anglican Church in India, Metropolitan Foss Westcott pressured him to recant these statements. On his refusal to do so he was expelled from Bishop's College and ostracized in Anglican & British social circles. He therefore sent his family to Kerala, and left for Gandhi's Sabarmathi Ashram, where he stayed for many months. His daughter's death constrained him to return to Kerala. Between 1947-50 he was Professor of English and subsequently Adhyaksha at Vishwabharati, Shantiniketan and from 1954 - 56 a member of the Christian Missionaries Activity Enquiry Committee headed by Dr. M.B. Niyogi. He died in May 1960.

In his 1939 book titled '*Gandhi's Challenge to Christianity*' he wrote "*I do not claim to be a great anything but I do claim to be a Gandhian and a Christian. That combination is to me vital and significant for the world today and specially so for India. The conviction came to me as a young man in the beginning of the Gandhian era in Indian politics, a conviction that has only deepened by the passage of years and a greater understanding of the message of both Jesus and Mahatma Gandhi, that a true Christian in India today must necessarily be Gandhian.*" For him Satyagraha was "*The Cross in Action*". He affirmed "*It is not sufficiently realized that Western Christianity is the result of a marriage between Hebraism, the Semetic heritage and Graeco-Roman culture. A real welding of Indian spirituality and Hebraic ethics might result in a Christianity that might enrich the whole world. An Indian Christianity that is really Indian and truly Christian, might give a lead to world Christianity.*"

Three decades later, Pope John Paul II echoed these ideas. In his book "*Crossing the Threshold of Hope*" he wrote : "*In Hinduism men explore the Divine mystery and express it through an endless bounty of myths and through penetrating philosophical insight. They seek freedom from the anguish of our human condition either by way of the ascetic life, profound meditation or by taking refuge in God with love and trust……Mahatma Gandhi, Hindu and Indian….was disillusioned with the ways in which Christianity was expressed in the political and social life of nations. Could a man who fought for the liberation of his great nation from colonialism accept Christianity in the form in which it had been imposed on his country by the same colonial power. The Second Vatican realized this difficulty and that is why the document on the relations between the Church and Hinduism and other relations of the Far East is so important."*

Sushil Kumar Rudra, Principal of St. Stephen's College, New Delhi was another strong, though quiet, Indian Christian supporter of Gandhi. His great contribution is best revealed in Gandhi's eulogy on his demise in January 1923. *"I would ask my reader to share my grief over the death of an esteemed friend and silent public servant, Principal Sushil Kumar Rudra. He was a first class educationist. As principal he made himself universally popular. There was a kind of spiritual bond between him and his pupils. Though he was a Christian, he had room in his bosom for Hinduism and Islam, for both of which he had high veneration. His was not an exclusive Christianity that condemned to perdition everyone who did not believe in Jesus Christ as the only saviour of the world. Jealous of the reputation of his own, he was tolerant of other faiths….Ever since my return home in 1915 I had been his guest whenever I had occasion to go to New Delhi…. The reader might not be aware that my open letter to the Viceroy giving concrete shape to the Khilafat claim was conceived and drafted under Principal Rudra's roof. He and Charlie Andrews were my revisonists. Non- Cooperation was conceived and hatched under his hospitable roof. He was a silent but deeply interested spectator at the private conference that took place between the Ali brothers, other Muslim friends and myself. He exemplified in his life the truth that religious perception gives one a correct sense of proportion, resulting in a beautiful harmony between action and belief."*

d). National Liberation, Anti-Racism and Anti-Dictatorship "Peoples Power" Movements.

USA.

Dr. William E.B.Dubois was the first African American to be won over by Gandhian Satyagraha. He appears to have initially learnt about it from John Haynes Holmes, his colleague in the National Association for the Advancement of Coloured people. In 1929, he wrote to Gandhi requesting a message to American Negroes. Gandhi obliged with "*Let not the 12 million Negroes be ashamed of the fact that they are the grandchildren of slaves. There is dishonour in being slave-owners. But let us not think of honour or dishonour in connection with the past. Let us realize that the future is with those who would be pure, truthful and loving. For as the old wise men have said: Truth ever is, untruth never was. Love alone binds and truth and love accrue only to the truly humble.*"

In his essay on '*Gandhi and the American Negroes*' written in 1956 Du Bois stated "*In Montgomery, Alabama, the former capital of the Confederate States which fought for years to make America a slave nation, the black workers last year refused any longer to use the public buses on which their seats had long been segregated from those of the white passengers, paying the same fare. .... The black workers led by young, educated ministers began a strike which stopped the discrimination, aroused the state and the nation and presented an unbending front of non-violence to the murderous mob which hitherto has ruled the South..... The American Negro is not yet free. He is still discriminated against, oppressed and exploited. The recent court decisions in his favour are excellent but are as yet only partially enforced. It may well be that the enforcement of these laws and real human equality and brotherhood in the United States will come only under the leadership of another Gandhi*".

The tragic past history of the American Negroes, and the Gandhi inspired liberation strategy **Martin Luther King** devised for them is best described in his own words. : "*For more than three centuries American Negroes have been battered by the iron rod of oppression, frustrated by day and bewildered by night by unbearable injustice. Forced to live with these shameful conditions, we are tempted to become bitter and to retaliate with a corresponding hate. But if this happens, the new order we seek will be little more than a duplicate of the old order. We must in strength and humility seek it with love. While abhorring segregation we shall love the segregationist.*

To our most bitter opponents we say "We shall match your capacity to inflict suffering by our capacity to endure suffering. We shall meet your physical force with soul force. Do to us what you will but we will continue to love you. We cannot in good conscience obey your unjust laws because non-cooperation with evil is as much a moral obligation as is cooperation with good... One day we shall win freedom, but not only for ourselves. We shall so appeal to your heart and conscience that we shall win you in the process and our victory will be a double victory".

Martin Luther King was won over to Gandhian Satyagraha after hearing Dr Mordecai Johnson speak about it at Fellowship House in Philadelphia. The latter, first African American president of Howard University in Washington D.C., was a great admirer of Gandhi and had visited India in 1950. King, then a student at Crozer, found this talk *"so profound and electrifying that I left the meeting and bought a half-dozen books on*

Rev Martin Luther King and Coretta King with Jawaharlal Nehru

Gandhi's life and works" In 1959, he visited India to personally learn from Gandhi's disciples how nonviolent resistance was planned and carried out. On his return, he wrote *"I left India more convinced than ever before that non-violent resistance is the most potent weapon available to oppressed people in their struggle for justice and human dignity. In a real sense, Mahatma Gandhi embodied in his life certain universal principles that are inherent in the moral structure of the universe and these principles are as inescapable as the law of gravitation".*

It was in the Montgomery bus boycott, which had been launched soon after Rosa Park's arrest, trial and imprisonment for refusing to vacate her seat for a white man on a bus, that King first tried 'satyagraha' in his struggle for racial equality. Using it consistently thereafter, he brought about more beneficial change for American blacks in eight years of non-violent struggle, than had come to them in the hundred years after the Civil War. The way non-violent struggle transformed his fellow blacks King described thus. "*When legal contests were the sole form of activity, the ordinary negro was involved as a passive spectator. His interest was stirred, but his energies were unemployed. Mass marches transformed the common man into the star performer he became. The Negro was no longer a subject of change; he was the active organ of change. The dignity his job denied him, he obtained in political and social action*".

For King : "*Mahatma Gandhi was the first person in human history to lift the ethic of love of Jesus Christ, above mere interaction between individuals and make it into a powerful and effective social force on a large scale If humanity is to progress, Gandhi is inescapable. We may ignore him at our own peril*". When an American churchman criticized him for this, he replied "It is ironic yet inescapably true that the greatest Christian of the modern world was a man who never embraced Christianity".

Next to Martin Luther King Jr., **Cesar Chavez** stands tallest as a nonviolent leader in the U.S. He was introduced to Gandhi by Fr. Donald Macdonald in San Jose, California. In the United Farm Workers movement he founded and led for more than thirty years, he applied Gandhian principles to the farm fields of America. He successfully combined Satyagraha, Catholic social teaching, and Fred Ross's and Saul Alinsky's organizational methods to devise a unique strategy that was part labor, part religious, and part social

When he launched *La Causa* in 1962, farm workers were paid just a dollar an hour. Mexican and Filipino farm worker families had miserable lives of backbreaking labor, job insecurity, abusive labor contractors and constant transfer from one work camp to another. They had no right to organize, no health insurance, no pensions or paid vacations. Many did not even have access to toilets or fresh drinking water. Educational opportunities were bleak. Many children, including Cesar (who went through 38 different schools), did not finish high school.

The United Farm Workers movement, by well planned use of fasts, strikes, picketing and boycotts won important victories. Wages increased and for the first time migrant workers gained medical insurance, pension benefits and the right to bargain collectively. The credit for all this goes to Chavez's nonviolent strategy. Robert Kennedy, who broke bread with him when he ended his widely reported 1968 fast, lauded him as, "*one of the heroic figures of our time.*"

South Africa

Gandhi's great contribution to South Africa is best encapsulated in **Nelson Mandela's** tribute to him on his 125th birth anniversary : "*Gandhi threatened the South African Government during the first and second decades of our century as no other man did. He established the first anti-colonial political organization in the country, if not in the world, founding the Natal Indian Congress in 1894. The African People's organization (APO) was established in 1902, the African National Congress (ANC) in 1912. So both were witnesses to and highly influenced by Gandhi's militant Satyagraha which began in 1907 and reached its climax in 1913 with the epic march of 5000 indentured workers on the coal mines of Natal. So the Indian struggle, in a sense is rooted in the African..... Though separated in time there is a bond between us, in our shared prison experiences, our defiance of unjust laws and in the fact that violence threatens our aspirations for peace and reconciliation*". Separately he also wrote "*I followed the Gandhian strategy for as long as I could but then came a point in our struggle when the brute force of the oppressor could no longer be countered through passive resistance alone. We founded Umkhonto we Sizwe and added a military dimension to our struggle. Even then we chose sabotage because it did not involve loss of life and offered the best hope for future race relations*".

However, as Colonel Laurent Du Plessis, former Chief of Military Intelligence of South Africa's Eastern Cape province clearly states in the *'Force More Powerful'* film titled *'Freedom in our Life Time'*, the "*armed struggle came to nothing..... It was the people's mass action, the economic boycott and international pressure, that brought about the change. De Klerk had no option but to take the action he did*" About the economic boycotts he avers "*They were very effective. Not to buy is not a crime. What do you do with people who do not buy ? You cannot shoot all of them. It is passive resistance. Gandhi started it, if I am not mistaken*". The boycotts of white shops and businesses led many of them to closed down. Neither declarations of States of Emergency nor imprisonment of innumerable Black activists during this period (1986-1989) ended them. They only tarnished South Africa's international image, gestated international sanctions and resulted in many multinationals, including Coca Cola, pulling out of the country. Because of this crisis President P.W. Botha was forced to resign in 1989. F. W. De Klerk who succeeded him, promptly lifted the ban on Black political parties and freed Nelson Mandela. These two then negotiated a new constitution based on universal adult franchise, whereunder South Africa's first free elections were held in 1994. The African National Congress won an overwhelming victory and Nelson Mandela became President. Far from showing any rancour for his 27 years of harsh imprisonment he announced that South Africans would now have to show that Whites, Blacks, Browns and Yellows could all live together in peace and harmony as "*Rainbow People*". Besides, he set up a Truth Commission to probe the brutalities of the Apartheid regime and provide an opportunity to victims and their tormentors to reconcile and establish new, amicable relationships.

From being Africa's pariah state, South Africa was suddenly transformed into its most admired nation. Nelson Mandela emerged as the new symbol of nobility and indomitable will for freedom. However, the heroes of the final "*mass action*" phase of the freedom struggle were Mkhuseli Jack, 27 year old, Port Elizabeth youth organizer and his collaborators Tango Lamani, Mike Xego & Janet Cherry, and Archbishop Desmond Tutu, who not only encouraged them but also ensured that their arduous struggle stayed non violent despite the unremitting brutalities of the Apartheid regime.

West Africa

In the preface to his autobiography, **Kwame Nkrumah** wrote "*After months of studying Gandhi's policy and watching the effect that it had, I began to see that, when backed by a strong political organization it could be the solution to the colonial problem.*" Ghana having secured its independence in 1957, the All African People's Conference was organized at Accra the following year. The provisional agenda prepared for it stated "*The main purpose of the All African People's Conference to be held at Accra, Ghana in December 1958 will be to formulate concrete plans and work out the Gandhian tactics and strategy of the African Non violent Revolution*". (This however was later deleted at the instance of the Egyptian delegation which argued that each country should decide for itself which strategy to adopt for its national liberation struggle.) Speaking at the 1960 Positive Action Conference for Peace and Security in Africa Nkrumah inter alia stated "*Postive action has already achieved remarkable success in the liberation struggle of our continent ..... If the direct action that was carried out by the* *international protest team were to be repeated on a mass scale, or simultaneously from various parts of Africa, the result could be as powerful and successful as Gandhi's historic Salt March. We salute Mahatma Gandhi, and we remember in tribute to him, that it was in South Africa that his method of non-violence and non-cooperation was first practiced in the struggle against the vicious race discrimination that still plagues that unhappy country".*

Patrice Lumumba, on the eve of his country Congo's independence, declared "*We have wrought our freedom by applying the principle of non violent action in our fight against colonialism. This we owe to Mahatma Gandhi.*"

In Nigeria, **Amino Kano**, a devout Muslim, according to his biographer Alan Feinstein, "*analysed Gandhi's success in lifting millions of Indians to a high level of dedication and endeavoured to adapt Gandhi's non violent techniques to Northern Nigeria*" and came to be called the "*Gandhi of Nigeria*".

East Africa

Jomo Kenyatta's biographer, Jeremy Murray Brown has written " *Kenyatta met the Indian Leader in November 1931 and Gandhi then inscribed Kenyatta's diary with the words 'Truth and non-violence can deliver any nation from bondage'. Kenyatta was to give much thought to reconciling that idea with African tradition*". Diwan Chaman Lal, who was his legal counsel, has revealed that when he visited Kenyatta in prison at Kapenguria, "*he took me into his barn-like cell and bending over his solitary suit-case searched in a corner for a little diary which he had treasured since 1931 because it contained an inscription in the hand-writing of Mahatma Gandhi" adding " A man who cherished Mahatma Gandhi's message of peace and non-violence even within the precincts of the gaol obviously cannot be accused of dictating a different course*".

About Gandhi's influence on **Julius Nyrere**, Russell Howe has written "*Greatly influenced by Asian leaders, and specially Gandhi, he sought to impose non-racialism on Tanganyika's revolution. This was a daring piece of wisdom*". Anil Nauriya sees Gandhi echoed in an important utterance of Nyrere : "*Fellow Africans, be on your guard. The enemy... has no argument against our cause. His only chance is to provoke violence so that he may use the gun. Do not give him that chance*".

North Africa & West Asia

When Gandhi undertook his '*fast unto death*' in September 1932, Nahas Pasha, Chairman of WAFD (Egyptian National Party) cabled him from Cairo on September 24 : "*Your resolve to sacrifice your own life, rather than tolerate any measure promoting disunion or caste prejudices amongst Indians has deeply stirred the heart of Egypt, which has, since the last decade, been linked with India by the holy bond of suffering for the same ideal of national self-expression and liberty..... In the name of Egypt and her people, I send you and the Indian people our brotherly love and heartfelt wishes for realization of ideals of truth, freedom and equality as embodied in the great example you are setting before the world.*"

Long considered a stable region under well entrenched authoritarian regimes three North African countries (Tunis, Egypt & Libya) and five West Asian ones (Yemen, Bahrain, Oman, Jordan and Syria) suddenly erupted with "*peoples power*" uprisings in early 2011. They were triggered on 17 December 2010, by Mohamed Bouazizi, a young, indigent, vegetable seller setting himself aflame on being humiliated and his cart overturned by an arrogant police woman. Soon thereafter long oppressed Tunisians came out nationwide in thousands, unarmed and fearless, demanding reforms and regime change. Unable to suppress or mollify this mass upsurge, President Zine El Abidine Ben Ali fled to Saudi Arabia on 14 January 2011 and submitted his resignation from there, thus ending his 23 years in power. This triggered similar uprisings and demands in all the other mentioned countries and in the following weeks led to the ousting of Egypt's "*pharonic*" president Hosni Mubarak on February 11, to Saudi Arabia sending a 1000 strong armoured contigent of its Peninsula Shield Force into Bahrain on March 13 to prevent its 200 year old Al Khalifa dynasty, from being overthrone and to Yemen's unyeilding President Ali Abdullah Saleh being badly injured in an RPG attack on his palace and flown to Saudi Arabia for "*Medical treatment*" on 4th June. The uprisings in Oman and Jordan have been brought under control through mollification but the ones in Libya and Syria, have transformed into brutal civil wars with NATO countries strongly supporting, the anti regime "*Rebels*" with ceaseless arial bombing in the former case and economic sanctions against its regime in the latter.

About the Egyptian revolution Niranjan Ramakrishnan in an article titled '*Gandhi on the Nile*' (Counter Currents, February 11, 2011) wrote "*The people of Egypt have just raised a political monument that will rank alongside their mightiest stone and mortar wonders of antiquity. They have shown the world a model exercise of peaceful, determined, and dignified people-power. Three hundred or more are said to have died in the struggle of the last eighteen days. All of them were protesters, not one a representative of the hated regime. They met assaults by horse and camel borne thugs with even more resolve, thousands more pouring into Tahrir Square in response. Instead of the suicide bombers for which the region has become renowned, this movement began with a single suicide. Instead of firebombing a building full of people, it began with a man (in Tunisia) setting fire to himself. Instead of clamouring for loaves and fishes, they stood firm on freedom, demanding nothing short of the dictator's exit. The people of Egypt have exploded something far bigger than an atom bomb — the myth that the Arab and Islamic worlds are unsuited for Satyagraha. The Egyptian people have enacted a revolution that would have made Gandhi proud. But their victory is all their own."*

In the New Yorker (The Inner Voice: Gandhi's real legacy, May 2, 2011) Pankaj Mishra quoted Jawaharlal Nehru's comment after the historic Salt March "*What the future will bring I know not, but . . . our prosaic existence has developed something of epic greatness in it.*" and wrote "*Many more people since then have known this exhilaration of effecting change through individual acts of courage and empathy. It is what young Egyptians and Tunisians feel today, and their Yemeni counterparts may experience tomorrow: the ever renewable power of coöperative action, which is a truer measure of Gandhi's legacy than his many failures.*"

Whereas all the mentioned uprisings (except in Yemen and Libya) are the determined and fearless handiwork of their own peoples Gene Sharpe the Gandhian scholar might indirectly have contributed to them. Sheryl Stolberg wrote (New York Times, February 16, 2011) "*When the International Center on Nonviolent Conflict, which trains democracy activists, conducted a workshop, in Cairo several years ago, among the papers it distributed was Mr. Sharp's "198 Methods of Nonviolent Action." Dalia Ziada, an Egyptian activist who attended this workshop said its trainees were active in both the Tunisia and Egypt revolts and that Mr. Sharp's message of 'attacking weaknesses of dictators stuck with them*". However Mr. Sharpe himself declared "*The people of Egypt did that — not me. It is straight out of Gandhi. If people are not afraid of the dictatorship, that dictatorship is in big trouble.*"

East Asia

The 1986 "*EDSA*" (People's Power) revolution in the Phillipines is particularly illuminating about the dynamics of non violent revolutions. It is therefore recounted in greater detail. The trigger for it was the assassination of the leading opponent of the Marcos dictatorship.

Benigno Aquino, an outstanding and dynamic politician, had started his professional life as a journalist and became mayor of Concepcion, his home town, at age 22. Six years later, he was governor of Tarlac province and in 1967, the youngest senator ever elected in the Phillipines. In 1973, when President **Ferdinand Marcos** was expected to step down on completion of his two terms, he decided to run for President. Instead of stepping down, Marcos declared martial law, suspended the constitution and jailed all political opponents. Benigno was charged with subversion and murder, tried by a military tribunal and sentenced to death. This was later commuted to life imprisonment. After seven years in prison he was permitted to go to the United States for emergency heart surgery. He could have continued living there, but decided to return home despite the grave threat to his life which his family and friends foresaw. On arrival at Manila on August 21st, 1983, as he was going from the aircraft to the terminal building, he was assassinated. The arrival statement he had prepared therefore could not be read. It is an important historical document and inter alia states " *I have returned on my own free will to join the ranks of those struggling to restore our rights through nonviolence. I could have opted to seek political asylum in America but I feel it is my duty, as it is the duty of every Filipino to suffer with his people especially in time of crisis. According to Gandhi, the willing sacrifice of the innocent is the most powerful answer to insolent tyranny that has yet been conceived by God and man."*

After his assassination, his wife **Corazon**, also returned from America. In the following months she united the fragmented opposition and courageously led a peoples' movement against the crimes and injustices of Marcos' martial law regime. In late 1985, when he called a snap election (in the confident belief he would win and thus silence his Filipino and American critics and banish Benigno's ghost) she, urged by one million signatories, decided to run for president. **Cardinal Sin** induced former senator **Salvador Laurel**, himself a presidential aspirant, to be her vice-presidential running mate. Though lacking political experience she proved a charismatic leader and skilled campaigner. Among the actions she took was to revive the *National Movement for*

Free Elections (*NAMFREL*) to monitor the elections. Its principal volunteers were parish priests and nuns all over the country. When the Marcos-dominated National Assembly proclaimed him the winner despite *NAMFREL* computing a majority for the Aquino-Laurel ticket, a national campaign of non violent resistance with civil disobedience was launched, which the Catholic Church endorsed. It received overwhelming response. On February 22, General **Fidel Ramos**, commander of the Philippine Constabulary called for Marcos's resignation. The latter ordered the army to quell his rebellion but Cardinal Sin appealed to the people on the Church-run *Radio Veritas* (which became the voice of the revolution) to non violently block pro-Marcos troop movements towards Camp Aguinaldo, Ramos' headquarters. Thousands, including priests, nuns and school children came onto the streets, linked arms and barricaded the tanks. In the face of this unexpected "*peoples power*" resistance many of the tank crew, as also those of seven helicopters, switched sides and supported the people.

Though Marcos went ahead with his formal inauguration on February 25, its boycott by foreign Ambassadors and the desertion of his trusted troops, made clear to him he had lost both national and international, particularly US, support. He therefore resigned and went into exile the same day. An hour later, Corazon Aquino and Salvador Laurel were sworn in as president and Vice President of the Philippines. The former thus became the first woman head of state in Asia. *EDSA*, the non violent struggle she had so courageously and effectively led, emerged as the first woman-led, People's Power Revolution in the world.

As president, Corazon Aquino promulgated a new constitution limiting presidential powers and establishing a bicameral legislature. She reformulated governmental policies, with strong emphasis on civil liberties, human rights, and dialogue with insurgents and secessionists. She had to confront many challenges, including nine coup attempts but succeeded in overcoming all of them and completed her full term in 1992. In just 30 months, EDSA succeeded in mobilizing the entire nation including its most conservative sections - the Church and armed forces - with the sacrifice of only one precious life. If violence had been used in the attempt to bring down the Marcos regime, hundreds of lives would have been lost with no assurance of success. EDSA re-establishes the validity of Gandhi's "*immutable maxim that government of the people is possible only so long as they consent either consciously or unconsciously to be governed*". When said consent is withdrawn, even a well entrenched and ruthless regime, like that of Ferdinand Marcos, overnight finds itself denuded of all power and authority.

South Asia

'Black Coat Revolution' of Pakistan

An amazing phenomenon in Pakistan in 2007-2008 was the determined, non violent struggle of its lawyers to reinstate Chief Justice Iftikhar Muhammad Chaudhry whom President Musharraf peremptorily suspended on 9th March 2007 on corruption charges. On 12th March, the lawyers stopped attending courts in protest against this suspension and held public rallies in Islamabad, Lahore, Karachi and Quetta. Babar Sattar, a leading lawyer declared : "*How do you function as a lawyer when the law is what the general says it is?*". For his temerity in asking this question he and many other lawyers were imprisoned and tortured. But the protest rallies continued, often opening with poet Faiz Ahmed Faiz's inspiring lines:

"These shackles, this burden around our necks,
Will turn into cotton and vanish into thin air,
And then we common people will stake a claim
On this land that is our very own.
Then the tyrant rulers will submit to defeat
At the hands of us simple folk.

On 6th October, just before parliament was dissolved President Musharraf got himself re-elected by the incumbent legislators. Among those who stood against him was Justice Wajihuddin Ahmed a former Supreme Court judge, whom the Supreme Court Lawyers Association sponsored. He secured only 8 votes against Musharraf's 671 but this was clear proof that the lawyers would continue to resist the latters rule.

On November 3, notwithstanding his overwhelming victory in the Presidential election, he declared a "*State of Emergency*", The Constitution was suspended, the January 8, 2008 general elections indefinitely postponed, the Chief Justice and other Supreme Court judges dismissed and put under house arrest. The international outrage these developments caused, impelled Musharraf to announce that elections would be held. In these elections, held on 18th February 2008, Pakistan Peoples Party and Pakistan Muslim

League(N) won the majority of seats and formed a coalition government with Yosaf Raza Gillani as Prime Minister. On 7th August, it took the bold decision to confront President Musharraf to either step down or face impeachment He was initially defiant and declared "*I will defeat those who try to push me to the wall.*" But on August 18, 2008, after an impassioned defence of his record as President, he announced his resignation and decision "*to proceed on pilgrimage to Mecca*".

This non violent struggle which achieved all its objectives, over a seventeen month period, now figures in the *Peoples Power* lexicon as the *Black Coat Revolution.*

Aitzaz Ahsan, Cambridge-educated lawyer and president, Pakistan's Supreme Court Bar Association, who principally inspired and led the nationwide lawyers struggle spoke of a "*grand new compact*" between the lawyers, judiciary and political parties to restore democracy and defeat extremist forces. He declared. "*The weapons to fight the war on terrorism are an empowered people who are assured that no man can arbitrarily impose his will upon their lives.*"

Whereas Gandhi might not be much known or revered in Pakistan today, Pakistan Times in its Editorial titled *Glorious Dust* , on the day after his assassination, *wrote* "*The people of India, and indirectly the people of Pakistan, for he was trying to befriend both, have added to their other losses, the most grievous loss of all - the loss of Gandhi. Let us hope that this most precious sacrifice to the demons of hate will placate them at last and the death of one will yet save the life of millions for whom this life was given. Once Hindus and Muslims mingled their blood to fight for freedom under Gandhi's banner during the Khilafat days; let us hope they will now mingle their tears over his glorious dust to retain their peaceful freedom under the independent flags of India and Pakistan*".

Aung San Suu Kyi of Myanmar (Burma)

Aung San Suu Kyi is an inspiring embodiment of Gandhi's maxims "*He who fears fails*" and "*Strength comes not from physical capacity but from indomitable will*". Daughter of Burma's assassinated national hero General Aung San, Suu Kyi spent her childhood in Rangoon. On her mother's appointment as Ambassador to India she accompanied her to New Delhi and studied at Lady Shri Ram College. Subsequently she studied at Oxford and the School of Oriental and African Studies in London where she met Michael Aris, a British Tibetan scholar. She married him in 1972 and lived in London thereafter. In March 1988 she returned to Burma to care for her ailing mother.

On July 23, 1988, Gen. Ne Win, in power since the March 2, 1962 coup, announced he was stepping down and that a referendum would soon be held on the country's future. This caused widespread exultation and a big rally for democracy was held on 8 August 1988 (8-8-88 being seen as an auspicious day). On 26th August, at a much bigger rally near Shwedagon Pagoda, Suu Kyi reiterated the call for democracy and soon thereafter founded the National League for Democracy (NLD), In the next twelve months she travelled all over Burma urging people to "*march unitedly, in a disciplined manner, towards the goal of democracy*". Pertured by the great impact she was making, the new military ruler General Saw Muang placed her under house arrest on 20 July 1989 and debarred her from further political activity. Nonetheless, in the May 27, 1990 national elections the NLD secured 59% of the votes and 392 of the 485 seats. Stunned by this, the Junta nullified the election results, imposed martial law and continued their rule.

Kept under continuous house arrest for almost 19 of the last 22 years and twice almost killed by Junta instigated hoodlums while travelling to north Burma towns, Su Kyi has refused to be intimidated or leave the country even when her husband was dying of cancer in London. The Junta offered her freedom if she left the country for good but she refused.

How deeply she has been influenced by Gandhi is revealed in her January 1, 1997 message to an International Youth Conference at Panchgani in India. In it she stated "*As Gandhi wrote 'In Truth, that Government is ideal which governs the least. It is no self government that leaves nothing for the people to do.' These words were written in 1925 yet could well be applied to present day Burma under a military dictatorship that leaves the people with no role to play in their own government. We remain in bondage after forty nine years of independence. There can be no real freedom unless the mind and spirit are free. Self Government that results in a crushed, intimidated people who have no control over their own destiny constitutes a betrayal of the struggle for independence, a struggle during which so much was sacrificed by so many."*

In her acceptance speech (read out by her son Alexander on her behalf) for the 1990 Sakharov Prize for Freedom of Thought she affirmed "*It is not power that corrupts but fear. Fear of losing power corrupts those who wield it and fear of the scourge of power corrupts those who are subject to it.*" In awarding her the 1991 Nobel Peace Prize the Committee stated "*Suu Kyi's struggle is one of the most extraordinary examples of civil courage in Asia in recent decades. She has become an important symbol in the struggle against oppression of many people throughout the world who are striving to attain democracy, human rights and ethnic conciliation by peaceful means.*"

During her many years of house arrest under the 1975 State Protection Act on grounds that she was "*likely to undermine community peace and stability of the country*", she lived with only two domestic maids.(her two sons live in London) and spent her time meditating, reading, writing, playing the old family piano. Because she made a brief appearance at her gate on 22 September 2007 to greet Buddhist monks rallying for human rights she was taken the following day to Insein Prison and kept there for seven days. When Cyclone Nargis struck in May 2008 the electricity supply to her home was disrupted and she had to live by candle light after dusk for many months. Yet, when finally released from detention on November 13, 2010 she greeted her supporters with a radiant smile and stated in true Gandhian spirit "*I do not have any antagonism towards the people who kept me under house arrest. The security officials treated me well. I want to ask the Junta to also treat the people well.*"

Suu Kyi, waves to supporters soon after her release

In an interview with BBC soon thereafter she expressed the hope for early talks with the Junta. "*I think we will have to sort out our differences across the table talking to each other, agreeing to disagree . . . or trying to remove the sources of our disagreement."* She made clear her National League for Democracy (NLD) would remain at the centre of her struggle for freedom and democracy, despite its dissolution by the Junta when it refused to participate in the Sham Nov. 7, 2010 national election. Asked how long it might take to achieve democracy she replied *"We are trying to achieve it as quickly as possible, but I don't know how long it will take."* .

Referring to recent events in Tunisia & Egypt in her Reith Lecture on BBC she said : *"Do we envy the people of Tunisia and Egypt? Yes, we do envy them their quick and peaceful transitions. But more than envy is a sense of solidarity and of renewed commitment to our cause, which is the cause of all women and men who value human dignity and freedom."*

Cynics of non violent struggle often point to Su Kyi's long and yet unsuccessful efforts to secure freedom and democracy for her people. They would do well to look at Afghanistan where over 100,000 soldiers from the US and several NATO countries have battled for over ten years, with the most sophisticated weapons, against a poorly armed Afghan resistance and yet are unable to "*pacify*" that country. They now appear ready to acquiesce in the return to power of the very regime they had overthrown. Meanwhile thousands of Afghans, most of them civilians, have been killed and their homes destroyed. In Burma, many have been imprisoned and have suffered greatly, but only a few have died. When freedom and democracy finally come Burma, as they undoubtedly will, the contrast with Afghanistan, will be stark. Success in the former case would have come through the inspiring leadership and indomitable will of a single, fearless, frail woman.

East Europe.

Peoples uprisings had occurred in Hungary in 1956 and Czechoslavakia ("*The Prague Spring*") in 1968 and initially achieved some success but as they had no well planned, nationwide strategy nor organization they could be ruthlessly suppressed. The credit for Eastern Europe's first successful non violent revolution goes to **Lech Walesa** and his fellow dock workers at **Lenin Shipyard** at Gdansk . Previously he had served in the army for two years and risen to the rank of corporal. He joined Lenin shipyard in 1967 as an electrician. In 1976, because of his pro-worker activities he was fired. He then began to organize non-communist trade unions in various shipyards. The security service kept him under constant surveillance and detained him from time to time. In August 1980 he led the Lenin shipyard strike which triggered strikes in all other shipyards. Their primary demand was workers' rights. The Gdansk Agreement of August 31, 1980, which conceded these rights as also the right to organize independent unions was Walesa's first big achievement. Soon thereafter he set up '*Solidarity*', apparently to safeguard the newly acquired rights but actually also to non violently resist Communist dictatorship and Soviet occupation of Poland. It soon emerged as a nationwide organization with 38 regional branches. The Catholic Church supported Walesa's efforts (he was a devout Catholic) and in January 1981 **Pope John Paul II** received him at the Vatican. In 1980-81, he travelled to Italy, Japan, Sweden, France and Switzerland as guest of the International Labour Organisation. In September 1981 he was elected Solidarity's Chairman at its First National Congress in Gdansk.

The pro-Soviet Polish Government of General Wojciech Jaruzelski. concerned at Solidarity's impressive growth and international repute sought to disband it in December 1981 by imposing martial law, banning Solidarity activities and arresting many of its leaders including Walesa. Though martial law was lifted in July 1983, many of the restrictions were continued through the civil code. In October 1983 the announcement of Walesa's Nobel prize raised the spirits of Solidarity members and strengthened their resistance which brought about a severe economic downturn. This forced the Jaruzelski regime to negotiate with Walesa and his colleagues, revoke the ban on Solidarity activities and agree to hold national elections. These elections, held in 1989, led to the installation of Poland's first Non Communist Prime Minister and opened the door to the formal demise of all Communist dictatorships imposed by Stalin on Eastern Europe after WWII. Under Mikhail Gorbachev the Soviet Union was no longer willing to use military force to keep communist parties in power in satellite states. In April 1990 at Solidarity's second national congress, Walesa was elected chairman with 77.5% of the votes. In December 1990 he was elected President of Poland.

Commenting on the earlier unsuccessful East European uprisings Walesa stated "*We didn't succeed when we tried to fight with arms, but we won when we adopted non-violence. I am a disciple of Mahatma Gandhi*".

Commenting also on the inspiration and moral support received from Pope John Paul II (a Pole) Lech Walesa stated : "*The Holy Father, reminded us how numerous we were and told us not to be afraid*". His portraits and those of the Virgin Mary were seen on several Polish factory walls during the period of struggle.

The success of Solidarity's non violent struggle in Poland gestated similar struggles (which Václav Havel aptly described as exercise of "*the power of the powerless.*") in other East European countries, the Baltic states, the Soviet Union and later also in the independent states born from it. Between 1989 - 2004, all East European Communist dictatorships, and the Berlin Wall (officially designated the *Anti-Fascist Protection Wall*) had been brought down and democracy established in Estonia, Latvia, Lithuania, German Democratic Republic, Czechoslovakia, Hungary, Bulgaria, Romania, Russia, Serbia, Georgia, and Ukraine. Besides, Germany had been reunified, the Warsaw Pact scrapped (November 24, 1990), and many of its former members admitted to the European Union.

Within sixty years of Gandhi's death over 130 countries had liberated themselves from colonialsm and more than 20 others had emancipated themselves from oppressive racist, Fascist and Communist regimes, in almost all cases non-violently. This is the most sweeping democratization of international political geography in history.

Berlin Wall being dismantled

West Europe

It is widely believed, as Martin Buber averred, that non violent resistance would never succeed against a "*diabolic universal steamroller*" like Hitler. In the New Yorker (May 2, 2011) Pankaj Mishra averred "*In advising European Jews to practice nonviolent resistance against Hitler, Gandhi was guilty of a grotesque misunderstanding of the Third Reich.*" In sharp contrast, Johan Galtung has written: "*That a demonstration against the Gestapo in favour of Jews actually took place and was successful seems absolutely incredible but it did happen and that too at a high point of war and terror in Berlin, the epicenter of Hitler's Nazism, at the beginning of March 1943* " Nathan Stoltfus, has dealt with this episode in detail, and indicated that in February 1943, the Gestapo arrested the approximately 10,000 Jews still in Berlin. Of these about 8000 were promptly transported to Auschwitz and never heard of again. As the other 2000 had German wives they were detained at the "*Collection Centre*" on Rosenstrasse Avenue. As soon as news of their husbands detention reached their wives many of them rushed to said collection centre and began to shout "*Give us our husbands back*". Their numbers swelled by the day and there were constant scuffles between them and Gestapo officials some of whom threatened to open fire unless they withdrew. The women were undeterred and kept up their chants. On the 8th day, to their great joy and relief their husbands were released. This was a triumphant climax not only to their seven day protests but also to their ten year stolid resistance to strong Nazi pressure to divorce their "*non-Aryan*" husbands. Nathan Stoltfus, who interviewed some of the officials about the unexpected release of these Jews wrote. "*The Nazi regime perpetrated an image of the German people as uniformly supportive of Nazism. Goebbels feared an action like the Rosenstrasse Protest that showed dissent publicly could spread quickly. These protesters represented personal interests yet the public nature of their opposition wrecked the regime's daily portrayal of reality, while the terror apparatus remained on the sidelines.... In a state that inhibited assembly, controlled information and portrayed dissidence as a fringe element in an otherwise unified populace, mass public protest was a political force, ...and poses an even more overt challenge to authority than does non compliance. It brings the conflict into public view* ". Stoltfus indicates that Goebbel's deputy Leopold Gutterer attributed the success of the Rosenstrasse protest "*to its openness and contrasted it with conspiratorial resistance, which the regime could more easily portray as an act against the people and the state. Unarmed actions avoided the appearance of treason and did not legitimize and unleash the crushing violence of the Nazi regime....*

The 'Rosenstrasse Monument' in Berlin

If the Rosenstrasse protesters had come armed the police would have had to shoot them".

The April - May 1943 Warsaw Ghetto uprising , which occurred just a few weeks after "*Rosenstrasse*", was a heroic but armed struggle in which some of the Jews resisted transportation to Treblinka "*work camp*" with revolvers, pistols, gasoline bombs and a few rifles received from the Polish resistance. In this uprising 17 Gestapo officials were killed and 90 wounded. However, the tragic and predictable end result was the brutal massacre of all the approximately 13,000 Jewish men, women and children in that ghetto.

The moral to be drawn from "*Rosenstrasse*" and the Warsaw uprising is that non violent resistance against Nazi terror not only worked it was the only form of resistance that had any chance of succeeding.

Mark Kurlansky has affirmed "*the Nazis are often cited as an example of an enemy against whom non-violence would be futile. This despite the success of several non violent campaigns. Amid some of the greatest violence the world has ever seen, it was little noted that more Jews were saved by non-violence than by violence.*" He gives examples of Denmark, Bulgaria, Raoul Wallenberg and Andre and Magda Trocme. Despite Nazi occupation the Danish Government refused to enact any anti-semetic laws. When the Nazi's took over, and on October 1, 1943 began to deport Jews "*the Danes hid almost the entire Jewish population of 6,500 including about 1500 refugees from Germany, Austria and Czechoslovakia. The hidden Jews were then secretly taken by boat to neutral Sweden. The Germans succeeded in deporting only 400 of them Theresinstadt".* Bulgaria, despite being a German ally saved its Jewish population by refusing to implement Nazi directives. Wallenberg, a Swedish Businessman, saved an estimated 100,000 Hungarian Jews, while serving as Sweden's Ambassador to Hungary, by issuing them with Swedish passports. The Tracmes, who had a school at Le Chambon-sur-Lignon in south eastern France, hid Jewish children there and smuggled them into Switzerland. Kurlansky concludes "*World War II abounds with such tales of non violent resistance and non-cooperation. Thousands of Jews were saved by individuals who risked their lives and those of their families, to hide a Jew or a Jewish family. Dictatorships are prepared to crush armed resistance, it is non-cooperation that confounds them."*

A sad aspect of the dreadful tragedy of European Jews during the 1938-45 period is that some Zionist leaders, ignoring the Gandhian imperative of always opposing and never cooperating with evil, collaborated with the Nazis. This is revealed by the reputed Jewish Scholar Hannah Arendt in her book '*Eichman in Jeusalem: The Banality of Evil"* She writes: "*To a Jew, the role of Jewish leaders in the destruction of their own people is undoubtedly the darkest chapter of the whole dark story. It had been known vaguely before, but it has now been exposed for the first time in all its pathetic and sordid detail by Raul Hilberg, in his book 'The destruction of the European Jews'..... In Amsterdam as in Warsaw, in Berlin as in Budapest, Jewish officials could be trusted to compile the lists of persons and of their property, to secure money from the deportees to defray the expenses of their deportation and extermination, to keep track of vacated apartments, to supply police forces to help seize Jews, and get them on trains until, as a last gesture they handed over the assets of the Jewish community, in good order, for final confiscation........ We know how the Jewish officials felt when they became instruments of murder - Like captains "whose ships were about to sink and who succeeded in bringing them safe to port by casting overboard a great part of their precious cargo"; like saviours who "with a handful of victims save a thousand people, with a thousand ten thousand. The truth however is quite gruesome. Dr Kastner in Hungary saved exactly 1684 people with approximately 476,000 victims. And who were those singled out for salvation? Those "who had worked all their lives for the "Zibur" (community) i.e. the Zioinst functionaries and the "most prominent Jews" as Kastner says in his report."*

e). National Defence and International Security Strategists

Gandhi's approach to national defence and international security was based on the maxim that for achieving security and peace it was the path of Truth, justice, non-violence training and mutually acceptable agreements that needed to be adopted and not that of amassing arms, invading and occupying countries and waging war. All actions which created fear and hate were to be averted and the contrary course followed. This approach is embodied in UNESCO's motto *"Since wars begin in the minds of men, it is in the minds of men that the defences of peace must be constructed"*.

Gandhi urged non-violent resistance to Abyssinia in 1935, to Czechoslovakia in 1938, to Britain in 1940 and even to India in 1942. *"If India were a free country, things could be done non-violently to prevent the Japanese from entering the country. Non-violent resistance could commence the moment they effected a landing. Non-violent resisters would refuse them any help, even water. If the Japanese compel resisters to give them water, they should refuse and be prepared to die in the act of resistance, for it is no part of their duty to help anyone to steal their country."* This has been greatly ridiculed as the height of absurdity. Yet, this was the strategy the Russians used against Napoleon in 1812. They even burnt their beloved and *"sacred"* Moscow to deny him and his troops shelter during the Russian winter. This strategy worked admirably for them! The *"Grand Armee"* of 690,000 men, with which Napoleon entered Moscow on September 14, 1812, was reduced to less than 50,000 frost-bitten and famished survivors when he reentered France. His Russian campaign is listed among *"the most lethal military operations in world history"*. Besides all the fighting men he lost through frost bite, starvation and desertions, he also lost about 200,000 horses and over 1,000 artillery pieces. This disaster was the decisive turning point of his spectacular military career and soon led to his final defeat, and subsequent transportation and imprisonment at the remote South Atlantic Island of St. Helena.

Napoleon entering a burning Moscow on September 14, 1812

Though Independent India summarily rejected Gandhi's ideas on nonviolent national defence they have been received quite favourably by national and international security analysts abroad.

Paul Wehr, in his article on *'Non-Violence and National Defence'* in the book *'Gandhi in the Post Modern Age'*, traces the development of the concept of civilian defence, subsequently termed social defence, based on Gandhi's non-violent resistance strategy. He points out that ***Walter Lippman*** was the first to write in its favour (1928) though ***William James*** had earlier (1910) urged the need to find a *"moral equivalent of war"* as an antidote for it. Whereas James had felt that military virtues like honor, courage, discipline, and efficiency should be promoted through a national non-military service Lippmann had argued that *"It is not sufficient to propose an equivalent for the military virtues..... What is needed is a Political Equivalent of War* i.e. *other ways of deciding those issues which have hitherto been decided by war",* However, Bertrand Russell, in his article on *" War and Nonresistance"* in the August 1915 *Atlantic Monthly* had proposed that nonviolent resistance be used if there was a German invasion of England.

In 1934, in his classic *The Power of Nonviolence*, Richard Gregg, like Gandhi, suggested nonviolent resistance as a *"substitute for war"* and made direct comparison between military strategy and nonviolent strategy. Barthelemy de Ligt in his 1935 book, *The Conquest of Violence* urged a *"campaign against all war and all preparation for war"* .

In 1937 ***Kenneth Boulding*** in his *'Paths of Glory: A new way with War'* argued that the technological revolution had made war dysfunctional and proposed that Britain, adopt a non-violent defence policy as a *"functional substitute for war"*. ***Lindberg*** in Denmark (1937), and ***Vrind*** in Holland (1938) urged similar action for their respective countries.

In 1955, ***Arne Naess*** and J***ohann Galtung*** in Norway enunciated the concept of *'non-violent social defence '* based on Gandhi's ideas and thus established a direct link between him and modern social defence theory. In the USA, ***Cecil Hinshaw*** (1956) argued that military defence in the nuclear age was too expensive and proposed social defence as a sensible option.

In 1959, ***Stephen King Hall***, in his book *'Defence in the Nuclear Age '* questioned the rationality of conventional military defence in the contemporary situation and urged that Britain renounce nuclear weapons, reject the US nuclear umbrella, devise non nuclear defence alternatives and also consider social defence. These proposals, "*coming from a highly esteemed military man, fourth lineal descendant of a family of naval officers, were startling and a turning point in the development of the civilian-based defense concept, the rationale now tending to shift from moral to strategic and military reasons and politicians and military men becoming involved as never before*" (Phillip Bogdonoff in November 1982 Association for Transarmament studies newsletter)".

Separately ***Johann Galtung*** in Norway and ***Gene Sharpe*** in USA analysed various non-violent resistance movements, particularly in Denmark and Norway under Nazi occupation and presented a credible case for Social Defence. Galtung, in his *Defense Without a Military System* (1959) developed eleven strategic principles for civilian defense. Sharpe pointed out that conventional military superiority enables an aggressor to invade and occupy a country but not to control it unless the victims cooperate or are coerced to do so. In the mentioned countries their peoples firmly resisted Nazi occupation by farmers destroying crops, workers adopting go-slow tactics, teachers refusing to teach Nazi ideology and newspapers resisting censorship. By doing so the impossible task of defending their countries borders was shifted to the populated areas where the invader's objective of occupying and exploiting these countries could be effectively frustrated.

The September 1964 Oxford Conference on Civilian Defence brought together military strategists, defence researchers, political analysts and people with direct experience of non-violent resistance. Among those at it were Gene Sharp, Adam Roberts, April Carter, Theodor Ebert, Alun Gwynne Jones (then *London Times* military correspondent and later, as Lord Chalfont, Minister of State for Foreign Affairs),Professor Ernest Bramsted, reputed researcher on totalitarianism and Colonel D.J. Goodspeed, military historian. The papers they presented were edited by Adam Roberts and published in 1967 as *The Strategy of Civilian Defense*. This book examined many historical episodes as also some ideas on "*transarmament*", a word to be a used instead of *"disarmament"* so as to clarify that countries would not be left defenseless but only their defense system transformed into a more effective one.

In the September 1967 follow-up conference at Munich, there was further consideration of *"transarmament"* and its implications in the international arena. A research group headed by **Theodore Ebert** was established to make an indepth study of it and related matters. It subsequently submitted a proposal for a German Social Defence strategy

The ruthless suppression of the 1968 Czech uprising by Soviet troops and the civilian resistance which continued thereafter stimulated further research in this field as also serious interest in government circles in civilian defence. *The Strategy of Civilian Defense* reappeared in paperback with a new introduction dealing with the Czech uprising. A Norwegian anthology of case studies was published in an enlarged edition. In 1969, *Gewaltfreie Aktion* (Nonviolent Action), a quarterly publication on nonviolent defense, edited by Theodor Ebert, was launched. Academic conferences on this topic were held at Tampere, Finland in 1970, at Uppsala, Sweden in 1972, at Brussels, 1976 and at Oslo, 1978.

The Norwegian Defense Research Establishment issued a report in 1976 on civilian defense as a component of overall security policy. It was titled *Non-Military Defense and Norwegian Security Policy* and edited by Johan Jorgen Holst (who became Norway's Minister of Defense, 1986-1989). In Denmark, the Minister for Education got the Institute for Peace and Conflict Research in Copenhagen to make an anthology of the literature on civilian defense. This, edited by Anders Boserup and Andrew Mack, was published in 1974 as *War Without Weapons*. Soon thereafter The Swedish Ministry of Defense supported a research program at Uppsala University's Peace and Conflict Research Department.

The Norwegian government was the first to officially study the merits of civilian defence. The ***Galtung and Hansen Commission*** set up for this purpose in 1987 recommended *'Total Defence'* whereby Norwegians would be trained for civilian as well as military defence. A similar study undertaken by Denmark recommended that in case of any future attack only Jutland should be militarily defended and the Danish islands prepared to rely only on civilian defence. Other European Governments that set up commissions to study the merits of such defence are Holland, Sweden, Austria and Finland. A study by the Finnish Psychological Defence Board led a parliamentary committee to conclude that civilian defence must be an integral part of national defence policy. By the mid 1990s Civilian / Social Defence had been incorporated as a component in the national defence policies of Norway Sweden, and Lithuania with Denmark, Holland and Finland moving in the same direction.

Paul Wehr concludes his historical survey of the evolution of '*Social Defence*' thus: "*Social Defence as a concept originated in the ethical principles of the Gandhian movement and in pacifist ideology. The Gandhian movement demonstrated the power of massive non cooperation with an occupying power in that case Britain. As the destructiveness of modern war became more evident, it was natural that the principles and techniques of Gandhian non cooperation would be applied to the problem of national defense. At first social defence research was non governmental. By the 1970s Governments were supporting it and political parties and peace movements were debating it. A quarter century of scholarly research has produced a respectable body of knowledge about the underlying principles, diverse methods and practical developments of social defence....Only time and events will tell whether Gandhi's ideas and practice will be as influential in the area of national defence as they have been in the field of social change.*"

In his book '*Waging Non-Violent Struggle - 20th Century Practice, 21st Century Potential*', Professor Gene Sharpe has analysed 23 separate 20th century non-violent struggles and indicated how this form of struggle operates in undermining sources of political legitimacy and power, and how it can be made more effective by strategic planning and systematic training. He affirms "*Today, if understood accurately and applied intelligently, wisely, and courageously, this type of struggle in fact offers great hope for a better future for our world*".

f) Peace, Spiritual and Social Activists / Movements

In the last five decades Gandhi has become a leading icon of peace, spirituality and social activists/movements all over the world. Glenn Paige, in his 1990 Gandhi Memorial lecture titled '*Gandhi contribution to Global Non violent Awakening*', has detailed his impact in the first two of these spheres : "*Without any doubt Gandhiji, supported by those who made his work possible is the principal contributor to global non violent awakening in the 20th century*". He avers that by fashioning Satyagraha as a "*profoundly spiritual*" tool Gandhi inspired diverse religious groups as also non-religious humanists to delve into their respective non violent spiritual resources and utilize them for bringing about peaceful non violent global change. Good examples of these are the following.

Writing from the Abbey of Gethsemani, Thomas Merton concludes his Foreword to '*Gandhi on Non Violence*' thus : "*Gandhi's principles are extremely pertinent today, more pertinent even than when they were conceived and worked out in practice in the ashrams and villages of India. They are pertinent for everybody but specially for those interested in implementing the principles expressed by Pope John XXIII, in Pacem in Terris. Indeed this Encyclical has the breadth and depth, the universality and tolerance of Gandhi's peace-minded outlook. Peace cannot be built on exclusivism, absolutism and intolerance; neither can it be built on vague liberal slogans and pious programs gestated in the smoke of confabulation. There can be no peace on earth without the inner change that brings man to his "right mind". Gandhi's observations on the prerequisites and disciplines involved in Satyagraha, the vow of Truth, are required reading for anyone seriously interested in man's fate in the nuclear age*".

Dr. John F. Kane, Denver area coordinator for Pax Christi, USA affirms "*For our "postmodern age" of seemingly unrestricted individualism, Gandhi stresses the overcoming of self and the rediscovery of humanity's essential unity. For a people preoccupied with the defence of rights and the protection of privilege, he stresses the primacy of duty and the necessity of service as essential conditions for the possibility of peace. For a culture continuously directed to the pursuit of pleasure and possession by an endless barrage of advertising propoganda, he stresses the need for simplification of life and real identification with the poor. For an increasingly confused and agnostic generation he stresses the absolute centrality of prayer and a living faith in God*".

'*Plough*', the publishing house of Church Communities International, has the following quote of John Dear S.J. (author of '*Dare to Imagine*') as the lead line of its Non Violence section "*To be visionaries of peace we need to be contemplatives of nonviolence, people who imagine the God of peace, who let God disarm our hearts, who allow the God of peace to show us the way to peace. As visionaries and contemplatives of peace, we can then become a prophetic people who not only denounce imperial violence as ungodly, immoral, and evil, but announce God's way of nonviolence, justice and peace".*

Glenn Paige also credits Gandhi's scientific approach, best testified by his *"Experiments with Truth"*, for opening up the possibilities of *"pursuing non-violent glolal transformation as a subject for interdisciplinary scientific investigation"* and gives the May 16, 1986 Seville *'Statement on Violence"* as an example. Issued by twenty distinguished anthropologists, ethologists and psychologists, it declares " *We conclude that biology does not condemn humanity to war......Just as "wars begin in the minds of men", peace also begins in our minds. The same species who invented war is capable of inventing peace. The responsibility lies with each of us."*

Glenn Paige also mentions Gandhi's emphasis on individual action, mass mobilization, focus on the poorest and weakest, and fearlessness as his other important inputs into global non violence awakening and lists Martin Luther King, Cesar Chavez, Dorothy Day, Mairead Corrigan and Betty Williams, Mother Theresa, Adolfo Perez Esquivel, Dalai Lama, Desmond Tutu, Amnesty International, War Resisters International, Peace Brigades International, Friends World Committee for Consultation, International Fellowship of Reconciliation, Humanitas International, Soka Gakkai International, Gruppe Schweiz Ohne Armee, United farm Workers Union, Shanti Sena, Lanka Sarvodaya Shramadana Sangamaya, Green Peace, Pax World Fund, Servicio Paz y Justicia as some of the many individuals and organizations deeply influenced by him, and affirms "*The work of all these, resonating with the Gandhian legacy as well as being rooted in their own spiritual and historical traditions, refuses to accept power striving, greed, hatred and ignorance as eternal obstacles to prevent worldwide cooperation for the well-being and happiness of all"*

The *'World Social Forum'* (WSF), also referred to as *'Global Justice Movement'* has emerged as a global *'people's resistance'* movement against exploitative capitalism and the "*Corporate Predator State*". It was conceived by Oded Grajew and born at Puerto Allegre, Brazil in 2000 with the support of Brazilian Workers Party. It defines itself as "*an opened space - plural, diverse, non-governmental and non-partisan - that stimulates decentralized debate, reflection, exchange of experiences, formulating proposals and building alliances among organizations and movement engaged in concrete actions towards a more democratic and just world.*" Its first three annual conclaves were held at Puerto Allegra in 2001, 2002 and 2003, with the participant numbers rising from 12,000 in 2001 to 66,000 in 2003, by which time it had established regional chapters in Europe, Asia and Africa . Its Asian chapter met in Hyderabad, the European Chapter in Florence and the African chapter at Addis Ababa in early 2003. The 2004 WSF, held at Mumbai January 16 -21 2004, was attended by 85,000 activists from over 100 countries. Nobel Laureate Joseph Stiglitz was key note speaker (Naom Chomsky was keynote speaker at WSF 2003). At WSF 2005 in Puerto Allegre, the participant number reached 155,000. WSF 2006 was therefore "*polycentric*" with separate meets in Caracas (Venezuela), Bamako (Mali), and Karachi (Pakistan). WSF 2007 at Nairobi , Kenya had 66,000 "*delegates*", representing 1,400 NGOs from 110 countries, making it the most impressive WSF so far. The eighth World Social Forum (2008) was "*global*" i.e., not organized at a particular place, but by thousands of local organizations all over the world, on or around January 26. It made a '***Global Call for Action***'. About these activists David Hardiman writes "*They stand for a human spirit that refuses to be crushed by the 'Leviathan' of the modern system of violence, oppression and exploitation. They aspire for a better, more equitable and non-violent future. In them, Gandhi - their model - still lives* ".

The ninth WSF took place at Belém, (in the heart of Brazil 's Amazon rainforest), in January 2009 and the tenth at Puerto Allegre January 26th-31st 2010. At the latter, Brazilian philosopher and sociologist **Candido Grzybowsky** declared "*Capitalism's unsustainability has never been so obvious. We need to create a system based on social and environmental justice*". **Hildebrando Velez Galeano**, head of the Colombian chapter of Friends of the Earth. drew raucous cheers when he urged developing nations to seize control of the global economy "*from the hands of the capitalist speculators who are destroying it. We have to decolonize our territory and declare it free of Coca-Cola and Monsanto*".

g). Playwrights, Composers, Lyricists and Film Producers

Indian playwrights have found the Mahatma a good dramatic persona. **Prasana's** powerful 1993 play *'Gandhi'* is, according to him, "*an effort to plumb the depths of Gandhiji's search for Truth*". Interviewed by Sobaila Kaur of the Sunday Times, he stated "*Gandhiji knew that the struggle for independence had to go through three stages : the struggle with oneself, the struggle with one's people and the struggle against the imperial power. This seemed more logical than all other ideologies, particularly Marxism of which I was a staunch adherent until I discovered Gandhi - and the Ram in him.*" Written originally in Kannada, this play, translated into Hindi by Devendra Raj Ankur, has been performed and acclaimed in New Delhi and other Indian cities. **Pradeep Dalvi's** Marathi play *'Mee Nathuram Godse Boltoi'* presented the assassin's justification for killing Gandhi. First performed in 1997 and banned after just six shows it was widely performed all over

Maharashtra after the pro-Hindutva BJP Government revoked said ban in 2002.

Ramu Ramanathan's 2002 play *'Mahadevbhai'* refuted the malicious imputations of 'Mee Nathuram Godse Boltoi'. The playwright averred " *Gandhi was being violated in more ways than one and I felt it was necessary to remind people about what Gandhi stood for*". This play, which has been staged in many Indian cities and been much acclaimed, presents an insight into Gandhi's mind through the jottings in his diary, which are narrated by Narayan Desai.

Premanand Gajvi's well researched play *'Gandhi Ambedkar'* was critically acclaimed but ran only for a few months in 1997. **Pratap Sharma's** play *'Sammy'*, directed by Lillette Dubey, presents select episodes of Gandhi's life from his South Africa days until his death and the mental and spiritual dilemmas he faced in his transformation from a timid young lawyer into an outstanding fearless leader. **Ajit Dahlvi's** 1995 Marathi play *'Gandhi Virudh Gandhi'* explores the troubled relationship between Gandhi and his eldest son Harilal and leaves the viewer bewildered as to which of them is more to blame for it. **Bangalore Little Theatre's** 2008 play *"The Prophet and The Poet"* presents the special relationship between Gandhi and Tagore based on their letters to each other. Directed by Vijay Padki this play, has been staged at Shantiniketan, Sabarmati Ashram, Rajkot, Bangalore and Mysore.

Ravi Shankar, the renowned Sitarist, composed "*Raga Mohan Kauns*" soon after Gandhi's assassination. This composition, played by him and accompanied on tabla by the great Alla Rakha was recorded in 1978 by *DEUTSCHE GRAMMOPHON*, and titled *Homage to Mahatma Gandhi*. Many thousands of this disc have been sold internationally since then.

Brian Boydell, Irish composer who had studied at the Royal College of Music and Royal Irish Academy of Music and later was Professor of Music at Trinity College (1962 to 1982) was deeply moved by Gandhi's assassination, who he considered the greatest figure of that age, He immediately began to compose *In Memoriam* and completed it by June that year. It was performed soon thereafter. The piece consists of a Prelude and Funeral March, with a Coda based on the ideas contained in the former. The Prelude sounds a note of human tragedy, and after the Funeral March builds up to a big climax, the final section transforms the mood into one of unearthly peace. This piece has become the most widely performed of Boydell's many compositions.

Philip Glass, widely acclaimed as the greatest modern music composer, acquired his distinctive "*minimalist*" style through his 1966 encounter with sitarist Ravi Shankar and discovery of the "*entirely additive rhythm*" of Indian music. In 1972 he met the Dalai Lama and since has been a

"Satyagraha" at Metropolitan Opera, New York

strong supporter of the Tibetan cause, non violence and vegetarianism. In 1978, soon after his impactful '*Einstein on the Beach*' (a "*metaphorical look at Albert Einstein..... whose theories led to the splitting of the atom*") which had nuclear holocaust in the climactic scene, he composed the opera *Satyagraha*, in which all vocal parts are sung in Sanskrit. It uses the Bhagavad-Gita as its source material, and presents Gandhi's spiritual and political awakening in South Africa. Leo Tolstoy, Rabindranath Tagore, and Martin Luther King Jr. are also included in the second and third acts. Its North American premiere was at Lewiston, NY, in July 1981 and the UK premiere at Birmingham. A new, joint production by English National Opera and Metropolitan Opera, New York premiered in London in April 2007 and at New York in April 2008. Interviewed soon thereafter by Asia Society President Vishaka Desai Glass spoke of the powerful impact Gandhi's ideas and the US Civil Rights Movement made on him in the 1960s.

Naresh Sohal, India born British music composer, dedicated his '*Satyagraha* ' symphony to Mahatma Gandhi. It has two movements. The first opens with Ram Dhun, a favourite hymn of Gandhi, played on the flute and is interrupted by the sudden burst of Rule Britannia in a different key. Gradually, it merges into a Ram Dhun variation. The second part is mellow and represents the joys and hopes of independent India, This symphony was first performed in March 1997 by the London Symphony Orchestra conducted by Zubin Mehta. Reviewing it, Nicholas Williams wrote in the Independent, "*Last evening's world premiere used*

Rule Britannia! and Ram Dhun as an allegory of the opposing parties in the independence struggle. Stressing the peaceful nature of the transition, Sohal so shocked native listeners with a strident version of Arne's nautical ditty that thereafter they were open to the work's many beauties, not least its magical opening for solo flute and the smooth link to the upbeat second section with its bracing trumpets and percussion. A worthy tribute to a lasting association that, as Nehru remarked, happens rarely in the history of nations."

Among well known songwriters/singers on Gandhi are **Bob Dylan** with '*They Killed Him*', **Pete Morton** with '*Gandhi and Jesus*', **Patti Smith** with '*Gandhi*', **Bob Livingston** with '*Gandhi and Sitting Bull*', **Plume Latraverse** with' *La Ballade De Sandale Et Gandhi* ', **Ange** with *'Et Gandhi l'indoux dit tout doux'*, **Aufwind** with *'Ahimsa* and *Mantra Mahatma'*, **Howard Carpendale** with '*Gandhi*', and **Bernd Stelter** with '*Mahatma*'.

The **US Public Broadcasting System's** six *'Force More Powerful'* films documenting successful non violent struggles during the twentieth century, as also **Richard Attenborough's** 1982 film *'Gandhi'*, have already been mentioned at page 3 of this book. Other notable films on Gandhi in the last five decades are **Mark Robson's** *1963 film 'Nine Hours to Rama'*, **Shyam Benegal's** 1996 film *'The Making of the Mahatma'*, **Kamal Hassan's** 2000 film *'Hey Ram'*, (in Tamil & Hindi), **Arun Patwardhan's** 2002 film '*War and Peace*', **Anupam Kher's** 2005 film '*Maine Gandhi Ko Nahin Mara*', **Vinod Chopra's** 2006 film '*Lage Raho Munna Bhai* ' *(original in Hindi with English subtitles, and subsequently in Tamil and Telugu)* , **Anil Kapoor's** 2007 film *'Gandhi my Father'*, **C R Manohar's** *2009* film '*Mahatma*' and **Amit Chheda's** 2009 film *'Road to Sangam'*. Among these films, Attenborough's 'Gandhi' and Vinod Chopra's *Lage Raho Munna Bhai* have made the greatest public impact, while Arun Patwardhan's '*War and Peace*' is the best presentation of the horrors of militarism and war, particularly nuclear weapons vis a vis Gandhi's gospel of Truth, non violence, universal brotherhood and peace.

h). Education and Academic Disciplines

Though Gandhi affirmed he was only a *"practical idealist"* and not a philosopher, his approach to every issue was so fundamental, that he has impacted substantially in diverse fields including education and academic disciplines without having any professional training for them.

Rousseau had lauded Plato's *Republic* as "*the finest treatise on education ever delivered.*" In said work, Plato had highlighted education as the "*one great thing*" essential for building his ideal society. Gandhi, who had read Plato's *Republic* and translated his '*Apology*' into Gujarati, placed equally high importance on education for creating his ideal Sarvodaya society. For him "*The education of the child begins with conception. The physical and mental states of the parents at the moment of conception are reproduced in the baby. Then during the period of pregnancy it continues to be effected by the mother's moods, desires and temperament as also by her ways of life. After birth the child imitates the parents and for a considerable number of years entirely depends on them.*" However his great contribution in this field was his innovative concept of Basic Education. He wrote "*The object of basic education is the physical, intellectual and moral development of the children through the medium of a handicraft. It is principally designed for village children and is meant to transform them into model villagers.*"

The fundamentals of Basic Education are:

"*Literacy is not the end of education nor even the beginning. It is only one of the means whereby man, woman or child can be educated. I would therefore begin the child's education by teaching it a useful handicraft and enabling it to produce from the moment it begins its training. I hold that the highest development of the mind and the soul is possible under such a system of education.*

All education to be true must be self supporting, i.e. in the end it will pay its expenses excepting the capital which will remain intact. In it the talent of the hand will be utilized even upto the final stage i.e. the students will be skillfully working at some industry for some period during the day. This will serve the double purpose of paying for their education and teaching them an occupation which they can later use to earn a living.

All education must be imparted through the medium of mother tongues or provincial languages. Students must also learn Hindustani, written in the Devanagari or Urdu script to facilitate Indiawide communication. They should translate into their own mother tongues all the new knowledge they learn and transmit it to the villages surrounding their respective schools.

There should be no sectional religious content in education but only universal ethics and a study of the basic tenets of all the great religious faiths other than one's own so that they cultivate a spirit of reverence for all of them.

The creation of a vital educational atmosphere is more important than the foundation of innumerable schools. Basic education links the students, whether from the villages or the cities, to all that is best and lasting in India. It cultivates their mental, physical and spiritual faculties and will spearhead a social revolution with the most far reaching consequences ....and go a long way towards eradicating some of the worst evils of the present social insecurity and poisoned relationship between the classes."

Separately Gandhi had affirmed "*Education is of no value if it is not able to build up a sound character*" ; and "*If we are to reach real peace in this world and if we are to carry on a real war against war, we shall have to begin with the children... Jesus never uttered a loftier or a grander truth than when he said that wisdom cometh out of the mouths of babes.*"

Glynn Richards draws attention to the similarities between Gandhi's educational ideas and those of Plato,Tillich, Montessori and Whitehead and writes " *What is most significant about Gandhi's philosophy of education is the way it reflects the teachings of other philosophers, theologians and educationists*" He explains that for Plato education did not consist in the accumulation of factual knowledge, but rather "*the contemplation of real existence: contemplation of the transcendental rather than the empirical, the realm of being rather then the realm of becoming*" and that Tillich "*sought to harmonize the three main aims of education, namely, the technical, humanistic and inductive, which stress the acquisition of skills, promotion of intellectual discipline and the preservation of social traditions respectively*". The Montesorri method of teaching "*combines the Platonic combination of music and bodily exercises and stresses the importance of a proper environment for teaching*" while for Whitehead, "*no curriculum could be considered complete without inclusion of technical subjects as acquisition of manual skills was as important as scientific knowledge and aesthetic appreciation*" In conclusion Richards writes "*Gandhi's Platonic spirit, his Tillichian approach, his Montessorian methodology and his Whiteheadian emphasis, places him in the vanguard of those who would propound an acceptable philosophy of education*".

Pitirim Sorokin, founder of Harvard Research Centre in Creative Altruism writes "*Unselfish love has enormous creative and therapeutic potentialities, far greater than most people think. Love is a life giving force, necessary for physical, mental and moral health; it is goodness and freedom at their loftiest; it is the finest and most powerful educational force for the ennoblement of humanity..... Supreme love transcends our conscious egos and their rational - hedonistic, utilitarian and endaemonistic - interests. If it remains ego-centred it is not supreme altruistic love but its low-grade modicum. No individual who consistently follows an ego-centric ethic can ever soar to the heights of supreme love and become either a Buddha or Jesus, a St. Francis of Assisi or a Gandhi.....Again and again Gandhi stresses that practically all his altruistic activity was motivated by the supraconscious,which he calls by the names of Truth, God, Love and so on. Mere rational knowledge of religion and ethics is quite insufficient for seeing Truth (God) and for following the path of supreme love. The grace of the supraconscious, activated through prayer, supplication, concentration, self surrender and humility is indispensable for such achievements."*

Whereas Gandhi's "*Basic Education*" has had only minimal impact on India's educational policy and edifice, which has promoted western style literary, technical and scientific education rather than primary education, the Gujarat Vidyapeeth at Ahmedabad (which Gandhi founded) and the Gandhigram Rural University near Madurai have dedicatedly kept alive this concept. Besides, over 100 universities in India have Centres for Gandhian Studies. The Indian Institute of Management in Ahmedabad has recently instituted a '*Project Ahimsa Shakti*' (non violence power) as part of its post graduate course in negotiations methodology. Harvard, Columbia and Chicago universities are offering courses in Gandhi's political and non violent conflict resolution strategies. As notable is Schumacher College in Dartington, Devon, UK. Named after E.F. Schumacher, author of the Gandhi inspired '*Small is beautiful*' book, it offers according to its Gandhian founder director Satish Kumar "*a radical blueprint for a new kind of learning respecting not only intellectual understanding but also the earth and a sense of the sacred*". People of many nationalities and backgrounds come here for a period of intensive study, practical activity, and contemplation. Arne Naess, Fritjof Capra, Deepak Chopra, Humberto Maturana, Wolfgang Sachs and Vandana Shiva are among the many reputed thinkers who have taught here.

j). Economic theory and methodology

Gandhi's economic ideas, which were principally motivated by the widespread and grinding poverty of India, have drawn severe criticism as primitive and impractical. One critic emphatically declared "*Gandhi does not understand economics*" and accused him of trying "*to put back the clock*". Yet even in the economic field Gandhi has had a notable impact.

For Gandhi there was no sharp distinction between economics and ethics. *"Economics that hurt the moral well being of an individual or a nation are immoral and therefore sinful. So also, the economics that permit one country to prey upon another are immoral...Swaraj has no meaning for the millions if they do not know how to employ their enforced idleness. Attainment of Swaraj is possible within a short time, but it is possible only by the revival of the spinning wheel."*

Gandhi wanted the village to be the basic economic entity and its economy geared to the people's innate talents, traditional avocations and easily available/replaceable natural resources. Where production of a particular item required a higher investment than the village could afford it would be located in the closest town. Those who chose to work in that town would continue to live in their own village. These small industrial townships would benefit from low cost rural labour and the capital generated by revived agriculture. Besides, they would motivate improvement of local communication networks and not need ordinary requisites to be brought in from far away cities.

Gandhi's ideas of simple living and manual labour reflected the views of Tolstoy, Ruskin and Thoreau. For him *"Civilization in the real sense of the term consists not in the multiplication but in the deliberate and voluntary reduction of selfish wants. This alone promotes real happiness and contentment and increases the capacity for service"*

Gandhi was quite opposed to state intervention in economic matters as it impinges on the individual's creativity. *"I look upon an increase of the power of the state with the greatest fear, because while apparently doing good by minimizing exploitation, it does the greatest harm to mankind by destroying individuality, which lies at the root of all progress. I know of many cases where men have adopted trusteeship, but none where the state has really lived for the poor."* He believed that moral suasion was an effective tool even in the economic field and could bring about beneficial change by getting individuals to change their economic behaviour e.g., stop buying foreign cloth. Vinobha Bhave's Bhoodan movement is a good example of successful moral suasion.

Though Gandhi wrote and spoke much about his economic ideas he neither had the time nor training to formulate a coherent economic theory. What came to be called *"Gandhian Economics"* was the outcome of the dedicated efforts of his remarkable disciple J.C.Kumarappa (JCK), who over a two decade period enunciated it in the columns of Young India and his book *'Economy of Permanence'*, published in 1945. In this book, JCK using simple examples of birds, animals and bees identified five types of economies: Parasitic, Predatory, Enterprising, Gregationary, and Service Oriented. It is only with the last mentioned, which is not profit oriented and acquisitive but, *"like nature, is dovetailed together in a common cause....and violence does not break the chain, that we have an economy of permanence"*. He blames the profit motive and mass production for most of the world's ills. *"Wars are started for capturing markets and creating customers for the surplus products. Production takes place first and the demand is then created at the point of a bayonet"*. Echoing Gandhi, he argues that only a village based and service oriented economy can ensure full employment, social welfare, nature conservation, true democracy and peace; Western civilization is "*like a Christmas tree, well decorated with tinsel and overladen with drums, bugles, dolls etc. ....But as the Christmas tree is cut off from the live plant, it cannot draw sap from mother earth; though it may retain its freshness for a while it will soon droop and dry and thereafter be of use only as firewood*".

Educated at Syracuse University, JCK was a thriving chartered accountant in Bombay, when in 1929, as advised by a friend, he went to seek Gandhi's opinion on his Columbia University doctoral dissertation on *'Public Finance and Indian Poverty'*. In the latter's hut he had to sit "*on the cow dung floor, regardless of the well kept crease of my silk trousers !*". However, he was amply compensated. Gandhi praised his dissertation - " *You are the first economist I have come across who thinks on the same lines as I do*" - and offered to publish it, in installments, in "*Young India*'. Thus began their close and long collaboration. Subsequently he got JCK to take up the editorship of Young India and become president of the All India Village Industries Association. The fact that Gandhi captivated the foreign educated, silk suited JCK at their very first meeting is another proof of the magical effect of his personality.

The first foreign economist to come out in support of Gandhi's economic ideas was Ernst Schumacher, the German economist who was adviser to the British Coal Board. In his book *'Small is Beautiful'* he described Gandhi as a *"People's Economist...who refused to treat economics as if people did not matter"* and argued *"The technology of mass production is inherently violent, ecologically damaging, self defeating in terms of non renewable resources and stultifying for the human person. The technology of production by the masses, making use of the best of modern knowledge and experience is conducive to decentralization, compatible with the laws of ecology, gentle in its use of scarce resources and designed to serve the human person instead of making him the servant of machines"*. He named this *'Intermediate Technology'* and affirmed it was vastly superior to traditional technologies and simpler and cheaper than modern ones. George McRobie followed Schmacher's lead with his book *'Small is possible'*. Separately, Ivan Illich, an Austrain Catholic priest in Mexico, echoed Schumacher's ideas in his books *'Tools for conviviality'* and *'Energy and Equity'*.

Narender Pani's book *'Inclusive Economics'* lauds Gandhi's economic methodology which unlike the conventional economic approach of constructing theoretical models and framing policies based thereon, focused first on the desired objectives and then on the requisites to achieve them. Pani argues that this approach is much better able to produce the intended results than abstract theoretical models which, as the ASEAN economic crisis of 1997 showed, often yield unexpected, calamitous results. He writes *"It is Gandhi's skepticism about grand theories that makes him relevant to the challenges faced by economists at the beginning of the 21st century. Gandhi emphasized the need to go beyond theories to understanding society. The method he developed was inclusive enough to deal with both the known and the unknown while reducing the scope for expediency. Once we shift the focus of theory to method, there is much wider acceptance of Gandhi's ideas. Even within mainstream economics there is some recognition of the value of the Gandhian method. .... Too often Gandhi's ideas are associated with his ascetic life style. There is in fact a tendency to believe that the Gandhian method would only be relevant to those who accept his ascetic lifestyle. But once we recognize that the method would be equally consistent with a variety of moral frameworks, it gains wider relevance".*

Gandhi's innovative Trusteeship concept that *"those who own money now are asked to behave like Trustees, holding their riches on behalf of the poor"*, sought to establish a link between ethics and economics and transform the inhumane capitalist order into a humane one by inducing moral transformation of capitalists. It also sought to avert the expropriations and killings which class wars engender. The 1917 Russian Revolution had shown how chaotic and brutal these turn out to be. He wrote *"It is my firm conviction that if the State suppressed capitalism by violence, it will be caught in the evils of violence itself. The state represents violence in a concentrated and organized form. The individual has a soul, but the State is a soulless machine and can never be weaned from violence to which it owes its existence. Hence I prefer the doctrine of trusteeship".*

Its essence is that wealth acquired either through bequest or through trade, industry and other means is *"God given"* and belongs as much to the community as to oneself and must be held in trust and used for the general welfare. During Gandhi's lifetime this concept evoked poor response. However, two Indian capitalists, Jamnalal Bajaj and J.R.D Tata adopted it. In the latter case it was partly because of family tradition but Gandhi's influence is undeniable as the following excerpt from one of JRD's letters reveals. *"I may say that I have always been basically in agreement with Gandhi's concept of trusteeship and have throughout my career tried to live up to it. In fact, our group of companies have, to the extent possible, officially adopted it as part of their credo. My only doubts have been in regard to the practical effect that can be given to such a concept, considering, on the one hand, the ethical standards, or lack of them, that seem to prevail today amongst large sections of the business community of our country, and on the other, the dogmatic view of socialism and the resultant hostility towards private enterprise adopted by our government".*

In recent years, as the sharp demarcation between capital and labour has faded with employee stock-options making labour part owner of the enterprise's capital, and corporate social responsibility has emerged as an integral element in good corporate governance, Gandhi's Trusteeship concept is being adopted by some of Indias new business tycoons like Narayan Murthy of Infosys and Azim Premji of Wipro. Multimillionaires though they are, their personal lives are remarkably modest and much of their surplus wealth is spent in providing education and toilet facilities for the masses. The most impressive example of the Gandhi's Trusteeship concept in action however is the Tata Steel plant and township in Jamshedpur about which the world's largest private steel maker Lakshmi Mittal has written *"For the breed that talks about corporate social responsibility and the role of corporate India, a visit to Jamshedpur is a must..... I have nothing to do with Tata Steel, but I strongly believe the message of hope and the message of goodness that they are spreading is worth sharing..... They have done so much more since I last visited Jamshedpur in 1992. The town has obviously got busier but the values thankfully haven't changed.... Greener and cleaner and a tribute to environment management. You could have been in the mountains. Such was the quality of air I inhaled! There was no belching smoke; no tired faces and so many more women workers, even on the shop floor. ..... There was spring in the air which came from a certain calmness which has always been the hallmark of Jamshedpur.... Jamsetji Nusserwanji Tata had created an edifice that is today a robust company and it is not about profits and about valuation. It is not about who becomes a millionaire and who doesnt'. It is about getting the job done with dignity and respect keeping the age-old values intact....."*

k). Environment and Ecology

Gandhi's leadership in the environmental and ecological fields is clearly seen in his insistence on leading a simple life, keeping one's surroundings clean, protecting animal life, avoiding all wastage and utilizing locally available, renewable materials to the maximum extent. Among his many statements on these subjects are the following :

"A certain degree of physical comfort is necessary but above that itbecomes a hindrance. Therefore, creating an unlimited number of wants and satisfying them is a delusion and a snare. Man falls from the ideal of plain living and high thinking the moment he multiplies his daily wants. His happiness really lies in contentment. I make bold to say that the Europeans will have to remodel

their outlook if they are not to perish under the weight of the comforts to which they are becoming slaves".

"Earth provides enough to satisfy every man's need but not for every man's greed. ..... The wars of our times spring from greed."

"Instead of having graceful hamlets dotting the countryside, we have dung heaps. The approach to many villages is not a refreshing experience."

"It has become a matter of absorbing interest to me to find out how best to save our people from the heinous sin of fouling Mother Earth every morning"

"The cow to me means the entire sub human world. Man through the cow is enjoined to realize his identity with all that lives"

"The real conflict is not between environment and development but between environment and the reckless exploitation of the earth by man."

Lauding his ecological wisdom Schumacher wrote *"Gandhi had always known, and rich countries are now reluctantly beginning to realize, that their affluence was stripping the world. The USA with 5.6% of world population is consuming upto 40% of the world's resources, most of them non renewable....Enough is now known about the basic facts of space ship earth to realize that its first class passengers are making demands which cannot be sustained very much longer without destroying the space ship"*

Judging from the still deplorable hygene and sanitary conditions in much of India it must be conceded that Gandhi's impact in this sphere has been limited but Dr. Bindeshwar Pathak's Sulabh Sauchalayas (referred to at page 86) is an impressive beginning in this respect. In the environmental field some of his devotees, particularly Sunderlal Bahuguna and Vandana Shiva have done impressive work. The former, who had met and been blessed, by Gandhi on the day before his assassination, dedicated his life to promoting Gandhi's message, and subsequently Vinoba Bhave's , in the Tehri region of the Himalayan foot hills. In 1973, when commercial tree cutting began in Chamoli district, the *Chipko* (literally "*to cling* " in Hindi) movement was initiated by a group of female and male activists to resist this and reclaim their traditional forest rights. Those who played pivotal roles in this were Gaura Devi, Sudesha Devi, Bachni Devi, Sunderlal Bahuguna, Chandi Prasad Bhatt, and Govind Singh Rawat. The movement soon spread throughout the Himalayan foothills. Its most notable feature was mass participation of women who, as the backbone of that region's economy, were directly affected by deforestation. Their anthem was :

'Laathi goley khayenge, apne paed bachatenge
(We shall face the batons and bullets, we shall save our trees)
Bhaley Kulhade chamkenge, hum paedon par chipkenge
(The shining axe will be raised, we will cling to the trees)

This brave struggle was waged for eight years and attracted both nationwide and international attention. It finally achieved its objective in 1981 when commercial felling of trees in the Himalayan foothills was banned.

The reputed ecologist, Vandana Shiva, chose the commencement date of Gandhi's Salt March for launching her '*Bija Satyagraha*' against genetically modified seeds, and declared *"Just as Gandhiji had made salt at Dandi to announce non-cooperation with the unjust British Salt Laws, the Bija Satygraha is an announcement of people's non-cooperation with the unjust patent laws that make seed saving by farmers a crime"*.

The international Green Movement clearly acknowledges his inspiration. Petra Kelly, a founder of the German Green party, has publicly stated: *"In one particular area of our political work we have been greatly inspired by Mahatma Gandhi. That is in our belief that a life style and method of production which rely on an endless supply and a lavish use of raw materials generates the motive for the violent appropriation of these raw materials from other countries. In contrast, a responsible use of raw materials, as part of an ecologically oriented life style and economy, reduces the risk that policies of violence will be pursued in our name"*. Like minded Green parties have been formed in a number of other European and Latin American countries.

That Gandhi has impacted substantially in the global environmental field is testified by the United Nations' Environmental programme making his maxim *"The world provides enough to satisfy every man's need, but not for every man's greed."* the prime slogan of its publicity campaign. The US Public Broadcasting service, in its RACE TO SAVE THE PLANET TV Series has done likewise.

The 1992 UN Conference on Environment and Development held at Rio de Janeiro, in June 1992, attended by 117 heads of state and representatives of 178 nations was the largest ever gathering of world leaders. The treaties and other documents they signed committed their nations to the pursuit of economic development in ways that would protect the Earth's environment and nonrenewable resources.

In September 1999, the UN General Assembly adopted a *'Declaration on a Culture of Peace'* calling upon governments, international organizations and civil society to promote this culture based on respect for life, freedom, justice, tolerance, dialogue, cooperation, democracy, equal rights and opportunities for all and sustainable development. The year 2000 was declared as '*The International Year for the Culture of Peace and the period 2001 - 2010 as the International Decade for a Culture of Peace and Non-Violence for the Children of the World*'. This was the first time that non-violence was made a clear and distinct component in a universal declaration and action programme.

On June 27, 2007, the UN General assembly adopted a resolution to observe 2 October each year as *International Day of Non-Violence* and called upon all Member States, United Nations organizations, NGOs and individuals to commemorate it in an appropriate manner and disseminate the message of non-violence by all possible means.

I). Management theory and practice.

Gandhi's impact in the field of management was not direct but through the change in the intellectual mindset on this subject gestated by the successful management of his many satyagrahas in which thousands of people, of diverse backgrounds participated, and by his Trusteeship concept.

In the throes of the world economic depression of the late 1920s, Britain's leading economist John Maynard Keynes in his 1930 '*A Treatise on Money*' had enunciated a remarkably amoral guideline for economic management. "*For atleast another hundred years we must pretend to ourselves that fair is foul and foul is fair; for foul is useful and fair is not. Avarice and usury and precaution must be our gods for a little longer still. For only they can lead us out of the tunnel of economic necessity into daylight*".

In sharp contrast, by the mid 1980s, the American management guru Peter Drucker had a very different gospel for managers. In his '*The New Realities*' he wrote: "*Because management deals with the motivation and direction of people in a common venture, it is deeply embedded in culture. A basic challenge managers therefore face is to identify those elements of the traditions and culture of their workers that can be used as management building blocks. Besides, as everyone like myself, who has worked with managers of all kinds of institutions for long years, have become aware, management is deeply involved with spiritual concerns - the nature of man, good and evil."*

In recent years concepts of Total Quality Management (TQM), Customer Relations management (CRM), Corporate Social Responsibility (CSR), Safeguarding the interests of all Stake Holders (SIASH), Frugal Engineering (FE), Lean Management (LM), Core Competence (CC), Building Scale at Lower Price Points (BSLPP), Culture of Innovative Thinking (CIT) and Visionary Leadership (VL) have come to be embodied in management theory and good corporate governance practices. Gandhi had urged practised all of these by the 1920 & 30s.

Concerning TQM, he had written "Students must all do spinning in a scientific manner. Their tools shall always be neat, clean and in good order and condition, then their yarn will naturally be of the highest quality".

On CRM, he had stated. "A customer is the most important visitor on our premises. He is not dependent on us. We are dependent on him. He is not an interruption in our work. He is the purpose of it... We are not doing him a favour by serving him. He is doing us a favour by giving us an opportunity to do so" .

His CSR is seen in his educational, health and sanitation efforts for the Champaran Indigo peasants, soon after he had secured a negotiated settlement of their grievances with the British landlords.

As for SIASH, he availed of his 1931 London visit for the Round Table Conference, to travel to Manchester to explain to textile mill workers and owners the rationale for the British textiles boycott he had launched in India. He did this despite the fact that just a few weeks earlier (in April

Gandhi with Lancashire textile workers in 1931

that year) eight thousand people had gathered in Blackburn "*to inform the Government that...unless a firm stand is taken which will stamp out Sedition, Lawlessness and Disorder [in India], there can be no hope for a revival of the Lancashire Cotton Trade.*" In an interview with the Press prior to this visit, he stated "*There is so much misunderstanding [in Lancashire] about what we have done with foreign cloth. If I went up there and talked with them I should be cross-examined, and would speak to them without reserve.*" He spent two days in this area (September 25-27) visiting many mills and meeting mill workers & owners, textile traders, journalists and the Mayor of Preston.

His FE and LM are seen is his choice of the charka for India's emancipation from colonialism and abysmal poverty, and his insistence on stringency in all expenditure and strict accounting of every rupee spent. He continued using the same pencil until it became so small that he could no longer write with it, and often used incoming post cards and envelopes to send replies and notes to associates.

CC according to J. Collins and J.I.Porras "*is a strategic concept that captures your best inherent capabilities*". Gandhi's knowledge of India's history led him to identify textiles as his people's core competence. For centuries India had clothed much of Europe with the finest cottons, muslins and "cashmeres". Fierce competition from machine made textiles and a taxation system that favoured imported rather than domestic textiles had ended this. The charka he advocated revived India's textile and subsequently other traditional industries. Since Independence, India is once again clothing millions of people all over the world. The Charka is also good testimony of Gandhi's BSLPP, CIT and VL.

Even before the new millennium dawned, Ashok Khosla, President of Development Alternatives, in an article in the Times of India (October 22, 1998) described Gandhi as the *'Prophet of Post Modernism'* extolled him as "*one of the greatest innovators of the 20th century*". He wrote "*Gandhiji was not for a primitive, back to the land life. Rather, he was a firm believer in technology as one of the means to improve the lives of our people. He was particularly sensitive to the need for improving the productivity of the workplace and the central role of technology in achieving this. He even offered one of the largest prizes of his time to a technological innovation.... His insights on technology, economics and governance may well be the most valuable resource for the wisdom we need to survive into the 21st century.*"

Anand David, Founder-Director, Manford Alliance, writing in the special "*The Leader Mahatma*' issue (October 2nd 2005) of Training and Management wrote "*After Peter Senge's 'Fifth Discipline' or Daniel Goleman's*

'Working with Emotional Intelligence', a scholar's book that genuinely stands out in the world of organizations and their development is Jim Collin's 'Good to Great' which states that in research studies of successful and enduring organizations the character of the leader consistently stood out. One key concept is Level 5 leadership. Level 5 leaders are a study in polarity in being both modest yet determined, humble yet bold.... Their primary driver is the larger cause of an enduring organization (read nation) rather than personal myopic gain. This is Gandhi to many of us".

Level 5 leadership is the pinnacle of People Capable Maturity Model (PCMM) developed by the Software Engineering Institute of Carnegie Mellon University in 1995. Whereas 1-4 leadership levels relate to basic management, work processes, environment, organizational competencies, skill analysis, team building and mentoring, level 5 is concerned with motivation and optimization of personnel and organizational competencies through inspired leadership and perfect teamwork.

C.K. Prahalad, does not mention Gandhi in his widely acclaimed book '*The Fortune At The Bottom of The Pyramid : Eradicating Poverty Through Profits*' but when he spoke at the INFOSYS Campus in Bangalore in 2008 he revealed that Gandhi's '*Talisman*' had impacted on him greatly. In the Preface to his mentioned book he writes "*This book is the result of a long and lonely journey for me. It started during the Christmas vacation of 1995. During that period of celebration and good cheer one issue kept nagging me : what are we doing about the poorest people around the world. Why is it that with all our technology, managerial know how and investment capacity, we cannot make even a minor contribution to the problem of pervasive global poverty and disenfranchisement. Why cant we create inclusive capitalism?*"

In his book he enunciates how companies, big and small, can serve the world's poorest people and yet make a profit. He also points out the new bottom of the pyramid resources and trends in technology, health care, consumer goods, finance etc. His gospel is that it is possible to build profitable businesses, create new eco-systems for wealth creation and reduce poverty and human misery, all at the same time. In other words : "*doing well by doing good*".

Among the many examples he gives of successful BOP enterprises are Nirma soaps/shampoos in mini bars/sachets, Jaipur rugs and prosthesis, Annapurna salt, Aravind Eye Care, ITC e Choupal, Bharti Airtel and Casas Bahia.

About this book Bill Gates has written "*C.K. Prahalad argues that companies must revolutionize how they do business in developing countries if both sides of that economic equation are to prosper. Drawing on a wealth of case studies, his compelling new book offers an intriguing blueprint for how to fight poverty with profitability*".

The greatest compliment to Gandhi's management insights, practices and achievements has come from Alan Axelrod, who had earlier written about these aspects of Queen Elizabeth I, Gen. George Patton and Winston Churchill. In his 2010 book, *Gandhi CEO: 14 Principles to Guide & Inspire Modern Leaders,* he affirms "*There is no doubt that Gandhi was a good man and an intensely spiritual man, but he was also a manager and executive, a supremely practical leader for change [management].*" .

His book has 14 chapters, each presenting one of the fourteen principles. Among them he gives prime importance to "*a humane and people-oriented approach*" - based on Gandhi's "*Talisman*". and to transparency to which he attributes Gandhi's moral stature and ultimate success. He urges CEOs to adopt these principles in all their decision-making processes and make their leadership an open book, since a "*closed book has little meaning and less value.*" He also urges them to be role models, demonstrate consistency in principles and give equal importance to means and ends.

He extolls Gandhi's non cooperation strategy and his vital insight that even oppressive governments derive their authority from the consent, voluntary or coerced, of the governed. He affirms that both these should be stark reminders to CEOs that businesses cannot be run by coercion and urges them to earn the cooperation and trust of their employees/stake holders, and welcome dissent because "*if everyone is thinking alike, no one is really thinking.*"

Lauding Gandhi's well planned, methodical approach in India's freedom struggle he avers that corporations too need to adopt such an approach as radical change merely for shaking things up is pointless. The challenge always is to change reality towards a desirable goal without creating chaos.

In a presentation at the '*Gandhi, Governance and the Corporation*' colloquium at IIM, Bangalore on October 2, 2008 Mr. R. Gopalakrishnan, CEO, Tata Sons, stated "*The business world is at an inflection point. At the time of the Industrial Revolution, for the business world, the basis of competitive advantage was physical assests; in the last thirty years we have heard a lot about competitiveness being based on information and knowledge assets: as we go forward into whatever the next age will be called, competitiveness in the world of business will be on ethical assets....... I have talked about this concept of Trusteeship and the way Tatas have practised it to managers of our acquired companies in Detroit, Norwich, UK and Singapore. Initially they just do not believe this is possible. Gradually the penny drops that ours is a very unique kind of organization which is actually doing this. I hope in course of time this will increase people's confidence that business can be humane and need not be an inhuman pursuit of greed*".

Now that other Indian companies have/are emerging as multinationals, they too should show the world that Gandhi's innovative management concepts and practices are compatible with and vital for their success. That this is perhaps happening already is revealed in "*The India Way*", a 2010 book authored by Peter Cappelli, Harbir Singh, Jitendra V.Singh and Michael Useem (all from Wharton School of Business). It shows how leading Indian companies are scoring remarkable successes not by adopting Western management concepts but innovative new ones rooted in their own historical and organizational cultures, and by looking beyond stockholders' interests to public mission and national purpose, by identifying products and services of compelling value to customers and improvising and adapting manufacturing processes to overcome endless hurdles.

m) Psychology and Psychiatry:

The reputed psychologist Eric Erikson has written "*The Freudian movement was not alone in emphasizing therapeutic persuasion as a cure for man's aberrations. The same period saw the development of a systematic concern with "the minds of men", as strategic for both peace and war, adaptation and revolution.*" He has averred that "*Gandhi's way is that of a double conversion. The hateful person, by containing his egoistic hate and by learning to love the opponent as human, will confront the opponent with an enveloping technique that will force or rather permit him to regain his latent capacity to trust and to love", that in all confrontations, the emphasis is not so much on the power to be gained over the opponent as on the" cure of an unbearable inner condition*" and that "*only the combined insight and discipline of Satyagraha can really give man the power that is stronger than all arms*". He has lauded Gandhi thus "*In a period when proud statesmen could speak of a "war to end War', when the super-policemen of Versailles could bathe in the glory of a peace that would make "the world safe for democracy" , when the Russian Revolutionaries entertained the belief that terror could initiate an eventual "withering away of the state", one man in India confronted the world with the strong suggestion that a new political instrument endowed with a new kind of religious fervour, may yet provide man with a choice.*"

n). Science and Technology

Because of Gandhi's emphasis on "*production by the masses rather than mass production*" some critics have alleged he was anti-science and anti-progress. Specifically asked in 1924 why he was anti-machinery his response was: "*How I can be anti-machinery when I know that even this body is a delicate piece of machinery? The spinning wheel is a machine, a little toothpick is a machine. What I object to is the craze for machinery, not machinery as such. The machine should not atrophy the limbs of man".*

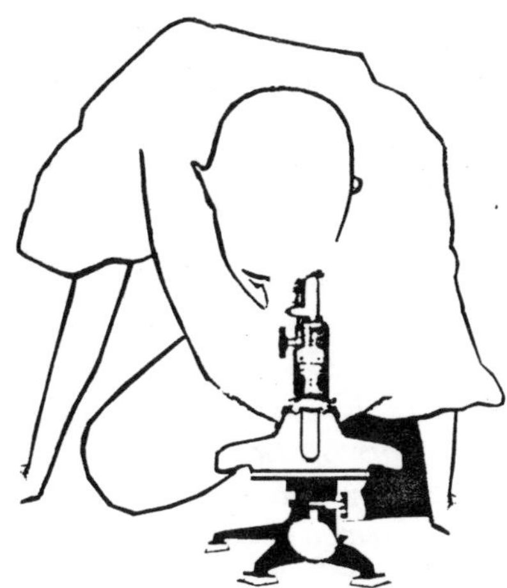

He held that machinery, by being *"labour saving"* makes thousands of workers redundant and lands them on the streets. He wanted people to be industrious, *"not like a machine, but like the busy bee."* and affirmed *"I would prize every invention made for the benefit of all and welcome the machine that lightens the burden of millions of people living in villages."*. The machine he extolled was the Singer sewing machine.

Johan Galtung comments " *In Gandhi's famous acceptance of the Singer sewing machine we see the acceptance of a machine that can be operated by one person and hence leads neither to exploitation nor to alienation. This leads to the interesting question of whether Gandhi would have accepted more machines of this kind (such as a lap top computer) that do not meet with the objections of machinism".* Galtung thinks he would have and states " *The crucial point is autonomy, in small decentralized units, not excluding all the fruits, bitter or sweet of modern, technical civilization."*

The devastating effects on India of mass production with modern machinery is well brought out by Paul Kennedy: *"India imported a mere 1 million yards of cotton fabric in 1814, but that figure had risen to 51 million yards by 1830 and to a staggering 995 million yards by 1870. The awful result, according to one calculation, was that whereas the British and Indian peoples had roughly similar per capita levels of industrialization at the onset of the Industrial Revolution in 1750, India's level was only one hundredth of the United Kingdom's by 1900".*

Claude Markovits has evaluated Gandhi's views on science quite accurately. He points out that whereas Gandhi was a severe critic of the way science was applied in the fields of industry, medicine and armaments, he was not opposed to science itself. *"In fact his whole approach, including to the Divine, was very scientific as he wanted to discover Truth through experimentation, as the title of his biography clearly indicates. One might even question if Gandhi's God was transcendent, since he believed so strongly in Truth only through experimentation".*

Michael Sonnleitner presents Gandhi's "scientific" formulation of Satyagraha thus : *"There is an indefinable mysterious power that pervades everything...a living power that is changeless, that holds all together, that creates, dissolves and recreates. That Power is God... This God is a Living Force. Our life is of that Force. That Force resides in but is not of the body. He who denies the existence of that great Force denies to himself the use of that inexhaustible Power and thus remains impotent. ...... Satyagraha is soul force pure and simple and whenever and to whatever extent there is room for the use of arms or physical force, there and to that extent there is so much less possibility for soul force. These are purely antagonistic forces and I had full realization of this antagonism even at the advent of Satyagraha....... Satyagraha connotes the living Law of Life. The law will work, just as the law of gravitation will work, whether we accept it or not. And just as a scientist will work wonders out of various applications of the laws of nature, even so a man who applies the law of love with scientific precision can work greater wonders"* Sonnleitner concludes "*A sufficiently developed satyagrahi could render venomous reptiles harmless or set a hungry tiger to peace. Gandhi's citing of numerous satyagrahi images thus include the exemplary figure of Daniel, who on entering the den of lions, was left unharmed by them.... No force could withstand the light of the world, the force of God embodied in human kind.... Whether or not Gandhi is correct in his formulations, however, must remain an issue of incredible importance, on which our more personal reflections may, in time, shed greater light."*

Gandhi had also stated: "*Scientists tell us that, without the presence of the cohesive force amongst the atoms that comprise this globe of ours, it would crumble to pieces and we would cease to exist. Even as there is a cohesive force in blind matter, so must there be in all things animate and the name of that cohesive force is love.....But we have to learn to use that force among all that lives.... Where there is love there is life; hatred leads to destruction.....I have therefore ventured to place before India the ancient law of self sacrifice... The rishis who discovered the law of non-violence in the midst of violence, were greater geniuses than Newton...*"

It is notable that Gandhi's "*Living Force*" which can provide "*inexhaustible power*" to every human soul, is remarkably akin to Einstein's $E = MC^2$ formula which reveals that even the tiniest particle of matter is compacted energy which when released could provide enormous quantities of power. Interestingly, the two concepts were enunciated within a year of each other - 1905 and 1906!. Also notable is that Gandhi described his "*theory*" as "*science in the making*" adding that "*My technique of nonviolent struggle is in the same stage as electricity in Edison's time. It needs to be refined and developed*".

In an article in Gandhi Marg on '*Gandhi as a Scientist*' T.S.Ananthu quotes Einstein as follows "*A human being is part of the whole, called by us "universe", a part limited in space and time. He experiences himself, his thoughts and feelings as something separated from the rest; a kind of optical delusion of his consciousness. This delusion is a kind of prison for us, restricting us to our personal desires and to affection for a few persons nearest to us. Our task must be to free ourselves from this prison by widening our circle of compassion to embrace all living creatures and the whole of nature in its beauty."* Ananthu concludes thus *"The above definition of a human being, and the goal of our life on earth, seems so much like a statement by Gandhi - yet, it has come from the pen of Einstein. It indicates the commonality of their world-view, and the Law of Love or Non-Violence as the foundation of the ultimate Law which governs the entire universe - the inanimate as well as the animate parts of it. Gandhi's understanding and personal experience of this ultimate Law of Life entitles him to be called a great scientist."*

o). Political philosophy and militant nationalism

Prof Gene Sharpe, besides crediting Gandhi with showing how to nonviolently yet effectively oppose injustice and oppression, also credits him with *"one of the most fundamental of all insights into the nature of Government - that all rulers in fact are dependent for their power on the submission, cooperation and obedience of their subjects"* and injustification quotes him *"In politics, its (Satyagraha's) use is based on the immutable maxim that government of the people is possible only so long as they consent either consciously or unconsciously to be governed".*

Dr. Joan Bondurant affirms that Gandhi made an *"inestimable contribution to political philosophy"* by challenging the basic assumptions of main stream political theory which assumes a separation of means and ends *"The Gandhian dialectic views means as ends-in-the-making. In contrast to the Hegelian and Marxian dialectics, the Gandhian is not descriptive of society but is a process to be applied by human beings in resolving basic conflicts and in producing an entirely new total circumstance .... The Gandhian experiments suggest that if man is to free himself from fear and threat alike, he pause in his flight from violence to set himself to the task of its conquest".*

Professor Dennis Dalton, who extols Gandhi for making a fundamental contribution to political theory with his concepts of Swaraj, rights and duties, writes *"European and American political theory has remained split since the 17th century in its conceptualization of freedom and obligation. The philosophies of Locke and Mill on the one side against Rousseau and Hegel on the other, mark a theoretical schism related to these two concepts so deep that it suggests, in Isiah Berlin's judgement, profoundly divergent and irreconcilable attitudes to the ends of life".* He argues that Gandhi by directly relating rights to duties and freedom to responsibility constitutes the *"different voice"* in political thought which *"merits inclusion in Western political discourse"*. Gandhi's linkage of rights to duties was based on the premise that all the individual's rights are provided by society and therefore their continuance had to benefit the individual and also society. Thus the right to free speech would survive only if individuals perform their duty by not using this right in an anti-social way. By society, he meant the collective entity of individuals and not the state. He was skeptical about the role of the state in this field.

Prof. Glenn Paige, in his 1990 Gandhi memorial lecture at Gandhi Smriti and Darshan Samiti, New Delhi stressed the need for an international, interspiritual, interdisciplinary global institution *"to help bring the legacy of Gandhiji and other non-violent resources to bear in global Satyagraha (non-violent action based on Truth and Love) for global Sarvodaya (nonviolent well being of all)"*. Having succeeded, against all odds, in establishing the Centre for Global Non-Violence at Honolulu in 2000, he thereafter embarked on his next, even more ambitious project of formulating a *'Non Killing Global Political Science"*. His book thus titled and published in 2001, surveys the evolution of political philosophy from Plato to the present day, lists the many successful non-violent struggles in recent decades and envisions a non-violent global community with *"no killing, no threats to kill and no weapons specifically designed to kill"*. Prof. William Smirnov, Vice President, Russian Political Science Association & International Political Science Association has extolled the book thus *"The basic ideas in this unique book can and should be accepted as the basis of common values for humanity in the 21st century as well as a program for their realization"*

More pertinent to the present terrorism-plagued global scenario is Gandhi's 1909 booklet *'Hind Swaraj'*, *"written in answer to the Indian school of violence"* and presenting *"the gospel of love in place of that of hate"*. Subsequently he wrote *"It (Hind Swaraj) was an attempt to offer the revolutionary something infinitely superior, retaining the whole of the spirit of self sacrifice and bravery that was to be found in the revolutionary"*.

Regarding the violent activities of militant Indian nationalists he wrote prophetically, in 1908 : *"The bomb now thrown at Englishmen will be aimed at Indians after the British are there no longer.....However much I may sympathize with and admire worthy motives, I am an uncompromising opponent of violent methods even to serve the noblest of causes....Acts of violence create bitterness in the survivors and brutality in the destroyer"*

In December 1928, in an article titled '*The curse of assassination*' he wrote: "*English books have taught us to applaud as heroic deeds of daring, even those of free-booters, villains, pirates and train wreckers. Newspapers fill columns with exciting stories, real or imaginary, of such deeds. Some of us have learnt this art of applauding anything adventurous. This cannot be regarded as anything but a bad omen. Surely there is nothing noble about a cold blooded robbery or murder*".

In September 1931, at the Emerson Club in London he averred that "*War demoralizes those who are trained for it. It brutalizes men of gentle character. It outrages every beautiful cannon of morality. Its path of glory is foul with the passions of lust and red with the blood of murder. This is not the pathway to our goal*".

If Gandhi's offer of "*the gospel of love in place of that of hate*" was/is accepted by India's militant nationalists and present day "jihadi" and other suicide bombers in various parts of the world, their respective agendas would have been/be far better served, and the world would have been infinitely better and safer today. That this "offer" was made over a hundred years ago, is a measure of Gandhi's extraordinary foresight, and insight into "*revolutionary heroism*". Johan Galtung extolls him thus "*Gandhi was certainly a revolutionary, much more revolutionary than the piecemeal revolutionaries of Western civilization..... Gandhi revolutionized revolution itself*".

"Non-Violence" sculpture at the UN building, New York

"The moral to be legitimately drawn from the supreme tragedy of the bomb is that it will not be destroyed by counter bombs...... Unless the world now adopts non-violence, it will spell certain suicide for mankind."

- Artwork by Nandalal Bose

Vindication of Gandhi's Vision and Strategy in the Global Scenario

Modern Civilization and WWs I & II:

In '*Hind Swaraj*' Gandhi' made devastating comments on Modern Civilization and the abhorrent dehumanization, violence and war inherent in it. Many critics have branded these as grossly inaccurate. Even Rajmohan Gandhi has described them as "*a slanted view*" and "*a warrior's manifesto*". However, he agrees with Devanesab that "*In the summer of 1909, Gandhi knew more about the realities of armed conflicts than any of the passionate revolutionaries who talked to him so earnestly*", and indicates "*The Gandhi of 1909 had seen the Boer and Zulu wars from close quarters ...... and there had been atleast three violent attacks on his person in South Africa.*" C.F.Andrews points out that Hind Swaraj was written when Tolstoy's influence was strongest on Gandhi and that in his '*The Slavery of our Times*' Tolstoy had linked violence with Modern Civilization. Besides, Gandhi had read Edward Carpenter's '*Civilization : Its Cause and Cure*', which had castigated it as a "*disease*".

Whatever the sources and degree of "*slant*" in '*Hind Swaraj*', the fact is that many of its assertions have come true almost exactly as stated : "*Formerly they wore skins and used spears as their weapons. Now they wear long trousers ...and carry revolvers containing five or more chambers....Formerly men travelled in wagons; now they travel in trains at the rate of four hundred and more miles per day. This is considered the height of civilization. It has been stated that, as men progress, they shall be able to travel in airships and reach any part of the world in a few hours. Men will not need the use of their hands and feet. They will press a button and they will have their clothing by their side. They will press another button and they will have their newspaper; a third and a motor car will be waiting for them....Formerly, when people wanted to fight with one another they measured between them their bodily strength; now it is possible to take away thousands of lives by one man working behind a gun from a hill. This is civilization.......Formerly men were made slaves under physical compulsion. Now they are enslaved by temptation of money and of the luxuries that money can buy. There are now diseases of which people never dreamed of before and an army of doctors is engaged in finding out their cures, and so hospitals have increased. This is a test of civilization. If anyone speaks to the contrary, know that he is ignorant. This civilization takes note neither of morality nor of religion. Its votaries calmly state that their business is not to teach morality...... This civilization is irreligion and it has taken such a hold on the people of Europe that those who are in it appear to be half mad. ....According to the teaching of Mohammed this would be considered a Satanic civilization. Hinduism calls it the Black Age ('Kali Yuga')."*

The fact also is that in less than forty years after *Hind Swaraj* was written, nearly sixty million people, mostly civilians, were killed and hundreds of cities and towns destroyed all over Europe, North Africa, East and South East Asia in the two world wars, and the Spanish and Greek civil wars. Every belligerent used the most destructive weapons they could lay their hands on, the Americans even dropping atom bombs on two Japanese cities. In Germany, during the last three years of the odious Nazi regime, 6 million Jews, gypsies, homosexuals and physically handicapped people, went up as smoke from highly efficient "death factories". These incredible crimes against humanity having been committed by highly "*civilized*" countries, Gandhi's views on and concurrence with Modern Civilization's categorization as "*Satanic*" is perhaps not as "slanted" as it initially appears. Today many people, particularly in Germany and Italy, readily concede that Hitler and Mussolini were "*half mad*".

Gandhi's strong opposition to the partition of India has also been amply vindicated. Soon after Lord Mountbatten had announced the decision to partition India he had warned him "*If you are not to leave a legacy of chaos behind, you have to make your choice and leave the government of the whole of India ....to one party.*" He had indicated that even a Jinnah led government could be this "*one party*" provided India was not divided and this government ruled in the interests of all the Indian people. Strongly opposing Jinnah's "*Two Nation*" thesis he had demanded to know : "*Why, is India not one nation? Was it not one during the Moghul period? Is India composed of two nations? If so why only two? Are not Christians a third, Parsis a fourth and so on? Are the Muslims of China a nation separate from the other Chinese? ....I make bold to say that Jinnah and those who think like him are rendering no service to Islam; they are misrepresenting the message inherent in the very word Islam.*" .Subsequently, when Pakistan was becoming a reality, he wrote "*The army is going to be divided.... This division of the army certainly fills the heart of every patriot with fear and misgivings. Why are two armies being created? Are they to defend the country against foreign aggression or are they to fight each other ....*"

Arthur Herman has written about Gandhi's great agony over partition, Jinnah's great admiration and awe for Churchill and the secret correspondence between them, under assumed names. He has quoted "*one recent historian*" thus : "*If Jinnah is regarded as the Father of Pakistan, Churchill must qualify as its uncle*".

The massacres that preceded and accompanied partition, resulting in the deaths of over half a million people and displacement of twelve million, the four India Pakistan wars (including Kargil) and Pakistan's blood drenched break up within 25 years proves, as Rajmohan Gandhi affirms, that "*Gandhi was prophetic in the future he painted*". He has pointed out that some years after India's independence Britain began to apply NIBMAR (no independence before majority rule) and adds "*If NIBMAR had been applied to India partition would have been avoided, but for India HMG's principle was no majority rule before an all Indian consensus*". This is what gave Jinnah a veto on all proposals unpalatable to him, and to secure the Pakistan he was so determined to get even though it was to be a "*truncated, moth eaten*" one. Starting off as a secular democracy, that too soon became truncated and moth eaten. Its first military coup occurred in 1958 and lasted 13 years. The two others that followed after brief spells of democracy lasted 11 and 8 years giving Pakistan only 29 years of democratic governance in its sixty two years of existence. Its military rulers, bereft of a political base of their own, wooed and supported Islamic fundamentalists with disastrous consequences. In his book '*Pakistan : Between Mosque and Military*', Hussain Haqqani, advisor to three Pakistani prime ministers and former Ambassador to Sri Lanka, has written frankly about the deleterious effects of feeding successive generations of youth on the "*Two Nation*" theory and of the close military-bureaucratic-Islamist nexus. He also reveals that the "*ideological tripod*" of Islamic nationalism, anti-India rhetoric and securing foreign military/economic assistance has been Pakistan's main plank in trying to achieve the elusive national unity and international role it persistently sought.

Since losing Bangladesh, Pakistan's rulers, both civilian and military, have covertly and consistently used terrorism in their efforts to detach Kashmir from India and secure "*strategic depth*" in Afghanistan. Their terrorist chickens have come home to roost. One of them assassinated former Prime Minister Benazir Bhutto in December 2007. Numerous other terrorist attacks have occurred since then in Islamabad, Lahore, Karachi, Peshawar and even in the army citadel of Rawalpindi, causing many deaths and much destruction. Many political and security analysts now consider Pakistan "*a failed state and prime incubator of terrorism*" . The latter is particularly so after Osama bin Laden and his family were discovered to have been secretly ensconced since 2005 in a high walled secure mansion in the garrison city of Abbotabad, a stone's throw from its prestigious Pakistan Military Academy. He was killed there by a helicopter borne, US Navy Seal team on May 2, 2011.

Gandhi's views on nuclear arms were explicitly expressed in the tragicaftermath of the atom bomb drops on Hiroshima and Nagasaki: "*The moral to be legitimately drawn from the supreme tragedy of the bomb is that it will not be destroyed by counter bombs. Non-Violence is the only thing the atom bomb cannot destroy...... Unless the world now adopts nonviolence, it will spell certain suicide for mankind.*" Albert Einstein made a similar affirmation. "*The unleashed power of the atom has changed everything but our thinking; thus we are drifting toward a catastrophe beyond comparison. We shall require a new manner of thinking if mankind is to survive*".

For four decades after its independence India had steadfastly opposed the production, testing, stockpiling and threats of use of nuclear arms, as *'crimes against humanity'*. At the UN General Assembly's Third Special Session on Disarmament (February 1988), Prime Minister Rajiv Gandhi declared "*Nuclear weapons threaten to annihilate human civilization and all that mankind has built through millenia of labour and toil. Nuclear weapon states and non nuclear weapon states alike are threatened by such a holocaust. It is imperative that nuclear weapons be eliminated...... Peace must be predicated on a basis other than the assurance of global destruction. We need a world order based on non-violence and peaceful coexistence.*" He outlined, and urged the adoption of a three stage Action Plan for elimination of all nuclear weapons by the year 2010.

Sadly, on May 11, 1998, a newly elected ultra nationalist Government peremptorily jettisoned India's long and ardous struggle for a nuclear free world, with five nuclear bomb explosions. Outlook Magazine described this as "*The Mother of all Gambles*" and asked whether it was done in the national or ruling party interest. Protagonists rationalized this step in terms of India's greatly endangered security environment. One of them, like "*devil quoting scripture*" invoked Gandhi and argued that Nonviolence could be practiced

Courtesy : Outlook Magazine

only by those with "*the strength of a giant*", and that "*Defiance of the nuclear hegemonic order and a declaration of no first use, together constitute a viable non-violent anti-nuclear resistance policy*". The then Home Minister boasted that acquisition of nuclear arms had transformed India's security environment and no country would ever dare attack it again. However, within two weeks Pakistan established nuclear parity with India with six of its own nuclear bomb explosions and a few months later clandestinely sent its troops into Kargil. The war which followed was comparatively minor in terms of past Indo-Pak wars. Yet, when the fighting began to go badly for it, Pakistan ominously hinted it might use its "*ultimate weapon*". Pakistani security analyst Hussain Haqqani and former US Deputy Secretary of State Strobe Talbot, in their books *'Pakistan between Mosque and Military'* and *'Engaging India'* have both confirmed the Pakistani threat was not an empty one, and in its final phase the Kargil conflict had definitely acquired a "*nuclear dimension*". Hence, far from improving India's security, its nuclear arms have created great new risks for it considering Pakistan's military dominated, Jihadist infiltrated and politically volatile scenario.

Former US Defence Secretary ***Robert McNamara***, in an article titled *'Nuclear Apocalypse'* in Foreign Policy (Spring 2005 issue), wrote that if the Bush administration and Congress would carefully study the military utility of nuclear weapons; the moral and legal considerations regarding their use and the risks of accidental use in the present global context, they would conclude, "*as I and an increasing number of senior military leaders, politicians, and civilian security experts have, that we must move promptly* *toward the elimination - or near elimination - of all nuclear weapons. For many, there is a strong temptation to cling to the strategies of the past 40 years. But to do so would be a serious mistake leading to unacceptable risks for all nations."*

Harvard Professor ***Noam Chomsky*** echoed the same idea in an article titled *'We Must Act Now to Prevent Another Hiroshima - or Worse '* in the 'Independent' (August 6th, 2005), "*The recent explosions and casualties in London are yet another reminder of how the cycle of attack and response could escalate, unpredictably, even to a point horrifically worse than Hiroshima or Nagasaki"*. He rued current US policy of "anticipatory selfdefense" and quoted President Jimmy Carter: "*The United States is the major culprit in this erosion of the NPT. While claiming to be protecting the world from proliferation threats in Iraq, Libya, Iran and North Korea, American leaders not only have abandoned existing treaty restraints but also have asserted plans to test and develop new weapons, including Anti-Ballistic missiles, the earth penetrating 'bunker buster' and perhaps some new 'small' bombs. They also have abandoned past pledges and now threaten first use of nuclear weapons against non-nuclear states"*.

With ***Barack Obama's*** assumption of office as US President in January 2009 a glimmer of hope has emerged that there might be a shift of US policy in this regard, as he has expressed the hope, and pledged his strenuous efforts, to rid the world of all nuclear weapons. The April 8, 2010 START Treaty signed by him at Prague with President Medvedev of Russia reduces their respective respective nuclear stockpiles by a about 30% and strategic nuclear missile launchers by 50%.

Sixtyfive years after Hiroshima and Nagasaki, the prophetic wisdom of Gandhi, Einstein and Bertrand Russell regarding the enormous threat nuclear weapons pose is now being acknowledged by a small but influential group in the world's only super power. Sadly, in Gandhi's own country, this is yet to happen. On the contrary some security analysts and scientists are calling for renewed testing, and plans have been announced for development of inter continental ballistic missiles. A former Naval Chief has urged a second strike capability that is "*overwhelmingly devastating*", and that India should shed its diffidence and "*find not just the ways and means, but the will to project power overseas*".

Those who glibly talk about an overwhelmingly devastating second strike capability ignore the fact that such a capability is more likely to motivate a preemptive strike. The great guru of nuclear arms policy ***Henry Kissinger*** pointed this out in testimony to the US Senate Foreign Relations Committee on SALT II: "*The nuclear age combines weapons of unprecedented destructive power, extremely rapid modes of delivery of intercontinental range and high vulnerability to a surprise attack. In these new and unprecedented circumstances, the conclusion seems inescapable that the side whose capacity for retaliation was vulnerable must react in crises in ways which would heighten the liklihood of cataclysm; a country whose strategic forces were not secure could be driven, even against its will, to strike first rather than await the opponents attack which it would know it could not survive*".

Protagonists of nuclear arms might also like to recall that a non-nuclear North Vietnam faced a nuclear armed America and subsequently a nuclear armed China, and emerged victorious on both occasions: a non-nuclear Egypt successfully confronted a nuclear Britain over Suez; and most importantly, in 1971, a non-nuclear India under the intrepid Mrs. Gandhi ensured Bangladesh's emergence as an independent nation in 1971 despite US nuclear blackmail. In all these cases it was right rather than might, courage rather than fear, and indomitable will rather than superior arms that triumphed.

Pakistan and India, both armed with nuclear bombs and on "*eyeball to eyeball*" confrontation on the issue of terorism have made South Asia "*the most dangerous place on earth*" and created a far more nightmarish senario than what Gandhi might have imagined when he asked the question why two armies were been created, "*to defend the countries against foreign aggression or to fight each other*".

India's success in safeguarding its democratic and secular polity since independence, in consistently empowering its woman and dalits and legislating the Right to Information and Right to Education Acts are commendable achievements. However, the ignoring by its constitution makers and leaders of Gandhi's ideas of a village based democracy of "*concentric circles* "and minimal state control of the economy and adopting a Westminster style one with a Soviet type economy, has had adverse consequences. Gandhian democracy, with indirect elections to the district, state and national "*panchayats*" would not have needed expensive electioneering which has become the most fecund cause of corruption. Most contenders for a parliamentary seat now spend almost 30 crore (300 million) rupees. Whereas only one of them wins, all raise money from some source or the other. The same applies to state, district and local elections though these are less expensive. Winners recoup their expenditures by diverse means as soon as they assume office. The scandals in arms purchases and army coffins, fake legal papers and revenue stamps and MPs demanding payments for releasing constituency development funds and even for asking questions in parliament, are some of the shocking proofs of this. Transparency International's 2004 'Global Corruption Barometer' put India's CPI (Corruption Perception Index) on its scale of 10 (very clean) to Zero (very corrupt) at the dismally low level of 2 .7! By 2008 it had marginally improved but only to 3.4. With the mega CWG and 2G Spectrum scams which have come to light in 2010 and shocked India and the world, said Index is sure to drop again.

Since the late 1980s,in open rejection of Gandhi's enlightened Sarva Dharma Samabhav (SDS) approach and the fundamental rights enshrined in the Indian constitution, ultra-rightist communal outfits have stridently propagated "*Hindutva*" and "*Hindu Rashtra*" concepts with "*Ratha Yatras*", "*Sant Sammelans*", verbal and physical attacks on Muslims/Christians and destruction of their places of worship, the most cataclasymic of which was the Babri Masjid demolition on December 6, 1992. Concurrently they have extolled "*Veer Savarkar*", the intellectual progenitor of "*Hindutva*", and the ideologue M.S.Golwakar, who in his book "*We or Our Nationhood defined*', elaborated and epitomized said concept thus : "*The foreign races in Hindustan (i.e. all Muslims and Christians) must either adopt the Hindu culture and languages, must learn to respect and hold in reverence the Hindu religion, must entertain no idea but the glorification of Hindu race and culture, i.e. of the Hindu nation, and must lose their separate existence to merge in the Hindu race, or stay in the country, wholly subordinated to the Hindu Nation, claiming nothing, deserving no privileges, far less any preferential treatment - not even citizen's rights. There is, or at least should be, no other course for them to adopt.*" The contrast between this vision and that of Gandhi of an India in which all religions, and their adherents, would be equally respected and have equal rights, is very stark. Unfortunately however, promoted under the pretext of building a magnificent Ram Temple at Ayodhya, this ideology did secure substantial political mileage for these communal outfits and enabled their political party to come to power in 1998, in coalition with 13 other parties. Though it fell within a year it came to power again, in another coalition, in the 1999 elections. It constituted a multi-community cabinet and promised good governance and "*development*" but law and order, social harmony and national security deteriorated considerably. In Gujarat, where this party ruled, gruesome anti-Muslim massacres occurred in February 2002 in Godhra, Ahmedabad and other cities, which amazingly enabled it to secure a larger majority in that state's election in December the same year. Similar anti-Muslim and anti-Christian strategies were subsequently adopted in Madhya Pradesh, Orissa and Karnataka and further political mileage obtained therefrom. The deleterous consequences of these nefarious policies for social harmony and national security have been clearly exposed by Virendra Prakash and Pratip Lahiri, both retired, senior Indian Administrative Service officers, in their books *Hindutva Demystified and Decoding Intolerance - Riots and the Emergence of Terrorism in India.* Since the 1992 Babri Masjid demolition, among the many places where terrorist attacks have occurred are Ahmedabad, Ajmer, Bangalore, Coimbatore, Hyderabad, Mumbai (1992, 2002, 2003, 2006, & 2009), New Delhi (at Parliament House on December 13, 2001) and Srinagar.

As ominous as politically instigated communal massacres, is the fact that Abhinav Bharat, a radical communal outfit of the '*Sangh Parivar*', has been discovered to have recruited serving armed forces officers for its nefarious activities. One of them was the mastermind of the Malegaon blasts as also of the earlier Hyderabad Mecca Masjid and Ajmer Sharief blasts. In all these cases it was Muslims who were initially suspected and arrested. Fortunately, the innate religious tolerance of the vast majority of Indian people, particularly Hindus, is a strong safeguard for India's secularism.

The 2004 and 2009 national elections and subsequent New Delhi, Rajasthan, Orissa, Bihar, West Bengal, Assam, Kerala and Tamilnadu assembly elections, have clearly shown that most Indian voters prefer social harmony, good governance and stability to hate, violence and shaky coalition governments. The BJP's vote share fell from 22.2 % in 2004 to 18.8% in 2009; the number of its MPs from 138 to 116. Its star campaigner, Gujarat chief minister Narendra Modi addressed 300 rallies and secured 37 seats for his party; the youthful Rahul Gandhi of the Congress party addressed 102 rallies and secured 75 seats, including Faizabad and 6 other seats in the Awadh region, from where BJP had risen to national prominence and power in 1998, with the emotive "*Build the Ram Temple*" issue. Among Rahul Gandhi's campaign statements the most heartwarming one, which echoed the Mahatma, was "*Poor people are the other ones who will make India great. India's power house is not in the cities, not in the metros. It lies in the villages*".

The other happy outcome of the 2009 national election was that the percentage of women Lok Sabha MPs rose from 8.7 to 10.7 and the parliamentary strength of the Communist Party (Marxist), whose govt. in West Bengal had opened fire on and killed 25 farmers at Singur and Nandiram, dropped from 35 to 15. However, its two unhappy outcomes were : the number of "*Crorepathi* " MPs jumped from 154 to 300 and that of "*tainted*" MPs from 128 to 150. Of the latter 73 have serious criminal charges against them and the MP from Porbandar, Gandhi's birthplace, has the largest number - 16!

Madhav Godbole has clearly brought out Parliament's "*Rapid Downhill Journey* " commencing with Indira Gandhi and accelerating thereafter. Indecorous behaviour, disruptions, absenteeism, defections, corruption, criminals as MPs (one even being brought from Jail to take his oath of office !) and legislation without even minimal debate have become the hallmarks of its present functioning. In 2008 it had a mere 46 sittings for the whole year; on the last date of Lok Sabha's Winter session, eight important bills were rushed through in 17 minutes. He has averred "*India may not get many Olympic medals, but if there was one for passing laws in a mindless manner, with the speed of lightning, it would certainly have won gold year after year* " and indicated that soon after Supreme Court's "*bombshell*" Judgement disqualifying Rajya Sabha member Jaya Bachan for holding the "*office of Profit*" of Chairman, UP Film Development Corporation, Parliament hastily passed the Parliament (Prevention of Disqualification) Amendment Bill to safeguard "*approximately 40 or more members from both Houses of Parliament* " from disqualification on similar grounds, giving said bill retrospective effect of 47 years ! When the President returned it for reconsideration, both Houses promptly passed it again leaving him no option but to sign it.

About MPs constituency development funds (MPLADS) Godbole indicates that the "*wily politician Narasinha Rao, facing the wrath of parliament for failure to protect the Babri Masjid introduced this scheme to placate MPs and provide a prop to his minority government* ". The annual "*largesse*" it provided them initially was Rs 50 lakhs. It was subsequently increased to Rs 1 crore, then to Rs 2 crores and recently to Rs 5 crores !

In April 2005 the National Advisory Council, chaired by Mrs Sonia Gandhi, had stated "*Ideally, local area development needs should be determined and interventions made by the elected local governments. Therefore MPALADS should be dispensed with and these funds should go directly to panchayats and muncipalities for the same purposes."* In February 2007, the Second Administrative Reforms Commission (ARC) headed by Mr. Veerappa Moily recommended abolition of MPALADS on grounds that this scheme *"seriously erodes the notion of separation of powers as the legislator directly becomes the executive".* It is amazing therefore that this scheme still continues and in July 2011 the *largesse* has been raised to Rs 5 Crores !

India's MPs, unanimously approving their own sizable salary, perquisites and MPLAD hikes, have become like Wall Street bankers who annually help themselves to mega bonuses for their "*vital work* "! Gandhi lived in a hut and dressed like a "*half naked* " peasant because he felt that unless he identified himself with and lived like the vast majority of the poverty stricken Indian people he could not speak and negotiate on their behalf.

The state dominated planned economy between 1950 - 1991 resulted in a mammoth *"license raj"*, which is turn spawned extensive corruption for securing much sought after industrial and import licenses. This spread like cancer into every sector of the economy and into every government department Enormous investments in agriculture, industry, education, health and housing notwithstanding, poverty, malnutrition, disease, unemployment, illiteracy, lack of housing, medical facilities and lack of infrastructure still continue to afflict over 40% of India's population. Though agricultural and industrial output increased, overall economic growth until 1990 hovered around 3% and was derided internationally as the *"Hindu rate of economic growth"*. Even ardent admirers of Jawaharlal Nehru and Indira Gandhi now concede the above mentioned approach has been more baneful than beneficial to India's economy.

The economic liberalization, and "*Reforms*" begun in 1991, released the enormous entrepreneurship of India's millions. By 2000 economic growth had spurted to 8%. By 2007 it had crossed 10%. Unfortunately however, Government policies during the 1998 -2008 period were tilted heavily in favour of the urban and corporate sectors and the foreign investor, because of which the rich - poor and urban - rural divides have greatly widened.

In the "*reform*" process trade and investment policies were liberalized, import duties brought down and many non tariff barriers eliminated. Even import of second hand capital goods was permitted even though this adversely effected its leading capital goods manufacturers like BHEL, HMT, SAIL, TATA, and Godrej. In the new scenario 30 MNCs such as Hindustan Lever,

Proctor and Gamble, ABB and Phillips promptly raised their equity in Indian joint venture firms to over 51% and took management control of them. A number of public sector enterprises were privatized. The most deleterious effect of all this liberalization has been on labour and employment. In 1990, the total employment in the organized sector was 26.35 million with the public sector accounting for over 71 % of the total. After 1997 there has been a consistent decline in employment both in the public and private sectors. In 2001 public sector employment was only 69% of total employment. Concurrently there was a growing "*casualization*" of labour and increasing numbers of child labourers which in 2000 was 10.2 million. In 2010 it had risen to 60 million.

According to the *2004* National Commission for Enterprises in Unorganised sector (Arjun Sengupta) Report about 836 million people (77% of India's population) subsist on Rs 20 a day (about 26 UK pence) or less. The commission pointed out that "*India is yet to evolve a comprehensive national social security policy with regard to its entire population*" and indicated that social security expenditure as a percentage of GDP is around 25 per cent in EU countries, 3.6 for China and only 2.6 in India. The Second National Commission on Labour pointed out that, "*the developed countries are spending up to 40 per cent of their GDP on safety nets. But, in India, the public expenditure on social security is a mere 1.8 per cent while even in Sri Lanka it is 4.7 per cent*". The 2006 -2007 National Sample Survey on Household Consumer Expenditure in India, reported that the average Indian spends just Rs 440 or less in a month on food ! That is the tragic condition of the "other India"

Nobel Laureate Amartya Sen has critiqued India's reforms thus "*The 'license raj' did make economic initiatives difficult, produced lots of inefficient industries and led to many allocational distortions but an under active govt in the social sector has bestowed on India the dubious distinction of having the largest number of poor in the world and also the largest middle-class on earth*" He has added that China's success story would not have been possible if it had not dealt with its educational and health challenges prior to embarking on economic liberalization. He rejects the argument that democracy is an obstacle to rapid economic development and holds that it is one of India's greatest assets.

As part of its policy of high economic growth with rapid industrialization and foreign investments the present Indian Government has actively promoted Special Economic Zones (SEZs) and provided numerous incentives to investors therein, In an article titled '*The Great SEZ Giveaway*' (Asian Age, December 3, 2007) Jayati Ghosh, has listed the plethora of benefits being granted to corporates in these SEZs despite their high costs to the national exchequer. On Gandhiji's birthday in 2007, 25,000 landless labourers and tribals marched from Gwalior to New Delhi, (reaching there on October 28) to non violently protest their displacement as a result of "*development*", for which their lands have been forcibly acquired to build SEZs, airports, highways, tourist resorts etc. They demanded the setting up of a National Land Reforms Commission. The eminent agricultural scientist Dr. M.S. Swaminathan endorsed this demand and urged that instead of SEZs, SAZs (Special Agricultural Zones) be set up " *If special export zones or special economic zones (SEZs) can be set up for promoting manufacturing and services sectors, why not special agricultural zones (SAZs) for the crisis-ridden farm sector to boost food production. Let the centre take the initiative to set up such SAZs in partnership with state governments, especially in the distressed states of Maharashtra, Andhra Pradesh, Karnataka and Kerala where hundreds of farmers have committed suicide due to debt burden and poor returns from low-yields. The government should make a beginning to develop SAZs in the 33 drought-prone districts identified in these states.*' Neither of these proposals have been implemented yet. Consequently, over 200,000 farmers have committed suicide since 1998 (when the seed market was opened to multinationals and their GM seeds) and Naxalism has now spread to over 180 districts. This is sombre proof of the extent of economic and social distress, and anger, in the rural areas over uneconomic prices for agricultural products, and state acquisition of farmers lands for SEZs etc.

India today has the world's largest middle class, its second largest technically trained manpower, some billionaires, many millionaires and sadly, most of its debt ridden and disposessed farmers, urban slum dwellers, illiterates, homeless, aids infected and armed rural and tribal militias. Unless India's economic policies are reframed to focus on the "*poorest and most helpless man*" of Gandhi's "*Talisman*", these problems would be further worsened. Dr. Arjun Sengupta, former Economic Adviser to Prime Minister/Deputy Chairman of the Planning Commission, in an article in the Deccan Chronicle (Sept. 21, 2009) titled "*Naxal Violence is a cry to be heard*', wrote "*On September 15, Prime Minister Man Mohan Singh sounded the most serious warning about Naxal Violence, calling it one of the gravest internal security problems the country faces*" and went on to affirm. "*The only way the*

Naxal problem can be resolved is by genuine negotiations and trying to provide answers to their age old problems. But before you even start these negotiations, you have to generate confidence among these vulnerable people that they are equal partners in the negotiations, that you are not out to grab their land and property and that you will respect their human rights". Lord Meghanand Desai, author of "*The Rediscovery of India* ", stated in an interview to Deccan Herald (January 10, 2010), "*The main issue in Naxalism is common property, which was nationalized. This is supposed to be development......Depriving people of common property is not a developmental thing but both the capitalist and socialist models of development are against common property."*

Sudeep Chakravarty, in his book '*Red Sun : Travels in Naxalite country*' writes " *The steady spread of Maoist radicalism in India is stunning. In 2004, according to the Home Minsitry's report, 55 districts in 9 states were effected. By 2008 the number had risen to 165 districts i.e. nearly 30% of the total of 602 districts....... There is little debate that the spread of Maoist influence is at its core the consequence of bad governance - or plain non-governance - and crushing exploitation in the world's next superpower."* He refers to a study/map made by economist Omkar Goswami of the CERG Advisory based on ownership or access to 11 amenities: a bank or post office, a pucca house, cooking gas, electricity, TV, telephone, scooter and separate kitchen/toilet/bathroom. Termed the Rural India District Score, districts with households having these amenities were shown in dark/light green for best/good, white for average and orange/red for bad/worst. Goswami avers "*Anyone going through the red and orange districts of eastern India can easily trace the hotbeds of Maoist insurgency. Getting the benefits of growth to these districts is the greatest challenge of development and political economy*".

That something effective **can** be done about this insurgency with a well planned, people-oriented approach, is revealed in a Forbes India (October9, 2009) article titled *The Peacemaker - A civil servant in a Naxal-dominated district in Madhya Pradesh shows how to stem the violence and win back the people.* The civil servant is Gulshan Bamra, Collector, 2006 - 2009 of the thickly forested, Naxal infested Balaghat district. The article states "*In those three years, what he has achieved is nothing short of spectacular. Road connectivity in the district shot up from 520 kilometres to 2,228 kilometres. About 28,000 hectares of new land came under irrigation. Tendu* *leaf (used in rolling beedis) collection and bamboo cutting restarted. Revenues from forest produce nearly doubled from Rs 28 crore in 2006-7 to 55 crore in 2008-09. Simultaneously migration dropped sharply from 4217 in 2005 to 2840 in 2008 as locals found work near their homes.* ***And the number of Naxalite attacks fell from 21 in 2005 to none in 2009".***

How did Bamra achieve this ? Since the Naxals had been helping the villagers with medicines he decided to organize medical camps at the weekly "haats" (markets) which many people from neighbouring villages attended. He took skin specialists, orthopaedics and gynaecologists to these camps as the ailments they treated were the ones most widely prevalent. He also took a big stock of medicines for free distribution. He used the "haats" for meetings with panchayat officials for ascertaining the most pressing needs of their villages. Thereafter, in coordination with all departments of his administration and pooling their funds/those of NREGP and other GOI schemes, he got roads, bridges, irrigation channels, schools and health centres built and cell phone, telegraph & TV towers erected. The Naxals viewed all this with concern and tried to induce the villagers not to cooperate. They failed. "Why should we try to stop it, when it will benefit us ?" the villagers asked.

Gulshan Bamra

The Forbes article ends drawing attention to Bamra's mission statement, a printout of which was stuck on his office wall. It read "Effectiveness (result-oriented approach), Sensitivity (respect for the individual) integrity (delivering on commitments) and Fairness (means should justify ends).

The 73rd constitutional amendment, enacted in 1992 to give formal recognition and backing to Panchayati Raj and the 2005 National Rural Employment Guarantee Act(renamed Mahatma Gandhi National Rural Employment Guarantee Act in October 2009) are good but much belated measures to ensure employment for India's rural population for at least 100 days a year and build rural infrasctructure. But what about the rest of the 265 days Gandhi would have asked. He would have strongly rued the many farmer suicides and the brutal firing on them at Singur and Nandigram in West Bengal, in January and March 2007, which killed twenty five of them. He would however have lauded what NGOs like ***Aarohi*** and ***Chirag*** (Central

Himalyan Rural Action Group) are doing in the Himalayan foothills in Uttarakhand and what Harva has achieved in Haryana.

Aarohi and **Chirag** have undertaken such innovative rural employment/ development projects as producing high quality body care products from apricot and peach kernels (which the villagers collect and bring to them), growing culinary herbs like parsley, mint, peppermint and rosemary as also fragrant herbs such as lavender, geranium, basil and chamomile for use in wardrobe and bathroom potpourris. They have also promoted community based plant nurseries, experimental farms, crop diversification, horticulture, animal husbandry, recharge of springs and watershed development. At Sitla, Chirag has set up a BPO where forty young rural women and men, with only high school education,are working on digitalizing Supreme Court judgements!

In Haryana, at Tikli and Aklimpur villages, women between 18-40 years of age, who early each morning cut and carry fodder for their cattle and collect cowdung, thereafter spend six hours working in a Harva (Harnessing Value From Rural India) BPO. Hemalatha Aithani wrote about them in Deccan Herald (July 8, 2010) under the title *Sickle in one hand and mouse in the other.* Ajay Chatterjee, a University of Pennyslvania MBA who set up Harva, states it is not an NGO but "*a business venture with a conscience and social responsibility*", in which women are employed not out of charity but because "*They are good at multitasking and can work at a stretch without taking many breaks.*" He cites the example of a 25 year old woman who studied only upto Standard VIII but "*mastered all the computer keyboard characters in just three hours which is not easy even for people like me*". These women working and earning at this BPO, have impacted substantially in enhancing their own status as that of other women, in a state notorious for its skewed sex ratio.

Gandhi's emphasis on the simple life and reduction of one's wants, is considered antediluvian by many. Yet, Paul Kennedy writes "*The overall consensus - with the exception of a few revisionists - is that the projected growth in the world's population cannot be sustained with our current patterns and levels of consumption..... Unlike animals and birds, human beings destroy forests, burn fossil fuels, drain wetlands, pollute rivers and oceans and ransack the earth for ores, oil and other raw materials...Developed northern regions place much greater stress per capita upon the earth's resources than do developing countries simply because the former consume much more.....According to one calculation, the average American baby represents twice the environmental damage of a Swedish child, three times that of an Italian, thirteen times that of a Brazilian, thirty five times that of an Indian, and 280 times that of a Chadian or Haitian because its level of consumption throughout its life will be so much greater. That is not a comfortable statistic for anyone with a conscience".*

Contrary to Gandhi's emphasis on village centred production and trade, globalization and foreign investments have been vigorously pursued / wooed in India since the early 1990's as the magic wand for eliminating poverty and stimulating economic growth. The result is the extensive corporatization of domestic production and Indian corporates blossoming into "*mega*" corporations and the rich becoming richer and the poor poorer as in other "*globalized*" countries . In the United States 5% of its people own 54% of its wealth ! In India, Bimal Jalan, former Reserve Bank of India governor pointed out in December 2009 that the total asset value of our top five billionaires (in US dollar terms) equalled those of the bottom 300 million Indians !. One of these billionaires has built himself a 27 stories mansion in Mumbai, which is reported to be the world's most flamboyant, expensive and hi-tech one.

India's present leaders often flaunt its high economic growth rates as proof of good governance and occasionally speak about "*Reforms with a human face*". The big question is whose "*face*"? That of the fat corporate CEO or "*the poorest and most helpless man*" Gandhi spoke about. In this context the big question that arises is, who will benefit from the much hyped Indo-US Nuclear Cooperation Agreement of 2009 - India's poor or those with shopping malls,multi-storeyed air conditioned homes, satellite TVs etc and the foreign/Indian corporates scurrying around for a share in this multibillion dollar nuclear pie? Will the electricity generated by these high priced nuclear power plants be affordable to the ordinary Indian ? The other big questions are: Will this agreement, on which the government won its vote of confidence amidst the most egregious turmoil ever seen in parliament and on which there still is no national consensus, get India involved, militarily or diplomatically, in America's ongoing wars in Iraq, Afghanistan, Libya and elsewhere ? Will it adversely effect its relations with China, since this agreement has been flaunted by some political and security analysts as capstone of a new US-India "*strategic architecture*" to "*contain*" China; How certain are the "*assured fuel supplies*" and enrichment and reprocessing technologies for the imported nuclear power plants as these are heavily anchored in the "*signing statement*" of the most untruthful President in US history, whose senior officials only a few days earlier had written to the US Congress that the fuel supply assurances were only "*political*" and "*not legally binding*".

India had exulted on the "*clean waiver*" it had secured from the the Nuclear Suppliers Group (NSG) in 2008. However at the NSG's 21st plenary meeting in the Netherlands on June 23-24, 2011, it has decided to "*strengthen its guidelines on transfer of sensitive enrichment and reprocessing technologies*". Though the US, France and Russia have subsequently announced these guidelines will not effect their bilateral commitments to India the fact remains that they concurred in the new guidelines. Besides this meeting legitimized China's supply of two additional nuclear reactors to Pakistan in violation of its own guidelines.

As former foreign secretary Kanwal Sibal wrote, in an article titled '*NSG approval of Sino-Pak nuclear pact*' (The Mail, July 12, 2011), "*China presented the NSG with a frontal challenge, and the NSG has buckled. This is a blow to our security interests......China had slammed the India-US nuclear deal as discriminatory towards Pakistan. It now wants to neutralize any political or strategic gain obtained by India from the India-US nuclear deal and the NSG exemption as a non-NPT country by treating Pakistan similarly. The US considers China's cooperation in dealing with proliferation concerns about Iran and North Korea more important than its Pakistan connection.*" Similarly, K.C.Singh, in his '*Nuclear Reality* ' article (Deccan Chronicle/ Asian Age, June 26, 2011) wrote "*American and Chinese interests may now be converging on the development of admission criteria to the four export control regimes i.e. Nuclear Suppliers Group, Missile Technology Control Regime and the Australia and Wassenaar Groups. The aim would be to technologically freeze India's semi-tested and rudimentary nuclear arsenal, slow down Pakistan's gallop towards a massive plutonium-based stockpile and open the door for Israel to emerge from its nuclear closet, perhaps in exchange for peace in West Asia. The West fears a loose nuke out of Pakistan and China fears a credible Indian deterrent.*" Therefore to secure NSG membership it now seems that India would have to sign the NPT, continue its moratorium on testing indefinitely and fully cooperate on the fissile material cut-off treaty. Besides, during Hilary Clinton's recent visit she urged India to work with IAEA to ensure its legislation was compatible with "*international practice*" which implies a watering down of its September 2010 Nuclear Liability law ! On the issue of Enrichment and Reprocessing technologies to India, which the June 2011 NSG meeting had made conditional to NPT signature, she evasively stated that none of the new conditions detract form the importance of the India-US nuclear deal nor contravene its provisions ! Has India been hiding from Hyde ?

Considering all these diplomatic and security hassles and the major challenges of protecting its nuclear power plants against natural disasters and terrorist attacks (the Kalpakkam reactor had a narrow escape when the Tsunami struck on December 26, 2004 and there have been mysterious "*accidents*" at Kaiga and Tarapur nuclear reactors in recent years) would not solar and wind energy and mini-hydels have been better and more eco-friendly for India? All these energy sources India has in abundance. Vandana Shiva, in her '*Nuclear Insanity*' article (Deccan Chronicle. May 21, 2011) has quoted Physicist Sowmya Dutta that the world has potential for 17 terra watt nuclear energy, 700 terra watt wind energy and 86,000 terra watt solar energy and asserted "*Alternatives to nuclear energy are thousand times more abundant and million times less risky. To push nuclear plants after Fukushima is pure insanity*". Likewise, Vice Admiral (Retd) Admiral Arun Kumar Roy has written (in *The Nuclear Limit,* Deccan Chronicle/Asian Age July 8,2011) "*Despite the obvious lessons of the latest nuclear disasters in Japan and the limitations of India's NLB, NDMS, NERT and TWS, I am amazed that our Department of Atomic Energy has reportedly projected a requirement of 655,000 MW of nuclear power by 2050. This would involve setting up about 655 additional imported reactors of 1000 MW each in "nuclear Parks" of about six reactors each. Given mainland India's 6000 km coastline it could have 109 nuclear parks about 55 km apart dotting its coastline. This would be a recipe for major disasters, given risks of tsunamis, earthquakes or a terrorist strike ...It makes no sense, it is not safe and it is not affordable*". The German Government, soon after the Fukushima disaster decided to shut down all its nuclear power plants by 2020 but the Indian Govt. is determined to pursue its ambitious target of 20,000 MW of nuclear power by 2020. The $22 billion, six reactor, 9,900 MW Jaitapur nuclear plant would be the world's largest and located on 968 hectares of fertile agricultural land belonging to five villages. The Villagers, strongly opposed to it, have refused to accept payment for their acquired lands. Ten gram panchayats have resigned in protest. On

April 18, 2011, the Maharashtra police opened fired on the protesting villagers killing one and seriously injuring eight others. India's pursuit of nuclear power is turning out to be a poisonous pie in the sky!

Fortunately, on January 12, 2010, the Prime Minster of India unveiled a $19 billion Jawaharlal Nehru National Solar Mission that is to generate 1,100 MW by 2013, 4000 MW by 1917 and 20,000 MW by 2020. Some mega projects are on the drawing board already, and a 35,000 sq.km area of the Thar Desert in Rajasthan has been earmarked for them. Separately Rs 900 crores has been allotted for a mega research programme, involving over a hundred scientists in eight national laboratories. Nonetheless, its ambitious Solar Mission notwithstanding, India is unlikely to catch up with China whose Golden Sun program, launched some years earlier has enabled it to produce 10,000 MW by end 2010. It is already the world's largest producer of solar panels.

Whereas globalization and liberalization are constantly harped upon by the Western countries and the World Bank as the magic wand that will eliminate poverty and usher in prosperity, the contrary has occured. David Korten has pointed out that globalization has concentrated enormous power in a few transnational and financial, industrial, mining and agricultural corporations and created a "*market tyranny that is extending its reach across the planet like a cancer, colonizing ever more of the planet's living spaces, destroying livelihoods, displacing people, rendering democratic institutions impotent, and feeding on life.*" The solution, he urges is to "*re-create societies that nurture cultural and biological diversity, get corporations out of politics...... and create localized economies*". The enormous economic power, nefarious activities and close linkages with power elites of most countries, of these transnational corporations has brought into vogue the term "*Corporate Predator State*".

Noam Chomsky describes globalization as "*the extention of transnational corporate tyranny.... they are huge commanding economy run from the top, relatively unaccountable and interlinked in various ways. Their first interest is profit. But it is does not end there. It deeper objective is to contruct an audience of a particular type, one that is addicted to a certain life style with artificial wants.*" This echoes Gandhi who had averred "*Formerly men were made slaves under physical compulsion. Now they are enslaved by temptation of money and of the luxuries that money can buy.*"

Nobel Laureate Joseph Stiglitz has rued the 2008 global financial meltdown, which as *"the fruit of a pattern of dishonesty on the part of financial institutions"*, is glaring proof of this. In greedy pursuit of profit maximization, investment banks and hedge funds have ventured into high risk, sub-prime areas and *"spread the risk"* to others with well packaged, superficially attractive *"derivatives"* which have been marketed globally. Warren Buffet has aptly described them as *"financial weapons of Mass Destruction"*. When these *"weapons"* exploded and mega firms like Bear Stearns and Lehman Brothers collapsed, the US Administration and Congress had no option but to bail them out with mega rescue packages. Nobel Laureate Paul Krugman castigated them as *"cash for trash"*. The highly *"privatized"* Iraq and Afghan wars have greatly enriched corporates well connected to high state officials. Former Portugese Prime Minister **Mario Soares**, has rued this *"promiscuous intermingling of politics and business"* and written in the New York Times *"Capitalism has to be rethought. It must be moved past this phase of speculation, past the "casino economy" to a form of ethical capitalism that respects the environment and the concerns of society"*. The same paper also carried a cartoon showing *Hurricane Ike* striking Texas and *Hurricane Greed* striking New York and Washington ! The greed continues unabated. About 3000 senior financial sector executives took home a total of US140 billion as 2009 year end bonuses.

The 2008 financial meltdown and the present global warming and food grains crisis validate Gandhi's affirmation of many decades ago that the *"Earth provides enough to satisfy every man's need but not for every man's greed"*. The ominous facts are : Herring, Cod and Anchovy shoals, heavily over-fished, are almost completely gone. The humpback and blue whales, already an endangered species, are still being harpooned by the Japanese for *"Scientific purposes"*. Elephant and tiger populations have been greatly attentuated because of the commercial value of their tusks, skins and bones. The most sordid such fact however concerns the American bison, also called *"Buffalo"*. Ray Allen Billington, in his book '*Westward Expansion*' writes : *"Probably 13,000,000 buffalo lived in the West when the first hunters arrived with their powerful long range rifles. They felled these stupid beasts mercilessly from train windows and horseback between 1867 -72 with no other reward than the sight of dying animals. The herds might have survived that onslaught but their fate was sealed when a Pennsylvania Tannery discovered in 1871 that buffalo hides could be used for commercial leather. With every hide worth upto $ 3, professional hunters swarmed over the* *plains to exploit the new source of wealth. Between 1872-74, 3,000,000 of these beasts were killed annually. By 1878, the southern herd was exterminated. By 1883 the Buffalo had vanished from the Northern Plains. By 1903 the number had dwindled to 34."*

Population increases and rising living standards have magnified the demand for meat, and for profits in its production and marketing. The shocking proof of this greed is the discovery of *"offal"* (produced from *"trimmings"* off the slaughter house floor, which include inedible parts and organs, cleaned entrails, fetuses, etc)in cattle feed. This has caused Bovine spongiform encephalopathy *("Mad Cow Disease)* in the US, UK, France, Canada, and other countries, which in turn has gestated a new form of Creutzfeldt-Jakob disease, which has killed several young people in Europe who ate the *"mad cow"* beef.

The skyrocketing of gasoline prices from US$ 14 per barrel in 1974 to US$ 140 per barrel in mid 2008, has led to millions of tons of corn and sugarcane being diverted to biofuel production and accentuated the global food crisis.

The exponential increase in land, sea and air transport vehicles (The single car American family of the 1920s, now has four cars and a speed boat, and in some cases a personal aircraft as well !) and extensive use of fossil fuels for these vehicles and for power generation, have resulted in unprecedented global warming. Nobel Laureate Albert Gore avers that *"the United States causes more environmental pollution than South America, Africa, the Middle East, Australia, and Japan put together"* and points out that *"20 of the hottest years on record have occurred within the last 25 years of which the hottest was 2005 when over 200 cities and towns in its western states set all-time heat records."* He lists the stark consequences of global warming: warmer ocean waters; more destructive hurricanes; increased drought, crop failures and forest fires; melting of Artic and Antarctic ice caps and glaciers worldwide; rising ocean levels and submerging of numerous islands, coastal cities and low-lying areas of many countries. All this would result in extensive human displacement and deaths, and loss of animal and plant diversity.

Since India has the highest mountain ranges in the world, the largest number of snow fed rivers and a 1.2 billion population, it more than any other country, needs to give top priority to combating global warming and the life styles that have caused it. Achieving high economic growth rates and *"prosperity"* is not half as important as this.

The recent and ongoing wars in the Balkans, Georgia, Iraq, Afghanistan and Libya have much to do with securing control of oil and gas resources, and access to territories through which their pipelines would be laid. They vindicate Petra Kelly's earlier quoted affirmation : " *A life style and method of production which rely on an endless supply and a lavish use of raw materials generates the motive for the violent appropriation of these raw materials from other countries.*"

Prince Charles, in his *'Facing the Future'* 2009 Richard Dimbleby Lecture in London stated " *So much, it seems to me, depends on how you define both "growth" and "prosperity." Most would agree, I think, that the main result of progress should be less misery and more happiness. But in our modern situation these "ends" have become dangerously confused with the "means," to the point where, now, wealth, innovation and growth have become the final goals. They have become the destination, when they were only at best a vehicle for getting there. It seems that through a drift of ethics, the direction of our economic system has ended up being an end in itself*".

He went on to list the various ways in which humanity has "*liquidated natural assets in pursuit of what we call 'progress'.*" He referred to the ancient Greek concept of "*harmonia*", to Adam Smith's *'Theory of Moral sentiments'*, to the deleterious effects of "*commercial structures that place an ever greater distance between the supplier and the consumer, because economies of scale can destroy the economics of localness*", to the *Stern Review on the economics of climate change*, to the *U.N.'s Millennium Ecosystem Assessment* - and stressed the urgent need, in view of the mushrooming global population and deepening ecological and economic crises to " *shift from a reductive, mechanistic approach*" to a new "*bottom up*" form of globalization "*for that is the way Nature operates.... from the roots up, not from the sky down*".

He concluded thus "*As Mahatma Gandhi pointed out, "The difference between what we do and what we are capable of doing would suffice to solve most of the world's problems. We must see that we are part of the Natural order rather than isolated from it; see that Nature is a profoundly beautiful world of complexity that operates according to an organic "grammar" of harmony, an interconnected, interdependent function of creation with harmony existing between all things*".

The three Arab Israeli wars and Israel's continued "existential threat" despite its massive military might vindicate Gandhi's 1938 assertion "*My sympathy does not blind me to the requirements of Justice. It is wrong and inhuman to impose the Jews on the Arabs. .... The nobler course would be to insist on a just treatment of the Jews wherever they were born and bred. The Jews born and bred in France are French precisely in the same sense as the Christians born in France are French. Every country is their home, including Palestine, not by aggression but by loving service...*"

Many reputed Jewish writers have acknowledged the "*requirements of Justice*" have not been met in Palestine. Tom Segev has exposed the falsehood that Palestine was "*A land without people for a people without land*" and quoted the British General Walter Congreve "*We might as well declare that England belongs to Italy because it was once occupied by the Romans*". Avi Shlaim has stated " *The history of the State of Israel is a vindication of Ze'ev Zabotinsky's strategy of the Iron Wall. Conflict accompanied the Zionist enterprise long before Hitler came on the scene.... There is no denying that the establishment of the State of Israel involved a massive injustice to the Palestinians.*" Amnon Rubinstein has critiqued the fundamentalist *'God-given-land'* claim to all of Palestine as "*a creation of the post-independence period*" and urged humane treatment of the Palestinians in keeping with traditional Jewish values, adding that since Jews today can "*flourish in democratic (non-Jewish) countries without having to relinquish their Judaism*", Israel should not deny to non-Jews similar rights and opportunities. Henry Seigman has urged (in a February 8, 2001 article in New York Review of Books) Israel to recognize its "*sacred obligation to a people that has been greatly wronged, a wrong compounded by keeping the West Bank and Gaza under occupation since 1967.*"

Gerald Kauffman, former British Labour Minister has written (in The Spectator, April 24, 2004: "*In the Seder service for Passover which is recited in religious Jewish homes in Israel and the Diaspora there is a telling reminiscence : Avadim hayinu b'Mtzrayim (we were slaves in Egypt). What the Egyptian Pharaoh did to the Jews, the Jews have now done to the Palestinians - except that the Palestinians have no Moses to bring them salvation and no Red Sea will part for them*".

Ilan Pappe has averred "*Never before, in the light of the Gaza tragedy, has the two fold strategy of BDS -Boycott, Divestment, Sanctions - and a one state solution, shined so clearly as the only alternative forward...... When the Wall of Apartheid is removed and the electric fences of Zionism dismantled, Gaza will become once more a symbol of Fernand Braudel's coastal society, able to fuse different cultural horizons and offer a space for new life instead of the war zone it has become in the last sixty years."*

Rabbi Michael Lerner, in his book *Healing Israel-Palestine*' has declared "*A state with many Jews in it is not a Jewish State unless it embodies an ethos of love and justice and becomes a living proof that healing and transformation is possible. Israel is not yet a Jewish state in that sense, so we will support the forces help evolve it in that direction..... We call upon the United States and other world powers to intervene with all their influence and economic power to put an end to the occupation and all acts of terror and create a de-militarized Palestinian state in all of the West Bank and Gaza,. And we call for all parties to adopt the non-violent philosophies of Martin Luther King and Mahatma Gandhi* "

Israel's persistent security concerns have led it to make preemptive strikes against Egypt and Syria in 1967, destroy Iraq's Osirak Nuclear reactor in 1981, invade and occupy southern Lebanon for 18 years and clandestinely arm itself with nuclear weapons (as revealed in 1986 by its nuclear scientist Mordechai Vanunu, who has been incarcerated ever since). Its 350 kilometre long, fifteen foot high *"security barrier"*, much of it within the West Bank and confining Palestinians to 16 disconnected enclaves comprising only 27% of their land, has been declared *"contrary to international law"* by the International Court of Justice.

Prime Minister Yitzhak Rabin, a wise, far sighted, pragmatic military hero saw that Israel's security could only be ensured with a *"land for peace"* agreement with the Palestinians. Initially a strong proponent of the *"Iron Wall"* approach, early in his second term as Prime minister, he decided to negotiate, secretly, with Yasser Arafat through Yair Hirschfeld and Ahmed Qurei. These negotiations are historic as they were the first face-to-face negotiations between them. The Norwegian government provided hospitality and ensured secrecy. The Accord that emanated from fourteen sessions of these negotiations was titled *Declaration of Principles on Interim Self- Government Arrangements* and

The historic hand shake between Rabin and Arafat

signed in Washington on 13 September 1993, by Mahmoud Abbas for PLO, Foreign Minister Shimon Peres for Israel. Secretary of State Warren Christopher for the United States and Foreign Minister Andrei Kozyrev for Russia, in the presence of PLO chairman Yasser Arafat, Israeli Prime Minister Yitzhak Rabin and US President Bill Clinton. Along with the Declaration of Principles. Both parties also signed Letters of Mutual Recognition - Israel recognizing the PLO as legitimate representative of the Palestinian people and the PLO recognizing Israel's right to exist and renouncing terrorism and other forms of violence against it. The Accord was expected to lead within a five year period to a permanent settlement based on UNSC Resolutions 242 and 338, and Israel and Palestine, as separate states living side by side in peace and mutual respect. Within a year thereafter (in July 1994) Rabin secured a peace treaty with Jordan's King Hussein.

Sadly, on November 4, 1995, at a mass rally in Tel Aviv in support of the Oslo Accords and soon after he had sung Shir Lashalom (Song for Peace) with Israeli singer Miri Aloni, Prime Minsiter was assassinated by a Zionist youth for *"agreeing to give up God given land"*. This was a great tragedy for Israel, Palestine, West Asia and the world. Among the many dignitaries at Rabin's funeral were the heads of state of Egypt and Jordan and foreign ministers of Morocco, Tunisia and Oman - proof of the great improvement he had brought about in Israel's relations with Arab countries. The many peace activists who annually gather on his death anniversary in Kikar Rabin (previously Kikar Malchei Y Israel i.e. Kings of Israel Square), to honour his memory is clear proof of the strong desire among Israelis and Palestinians for peaceful coexistence based on his *"land for peace"* approach.

Hard Line Likud Leader Benyamin Netanyahu who won the May 1996 elections, disparaged and ignored the Oslo Accord. His successor. Labour leader Ehud Barak, Prime Minister from 1999 -2001, resumed negotiations with Yasser Arafat in July 2000 at Camp David, with President Clinton's good offices, These talks continued at Taba, January 22 - 28, 2001 and concluded with a joint statement indicating progress had been made but that more negotiations were needed. Shortly thereafter George Bush took over as US president and Ariel Sharon as Israel's Prime Minister. Both rejected all contact with Arafat, who ailing and completely isolated, died on November 11, 2004. Thereafter, with Hamas' impressive victory in the 2006 national election, its subsequent break with Fatah and expulsion of its bureaucracy from Gaza in June 2007 and coming to power in March 2009 of an extremely right wing govt. led by Benyamin Netanyahu as Prime Minister has further complicated the Israeli - Palestinian problem. The

February 2011, a "*people's power*" overthrow of President Mubarak, a close US, Israel ally in the last three decades; the May 4, 2011 Fatah and Hamas have signed a unity agreement at Cairo brokered by the new Egyptian govt; on May 15th, "*Nakba*" (catastrophe) Day, coordinated protest marches well by hundreds of Israeli Arabs and Palestinians from the West Bank, Gaza Lebanon, Syria and Jordan had within Israel and onto its borders are all unexpected and worrisome developments for Israel, despite its overwhelming military superiority.

62 years after its birth Israel still has no formally defined national borders. Its polity is highly splintered and its relations with most Arab and Muslim countries (including Turkey, since May 31,2010 when Israel boarded its humanitarian aid convoy to Gaza and killed seven of its onboard citizens) are quite strained. Ever since Iran commenced uranium enrichment and its President Ahmedinejad declared that Israel "*deserves to be wiped off the map*", Israeli Prime Ministers have been hinting that they might be compelled to destroy Iran's nuclear installations. If it embarks on this risky venture a West Asian conflagration would undoubtedly erupt as Iran is a large (1.65 million sq. km.) country of 80 million people and well equipped with modern weaponry including missiles of upto 2000 km. range. In 2007 President Bush had ominously spoken of the possibility of World War III erupting in this region. Fortunately President Obama's approach has been a more sedate one and favours diplomacy and economic sanctions to induce Iran to give up uranium enrichment.

In his book "*Peace Not Apartheid* **Jimmy Carter** has written " *Since the 1979 Israeli - Egyptian peace treaty was signed, much blood has been shed unnecessarily and repeated efforts for a negotiated peace between Israel and her neighbors have failed. Despite its criticism by some Arab sources, this treaty stands as proof that diplomacy can bring lasting peace between ancient adversaries.*" He has pointed out the 1978 Camp David Accord, 1982 Reagan statement, 1993 Oslo Agreement, 1994 Israel Jordan Peace Treaty, 2002 Arab peace proposal, 2003 Geneva Initiative and the International Quartet's Roadmap have good peace making elements in them, and concluded thus "*The bottom line is this : Peace will come to Israel and the Middle East only when the Israeli Government is willing to comply with international law, with the Roadmap for Peace, with official American Policy, with the wishes of the majority of its own citizens and honors its own previous commitments by accepting its legal borders. All Arab neighbors must pledge to honor Israel's right to live in peace under these conditions. The United States is squandering international prestige and goodwill and intensifying* *global anti- American terrorism by unofficially condoning or abetting the Israeli confiscation and colonization of Palestinian territories".*

In his impactful June 4, 2009 Cairo speech, **President Obama** declared : *"For decades, there has been a stalemate: two peoples with legitimate aspirations, each with a painful history that makes compromise elusive. It is easy to point fingers - for Palestinians to point to the displacement brought by Israel's founding, and for Israelis to point to the constant hostility and attacks throughout its history from within its borders as well as beyond. But if we see this conflict only from one side or the other, then we will be blind to the truth: the only resolution is for the aspirations of both sides to be met through two states, where Israelis and Palestinians each live in peace and security. That is in Israel's interest, Palestine's interest, America's interest, and the world's interest. That is why I intend to personally pursue this outcome with all the patience that the task requires. For peace to come, it is time for them - and all of us - to live up to our responsibilities."*

Commenting on this speech Israel's leading peace activist **Uri Avnery** wrote *"While Obama proclaims the 21st century, the government of Israel is returning to the 19th. That was the century when a narrow, egocentric, aggressive nationalism took root in many countries. A century that sanctified the belligerent nation which oppresses minorities and subdues neighbors. The century that gave birth to modern anti-Semitism and to its response - modern Zionism. ... The underlying collision is between two mental worlds which are as distinct from each other as the sun and the moon.".*

Majida Abu Rahmah's January 8, 2010 letter in the Huffington Post movingly epitomizes the non violent struggle of her people for justice. It is therefore quoted in extenso: *"On International Human Rights Day in 2008, my husband Abdallah Abu Rahmah was in Berlin receiving a medal from the World Association for Human Rights. Last year on the same day, 10 December, he was taken away at 2am by Israeli soldiers who broke into our West Bank home. Abdallah was arrested for the same reasons he received the prize — his nonviolent struggle for justice, equality and peace in Palestine/Israel.*

My husband is a school teacher and farmer from the Palestinian village of Bilin. When Israel built its apartheid wall here, it separated Bilin from more than half of its land, in order to facilitate the expansion of the illegal settlement of Mattityahu East. In response, Abdallah and fellow villagers began a campaign of nonviolent resistance. Every Friday for the past five years, we've marched, with Israeli and international supporters, to protest the theft of our land and livelihoods. In September, 2007 Israel's Supreme

Court ruled that the route of the wall in Bilin was illegal and should be changed. Over two years later, the wall remains, unmoved. Many were discouraged, but Abdallah told them that the pressure of our campaign and international support could bring down the wall.

As the grassroots struggle grows here, the efforts to end it have intensified. Our beloved friend, Bassem Abu Rahmah, was murdered by Israeli soldiers as he tried to talk with them, while participating in a demonstration. Leaders like former President Jimmy Carter and Archbishop Desmond Tutu, have visited our village. They stood with Abdallah at Bassem's grave last August. Tutu told us, Just as a simple man named Gandhi led the successful nonviolent struggle in India and simple people such as Rosa Parks and Martin Luther King led the struggle for civil rights in the United States, simple people here in Bilin are leading a nonviolent struggle that will bring them their freedom."

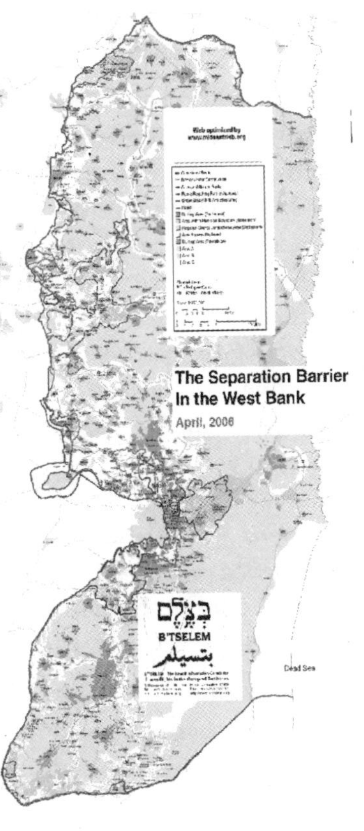

Twelve hours after Abdallah was taken to a military jail from our home, I listened as President Obama received the Nobel Peace Prize and spoke of "the men and women around the world who have been jailed and beaten in the pursuit of justice." I thought of Bassem, Adeeb and my husband, and wondered if President Obama will take action to support our struggle for freedom."

President Obama did take action. He named George Mitchell, architect of the 1998 Northern Ireland Peace Accords as his Middle East Envoy. After much effort Mitchell did manage to get "proximity" (intermediary) talks started between Israel and Palestine (direct face - to -face talks having broken down in December 2008, because of Israel's illegal construction activity in East Jerusalem). However these talks too ceased when Prime Minister Netanhayu refused, despite strong US urging, to extend the six month suspension of construction activity he had ordered in March 2010. In early May 2011 Mitchell, obviously frustrated by his 30 months of fruitless effort submitted his resignation to President Obama.

On the eve of Prime Minister Netanyahu's visit to the US, President Obama, publicly urged recommencement of peace talks and the two state solution based on 1967 borders with mutually agreed land swaps. The latter, in his May 24th speech to the US Congress emphatically rejected this declaring *"Israel will not return to the indefensible lines of 1967"* and adding *"In Judea and Samaria, the Jewish people are not foreign occupiers. We are not the British in India. We are not the Belgians in the Congo. This is the land of our forefathers, the Land of Israel, to which Abraham brought the idea of one God, where David set out to confront Goliath, and where Isaiah saw a vision of eternal peace. No distortion of history can deny the four thousand year old bond, between the Jewish people and the Jewish land".* The only hope he held out to the Palestinians was a hopeless one *"So I say to President Abbas: Tear up your pact with Hamas! Sit down and negotiate! Make peace with the Jewish state! And if you do, I promise you this. Israel will not be the last country to welcome a Palestinian state as a new member of the United Nations. It will be the first to do so."*

President Abbas, in a May 16, 2011 International Herald Tribune article wrote *" We have been negotiating with the Israel for 20 years without coming any closer to realizing a state of our own. We cannot wait indefinitely while Israel continues to send more settlers to the occupied West Bank and denies Palestinians access to most of our land and holy places, particularly in Jerusalem. Neither political pressure nor promises of rewards by the United States have stopped Israel's settlement program We have therefore decided to request international recognition of the State of Palestine on the 1967 border and to be admitted as a full member of the United Nations".* Whether this Palestinian move will succeed is a moot question, considering the probability of a US veto in the Security council. However, the fact is that in the UN General Assembly 118 states have already recognized the Palestinian National Authority and 130 is the figure for a 2/3 majority. Besides following publication of Justice Richard Goldstone's critical report on Israel's 23 day military offensive against Gaza in December 2008 (which killed over 1400 Palestinians), the international outrage over its May 31st 2010 attack on the Gaza aid flotilla in international waters. Israel's standing and "*legitimacy*" in the international arena have considerably declined.

There is much NGO activity, within Israel and the US, to get the Netanhayu government to recommence peace talks, stop housing construction in occupied territories and seek a mutually acceptable settlement with the Palestinians on the '*Land for Peace*' basis. Among those actively involved in this effort are Gush Shalom, Rabbis for Human Rights, Taayush, Coalition of Women for Just Peace, Combatants for Peace, Americans for Peace Now and Network of Spiritual Progressives Most members of these organizations are Israeli and American Jews who support a two-state solution with 1967 borders and Rachel Corrie, the heroic young who was run over by an Israeli army bull dozer at Rafah in March 2003 while trying to prevent demolition of a Palestinian home, was Jewish American. Many of the mentioned NGOs, are also involved in promoting and supporting non violent struggle against Israeli occupation and oppression.

Writing about this form of struggle from Bilin in the West Bank, Nicholas Kristoff wrote in the New York Times (July 9, 2010). "*Despite being stoned and tear gassed on this trip, I find a reed of hope here. Its that some Palestinians are dabbling in a strategy of non violent resistance that just might be a game changer*". He goes on to indicate that whereas Palestinians do not yet have a Gandhi, Ayed Morrar, strategist of the successful non violent struggle at Budrus might be emerging as one such and quotes him thus "*With non violent struggle we can win the media battle. They always used to say that Palestinians are killers. With non violence we can show that we are victims, that we are not against Jews but are against the occupation*". Kristof mentions Morrar's daughter Iltezam who has been organizing the women for such struggles, one of which was very successful, and comments "*Israeli security forces knew how to deal with bombers but were flummoxed by peaceful Palestinian women. Even when beaten and fired on with rubber bullets the women persevered. Finally Israel gave up. It re-routed the security fence to by pass all of Budrus. The saga is chronicled in this year's must-see documentary Budrus, a riveting window into what might be possible if Palestinians adopted civil disobedience on a huge scale. In a sign of the interest in non violent strategies, the documentary is scheduled to play in dozens of West Bank villages in the coming months as well as at international film festivals*".

Writing in the same strain, Thomas Friedman in an article titled "*Lessons from Tahrir Square*", (New York Times, May 24, 2011) wrote "*To the Palestinians I would say: Your dilemma is how to move Israel in a way that won't blow up in your face or require total surrender. You have to start with the iron law of Israeli-Arab peace: whichever party has the Israeli silent majority on its side wins. Anwar Sadat brought the Israeli majority over to his side when he went to Israel, and he got everything he wanted"*..... Ironically, it is the Israeli's who have inbibed lessons from Tahrir Square . Since mid July they have taken to the streets, first in hundreds and by early August in their thousands. On Saturday, August 6th over 300,000 were in protest rallies nationwide - 250,000 in Tel Aviv, 30,000 in Jerusalem and about 3,000 each in Ashkelon, Haifa , Tzemach, Petach Tikva, Raanana, Dimona, Hadera, Rosh Pina, Kiryat Shomna and Eilat. Gil Sasson, one of the leaders of these protests told reporters "*We have here an unprecedented collective awakening. What started as a battle for affordable housing has turned into a protest movement that is snowballing and is now aiming for a system-wide change.*" To dramatize their complaint of unaffordable housing a sprawling "*tent community*" has been planted on Rothschild Boulevard in Tel Aviv with many protesters taking turns to live in it. "*Midan Tahrir comes to Kikar Rabin*" one protester proudly declared..

President Sadat addressing the Israeli Knesset, Nov. 20, 1977

President **Anwar Sadat** may or may not have been inspired by Gandhi but in 1977 faced the truth that Egypt's 1948, 1967 and 1973 wars with Israel (in the last of which it had notable initial success) were disastrous for it. He abjured war and took the path of non-violent conflict resolution. At considerable risk to his political future as also his life, he made the historic journey to Jerusalem in November 1977. This opened the door to negotiations with Prime Minister Menachem Begin and led, with President Carter's good offices, to the historic Camp David Accord of September 1978. In March 1979, Egypt and Israel signed a peace treaty that formally ended the state of war that had existed between them for 30 years. Soon thereafter, mutual diplomatic relations were established. By June 1982 Egypt had regained from Israel all territory it had lost since the 1967 war, *"without firing a shot!"*.

This treaty, respected by both sides and hailed by the world, has endured but President Sadat paid for it with his life. Mubarak who succeeded Sadat, imposed emergency rule soon after the latter's assassination and ruled with it, oppressively and corruptly, for three long decades until he was finally overthrown with a non-violent "Peoples Power" revolution on February 11, 2011.

In August 1994, after many decades of armed resistance to British presence in Northern Ireland, *Sinn Fein* and its President **Gerry Adams**, (who organized the 1981 hunger strikes by IRA prisoners and galvanized the Northern Ireland Catholic community) announced a unilateral 18 month ceasefire, subsequently extended it and in April 1998 signed the historic *"Good Friday Agreement"*. He publicly acknowledged the Truth that violence had not achieved their objectives and the non-violent approach was more likely to do so. In the June 1998 elections Adams won a seat in the Northern Ireland Assembly and subsequently became a member of the British Parliament. A new chapter in Northern Ireland's long and painful struggle for national reunification was thus opened.

Las Madres De Plaza De Mayo in Arjentina:

A small group of women - only fourteen originally - fearlessly took on the brutal Argentine military junta on 30 April 1977. They were the mothers of fourteen of the very many who "*disappeared*" during the Juntas seven year (1976-1983) rule particularly in the initial years, They gathered in the Plaza de Mayo, in front of the Casa Rosada, (Presidential Palace), wearing white head scarves with their childrens names embroidered on them. Thereafter they came every Thursday afternoon. By the end of 1977 their number had risen to 150. Describing themselves as '*Las Madres de Plaza de Mayo*' (MPM) they presented petitions demanding information about their children and also inserted ads in newspapers. In February 1978, when three of the MPM founders (Azucena Villaflor, Esther Careaga and María Eugenia Bianco) also "*disappeared* ", wide national and international revulsion against the Junta erupted and other dissident organizations joined MPM. Before long there was a national network of such organizations and opposition to the Junta steadily increased all over the country. Some political analysts have opined that the Juntas decision to invade and occupy the Malvinas (Falkland) islands in early April 1982 was motivated by its calculation that this would defuse the widespread opposition to it and regain the peoples support. Its humiliating defeat by the British forced it to retract the ban on political parties and restore civil liberties. On December 10, 1983, a civilian government under **Raul Alfonsin** assumed power and initiated action to established civilian control of the armed forces, consolidate democratic institutions and investigate the cases of those who had "*disappeared*". This was carried forward by his successor **Nestor Kirchner** who ensured that those military officers involved in these crimes were prosecuted and sentenced to life terms.

The mothers with President Néstor Kirchner

Rita Arditti, in her book *searching For Life*, has stated: "*These Mothers have created a new form of political participation, outside the traditional party structures and based on the values of love and caring. Motherhood allowed them to build a bond and shape a movement without men.*" **Mark Kurlansky**, has affirmed "*Many factors led to the collapse of the Argentine regime in 1982. But these women were one of the important catalysts for change.*"

In 1999, the MPM was awarded the United Nations Prize for Peace Education.

In Chile **General Augusto Pinochet** overthrew the democratically elected **Salvador Allende** government on September 11, 1973. **Priscilla Hayner** in her book *Unspeakable Truths'* has recounted the horror that followed with over a hundred thousand tortured and many never seen again thereafter, and the non violent struggle adopted to resist and exposed these brutalities. "*Some of us wondered, could Gandhian insights about the power of nonviolence help the struggle to defy the terror? A few of us decided to try to inspire others to speak up against the dictatorship by "crying out the truth." Clandestine pamphlets and leaflets were printed. Slogans were painted on the walls at night at great risk. Underlying these actions was the principle of active nonviolence: since there is injustice, the first requirement is to report it, otherwise we are accomplices. The clandestine actions helped spread the principle of telling the truth and acting on it. Yet, despite the risks, we needed to move beyond clandestine protests into the public arena*".

José Aldunate, a Jesuit priest who became the leader of the *Sebastian Acevedo Movement Against Torture in Chile*, has written " *We educated ourselves about torture and about the dynamics of nonviolence. We watched a film on Mahatma Gandhi. We deliberated and decided to undertake a nonviolent demonstration to denounce torture... We had an obligation to denounce it in public. We needed to shake the population's conscience.*"

On September 14, 1983, the anti-torture campaign was launched in front of the National Investigation Center, 1470 Borgoño St., in Santiago with 70 persons interrupting traffic. unfurling a banner with "*Torturing Done Here.*" and singing a hymn to liberty. The group returned here every month to denounce the regime's crimes against humanity. It had no meeting place, no secretariat, no infrastructure. It met in the streets and plazas when it was time to act. It had no membership list. Participants came by personal invitation, as the movement had to avoid infiltration from the secret police and other repressive institutions. Instructions were passed from person to person. Participants were mainly trained during the actions themselves, and each action was evaluated on the spot.

When **Pope John Paul II** visited Chile in April 1987 he called upon its Catholics and 31 bishops not only to pray, but to actively strive for the restoration of democracy in Chile emphasizing that "*the Gospel consistently urges respect for human rights.*" He found the time to go to the Vicariate of Solidarity, the Church-led pro-democracy, anti-Pinochet organization and encourage its workers to continue their "*noble work*". In 1988, when Pinochet announced a plebiscite designed to extend and ratify his rule for a further eight year period, a nationwide "*Chile Sí, Pinochet No*" campaign was launched. To Pinochets great surprise and dismay, the "*No*"s secured the majority and the three armed services chiefs advised him to resign, which he did. On

March 11, 1990 national elections were held and soon therafter Patricio Aylwin Azócar assumed office as the first democratically elected President after the 17 year military dictatorship.

In 1973, when the military coup took place **Michelle Bachelet's** father, a General, was in charge of the the Food Distribution Office of the Allende government. He was charged with Treason and tortured as a rersult of which he suffered cardiac arrest and died on March 12, 1974. In January 1975, his wife and daughter Michelle, who had worked as couriers for the underground Socialist Party and assisted in organizing a Resistance movement were arrested and taken to Villa Grimaldi, the notorious secret detention center in Santiago, interrogated, tortured and imprisioned at *Cuatro Alamos* detention center. In June 1975, thanks to military friends, they were released and exiled to Australia. In May that year Micehelle left for East Germany to continue her medical studies. In 1979 she was permitted to return to Chile. She began to work at **PIDEE,** an NGO for children of those tortured and killed by the Pinochet Regime. She also supported the movement against torture and for re-establishment of democracy. On March 11, 2000 Bachelet—virtually unknown on the national scene at the time — was appointed Minister of Health and on January 7, 2002 as Defense Minister. In the latter capacity she secured the historic 2003 "*Never again*" declaration by Army Chief General **Juan Emilio Cheyre**, about subverting democracy in Chile. This earned her great admiration and much respect.

In January 2005, she was named the Socialists Party's presidential candidate. A year later, in the runoff election, she won the presidency with 53.5% of the vote, and became Chile's first female president and first woman not the wife of a previous head of state or political leader to reach the presidency of a Latin American nation.

In her victory statement she echoed Gandhi and said "*Violence came into my life, destroying what I loved, because I was a victim of hate. I have dedicated my life to reversing that hate and converting it into understanding, tolerance and love*". Also in keeping with a Gandhian maxim, she took the unprecedenteded step of appointing women to half of all the cabinet posts.

Evo Morales, an Aymara (indigenous Bolivian) coca farmer and leader of the Movement toward Socialism (MAS) had kept track of the *"peoples power"* movements in the US, South Africa and Eastern Europe and taken lessons from it. In 2003 he led thousands of coca farmers and other peasants, on a 120-mile march from Cochabamba to La Paz to demand that foreign companies be made to pay a fifty percent royalty to Bolivia for the natural gas they extract from it. This uprising forced President Gonzalo Sánchez de Lozada out of office. Carlos Mesa, who succeeded him was harried with the same demand and many more sections of the population including teachers and street vendors joined the movement. In March 2005, the Bolivian Congress finally enacted a law imposing a 32-percent tax in addition to the 18 % royalties that foreign companies had been paying. Bolivia's natural gas reserves are second only to Venezuela but it had been benefiting very little from them. In early January 2006, Evo Morales was elected President of Bolivia and became the first Aymara to lead his country, thus ending almost 500 years of his people's subjugation by the Spanish Conquistadores and their descendants. Bolivian style Satyagraha achieved this miracle!

In his book, *The End of Prehistory*, Tomás Hirsch narrates the moment when Evo Morales took on his role as the first indigene ruler: *"In Bolivia, Evo Morales led the peasant and indigenes world to government. Evo takes on the Presidency at the Gateway of the Sun, wearing the unku, a coat used by the ancient priests of Tiwanaku 1,000 years ago; the chuku, a four-pointed cap representing the 4 cardinal directions, and there it flames the wipala, with the rainbow colors, officially established in 1975 as the banner of the Tawantinsuyo. A leader that emerges from the heart of his people, carrying a ceremonial staff containing two condor heads, which was delivered by the amautas (ancestral priests, kallawayas shamans)"*.

In November 2007 Evo Morales hosted, and inaugurated, the Second Pan American Humanist Forum at which he declared *"And what do I ask for Bolivia, for every Bolivian brother? I ask for peace, and request serenity for the moments Bolivia is living now. I ask my guide, the highest of the poets, to help to shed light on the way the Bolivian people decided to follow with dignity. I ask the answer to be non-violent."*

"Power of the original Mandate"

Chiara Lubich, founder of *'Focolare'*, is an amazing and inspiring vindication of Gandhi's affirmation that *"Non-Violence is the only thing the atom bomb cannot destroy"*. For him the essence of non violence was unconditional love even of one's enemies. Born as Silvia Lubich in Trent, Italy in 1920, she grew up in extreme poverty and financed her studies upto university by giving tuitions. During World War II, while bombs were being dropped on her home town, she "*discovered*" that Love, which is a manifestation of God, is *"stronger than the bombs that were falling on Trent"*. She decided to dedicate her life to God and strive for human unity and world peace. She was just 23 years old when she took this decision on December 7, 1943. She changed her name to Chiara in honour of Saint Clare (Chiara) of Assisi, one of the first followers of Saint Francis of Assisi, who founded the Order of Poor Ladies, (now known as the Order of Saint Clare) a monastic religious order for women. Even though her own home was destroyed in the bombing and her family left Trent she stayed on to tend the homeless and the wounded. Her *"divine adventure"* began when she found a woman driven to insanity by the bombing that had killed four of her children. She was joined by twelve of her friends and they stayed together in a little home they named "*the little house of Nazareth* ". Its limited accomodation and resources were shared with all those in need. They let it be known that if killed in the bombing, the only inscription they wished on their graves was *"And we have believed in Love"*.

Focolare (small communities of lay volunteers), is a lay spiritual movement, initially of celibate women, but later also of celibate men and married couples and their children, strives to promote human unity and world peace through spirituality and loving service to everyone in need of it. It has grown slowly but surely. In 1948 Chiara secured the whole hearted support of Igino Giordani, writer, journalist, ecumenism and peace activist and member of the Italian parliament, which enabled access to the highest levels of the Catholic Church, the Italian government, parliament and the media. In 1949, Pasquale Foresi became the first Focolarino to be ordained a priest. He helped to institute the Movement's theological studies and to start the *Città Nuova, Focolare's* Publishing House. The same year, the practice of retreating to the Dolomite Mountains for a week for reflection and strengthening community bands was commenced. These retreats were named *'Mariapolis'* in honour of the Virgin Mary. They attracted increasing number of people each year. At the 1959 Mariapolis, attended by more than 10,000 people from 27 nations Chiara added an important new dimension to *Focolare's* peace efforts by urging participants to "*love the nation of the other as you love your won*". A spiritualized internationalism thereafter became the hallmark of the movement.

In 1962 Focolare received formal approval from the Pope as an *Ecumenic Lay Congregation of the Catholic Church*. In 1967, its *New Families and New Humanity Movements for a United World* were launched In 1970 the *Gen 3* (youth) Movement was launched with the motto *Young People for a United World*. In 1976, *Bishop Friends of Focolare* was launched by Bishop Klaus Hemmerle of Aachen in Germany, "*to deepen the spirituality and collegial unity*" of his fellow Bishops.

In 1984 John Paul II visited *Focolare's* International headquarters at Rocca di Papa in Italy and lauded its "*radicalism of love*".

In 1991, during a trip to Brazil, Chiara was deeply moved by the plight of those living in sub-human conditions in Sao Paolo's favelas (slums),enunciated the "*Economy of Communion in Liberty*" and urged industrialists and businessmen among Brazils 250,000 *Focolare* members to invest in poverty stricken villages and small towns, make their residents share holders in their enterprises and use part of their profits to promote a "*culture of giving*" by building schools, hospitals and infrastructure there. Chiara explained it thus "*In contrast to the consumerist economy which is based on a culture of having, the economy of communion is an economy of giving. This would seem difficult, even heroic, but this is not so since man, who is made in the image of God who is love, finds fulfillment in loving, in giving. It is this consideration, backed by our experience, that gives us the hope that the economy of communion will spread universally*".

By September 2001, 761 business enterprises had joined the "*Economy of Communion*" (EC) all over the world, with Italy topping the list with 246, followed by Western Europe (172), Brazil (82) and Eastern Europe (60). It is estimated that EC businesses worldwide now are approximately 1000. In some of these enterprises slum dwellers have become share holders by investing as little as $ 5. Main items produced are clothing, food items, household goods, building materials and agricultural requisites. Main items traded are clothing, groceries, household items and healthcare products. One of the EC businessmen explained this new economic activity thus "*It is a vision of the economy based not on the struggle to dominate but on a commitment to grow together, risking economic resources, creativity and talents, to share profits with those excluded from the current economic system, because they are 'unproductive'* ". Professor Adam Biela of Lublin Catholic University, Poland has lauded it as a "*Copernican revolution in the Social Sciences*".

In 1996 Chiara was awarded the UNESCO Prize for Education for Peace, in Paris, and Focolare was lauded thus: "*In an age when ethnic and religious differences too often lead to violent conflict, the spread of the Focolare Movement has also contributed to a constructive dialogue between persons, generations, social classes and peoples*". Speaking to the Catalan Parliament in December 2002 on '*Fraternity in Politics*' she stated that this was "*not a new party, but the contribution of a new political culture and praxis,*" which Mahatma Gandhi, Martin Luther King and the Dalai Lama had urged earlier but Jesus Christ was the first to give "*as a special gift to humanity, with his prayer: 'Father, that they may all be one'* ".

With Pope John Paul II

Every summer *Focolare* organizes '*Mariapolis* ' retreats - more than 100 worldwide -, where members and newcomers come together to discuss the movement and its spirituality while putting it into practice. More than 200,000 people worldwide attend them each year.

Focolare today is in 180 countries and has over two million members. It has 23 regional branches in various parts of the world. It emphasizes individual spirituality, but also places high importance on "*trying to help each other in our journey towards God.*" Though theologically Roman Catholic, *Focolare* has established strong links to all the Christian churches and other religions particularly Judaism, Buddhism and Hinduism. In the context of inter-religious dialogue and the '*Charism of Unity and Politics*' Chiara has quoted Mahatma Gandhi, whom she lauded as "*one of the rare giants of the spirit* ", as follows : " *The Golden Rule is to be friends of the world and to consider the whole human family as 'one'. Whoever distinguishes between the faithful of his own religion and those of another, misinforms the members of his own and opens the way to rejection and irreligion* ".

Chiara died at Rocca di Papa in Italy on March 14, 2008, at the age of 88. Her funeral was attended by 25,000 people, 17 Cardinals, 49 Bishops, 1200 priests as well as representatives of all the world's main religions. A well deserved honour for someone, who 65 years earlier, had started off alone on her "*Divine Adventure*" .

Tsunesaburo Makiguchi and Soka Gakkai

Tsunesaburo Makiguchi (1871-1944), author and educator is a good vindication of Gandhi's affirmation "*If we are to reach real peace in this world and if we are to carry on a real war against war we shall have to begin with the children* ". Deeply inspired by Nichiren Buddhism, he dedicated himself to reform Japan's hidebound educational system. His Theory of Value-Creating Pedagogy was published in book form in 1930 under the title *Soka Kyoikugaku Taipei.*

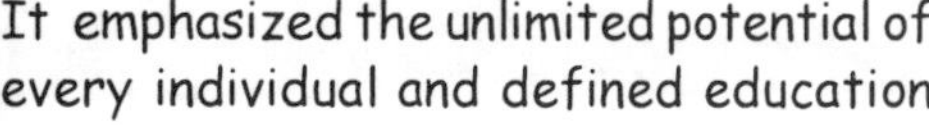

It emphasized the unlimited potential of every individual and defined education as the lifelong pursuit of self-awareness, wisdom and development. In 1930 he founded the Soka Kyoiku Gakkai (Society for the Creation of Value) as a study group of reformist educators. His objective was to create an educational system which would be a partnership of school, home and community, in which each had responsibility for a specific part of the education. In this system, a child would spend half a day in school and the other half in apprenticeships and other types of work, at home and in the community, befitting the nature and needs of each child and instilling in him/her the highest personal/societal values. It would also change all of them from being bored, apathetic rote-learners into eager, self-motivated students. This however was quite contrary to what Japan's then autocratic fascist authorities wanted viz. an educational system that produced ultra-nationalist, ever obedient citizens.

In the early 1930s ultra-nationalism had gestated in Japan. Its militarist government had reintroduced the ancient Shinto ideology which deified the emperor and suppressed all forms of dissidence. The refusal of Makiguchi and his close associate ***Josei Toda*** (1900-58) to renounce or alter their innovative educational ideas led to their imprisonment in 1943 as "*thought criminals.*" Makiguchi died in prison in 1944 at the age of 73. Josei Toda survived the prison ordeal and was released when the war ended. Soon thereafter, he embarked on rebuilding Soka Gakkai and enlarged its mission from education for youth to education for betterment of society as a whole. He utilized a form of Buddhism focussed on social harmony for overcoming post-war despair and promoting self-empowerment. This resonated well among the people, traumatized by the complete devastation of Hiroshima and Nagasaki.

In 1957, Toda made an impassioned call on his followers to strive for the abolition of nuclear weapons. This thereafter became the capstone of the Soka Gakkai's peace activities. By the time Toda died in 1958 Soka Gakkai had approximately one million members.

Makiguchi and his pupils

Toda's successor, **Daisaku Ikeda,** who had experienced the horrors of war as a youth, decided to dedicate his life to building social harmony and international peace. He was just 32 when he became Soka Gakkai's president in 1960. Under his dynamic leadership, the organization has expanded globally. In 1975, he founded Soka Gakkai International (SGI). Today it is a global network of 82 constituent organizations with activities in 192 countries and territories.

Daisaku Ikeda's great respect for Gandhi is indicated in the article titled '*Gandhism and the 21st Century*' published in the Journal of Peace and Gandhian Studies (April-September 1997 issue). In it, he affirmed "*Buddhism's contribution is its discovery that it is "ignorance" that lies at the heart of mutually enthralled unfolding of the individual and the world. Mahatma Gandhi worked tirelessly toward the conquest of that inner darkness. The fact that Gandhi used the term Satyagraha to characterize his non-violent resistance is of great interest. His was a movement of social engagement which at the same time embodied the philosophical struggle to overcome the negative inner forces that Buddhism describes as ignorance. In Gandhi's life we can observe an absolute consistency between action and philosophy, spirit and body.*"

President Luiz Inácio Lula da Silva of Brazil

Brazilian president **Luiz Inácio** Lula, fondly hailed by millions of his countrymen as "*Lula, Papai* " (Papa Lula) has convincingly demonstrated that Gandhi's *Talisman* about policy makers recalling the face of the poorest man while formulating their policies can and do work in actual practice.

Lula's mother, unable to eke out a livelihood in Brazil's impoverished, drought plagued north eastern Sertão region,travelled with her children to São Paulo, 2,000 kilometers to the south,to find work there for all of them as domestic servants, waiters or construction workers. Lula's eventual rise to power began in that city's industrial suburbs, through the Brazilian Workers Party.

Brazil was once called "*Belindia,*" a term coined by a businessman who saw the vast country as a cross between Belgium and India, a place of European wealth and Asian poverty, where the chasm between rich and poor seemed insurmountable. President Lula was the first to attempt to bridge that gap.

When he was elected president in December 2002 he continued to speak the language of ordinary people, recounting events of his youth and how at age 5 he had to fetch water balancing the heavy bucket on his head. As President, he decided to do something about giving water to the Sertao region even if a mega project was required to achieve it. The 2,700-kilometer long São Francisco river provides water to five states but makes a big loop around the Sertão region denying its waters to it. With the mega project, which some have described as "*Pharonic*", two canals 400 and 220 km long are being constructed to transport 26.3 m3/s of water from this river into the Sertao region. The sizable difference in altitude is being overcome by pumping water 165m into the northern canal and 364m into the eastern canal, with nine pumping stations, 27 aqueducts, eight tunnels, 35 water reservoirs and two hydroelectric plants. 70% of this water is to be utilized for sugar cane cultivation, horticulture and shrimp farms, 26% for urban use (mainly for Fortaleza city) and the remaining 4% for use by rural populations. To keep down the project's estimated 6.6 billion Real (approx. $ 4 billion). cost, battalions of soldiers have been deployed to excavate the canals with heavy earthmoving equipment. Eight thousand labourers are toiling at construction sites. If all goes well, 12 million, mainly rural Brazilians would benefit from this project, scheduled to be completed by 2025. Lula's ardent supporters liken him to President Franklin Roosevelt, who launched the Tennessee River Valley project. His critics castigate him as a megalomaniac.

As "Worker-President" Lula became as much a darling of foreign investors as idol of the poor. His predecessor, Fernando Henrique Cardoso had given Brazil a solid platform for growth, with inflation tamed, fiscal discipline imposed, many public sector enterprises privatised and incentives for foreign investments introduced. Lula made the best use of these benefits to create new jobs and industries and better economic conditions for all particularly the poor and lower middle class.

To strengthen the domestic industrial base he called upon Brazil's industrial giants, Petrobras, the national oil company, Vale, the mining giant and Gerdau, the privately owned steelmaker to produce all their oil and mining industry requirements,from pipes to ships, within Brazil. This attracted much foreign investment into these new industries and created thousands of new jobs. The economy group at 5% with substantial exports, besides the usual coffee, soybeans, sugar, beef and iron ore also cellulose, cars and aircraft. As China replaced the United States as Brazil's biggest trading partner in early 2009, it has been less severely affected by the 2008 US recession than most other countries.

Since President Lula assumed office on January 1st 2003, Brazil's middle class has grown by 29 million creating a powerful domestic consumer market. Another 20 million people have been lifted out of abject poverty. The income of the poorest 10 percent has grown five times faster than that of the richest 10 percent. Unemployment and illiteracy have dropped substantially.

Brazil has repaid all its foreign debt. In early 2002 it needed an emergency $30 billion bail out from IMF. In 2009 it provided $5 billion to it for providing loans to developing nations. Its foreign currency reserves now exceed $200 billion and the Real is now a strong currency. Since 2008 the Real has gained almost 50% against the dollar. All this is partly due to President Lula being as lucky as good a president. During his tenure Brazil has benefited greatly from the commodity boom.

Writing about all these achievements under the title '*Brazil Takes Off*' the Economist wrote in November 2009 "*When, back in 2001, economists at Goldman Sachs bracketed Brazil with Russia, India and China as the economies that would come to dominate the world, there was much sniping about the B in the BRIC acronym. Brazil? A country with a growth rate as skimpy as its swimsuits, prey to any financial crisis that was around, a place*

President Lula with Brazil's poor students

of chronic political instability, whose infinite capacity to squander its obvious potential was as legendary as its talent for football and carnivals, did not seem to belong with those emerging titans. Now that scepticism looks misplaced.......Forecasts vary, but sometime in the decade after 2014—rather sooner than Goldman Sachs envisaged—Brazil is likely to become the world's fifth-largest economy, overtaking Britain and France. And, in some ways, Brazil outclasses the other BRICs. Unlike China, it is a democracy. Unlike India, it has no insurgents, no ethnic and religious conflicts nor hostile neighbours. Unlike Russia, it exports more than oil and arms, and treats foreign investors with respect. Under the presidency of Luiz Inácio Lula da Silva, a former trade-union leader born in poverty, its government has moved to reduce the searing inequalities that have long disfigured it. Indeed, when it comes to smart social policy and boosting consumption at home, the developing world has much more to learn from Brazil than from China."

In November 2010 President Lula was awarded the prestigious Indira Gandhi Prize for Peace, Disarmament and Development for having *"championed the cause of the global south and worked to strengthen bonds among the developing countries"* and for *"his priority from the start being inclusive growth and the consolidation and expansion of social programmes,"*

International Terrorism

Gandhi had declared "*The world rests on the bed rock of Satya*" and "*Peace will come when Truth is pursued and Truth implies justice*". The spate of corporate scandals in Enron, Worldcom, Bear Sterns, Lehman brothers and other mega firms, resulting in their bankruptcies and impoverishment of their very many stake holders, are the calamitous consequences of their CEOs deviating from the path of Truth for personal gain or for maximizing profits by dishonest means. The same is true for political leaders who indulge in corrupt practices, promise to protect but permit destruction of places of worship (i.e. Babri Masjid), invade countries on the basis of blatant falsehoods (of which Iraq is the starkest example), undertake targeted assassinations and pre-emptive strikes and embark upon regime changes in countries that oppose their dictates. The spate of terrorist attacks in New York, Washington, Tel Aviv, Jeddah, Bali, Mumbai, New Delhi, Srinagar, Istanbul, Rabat, Baghdad, Djakarta, Madrid, London, Sharm al Shaik, Amman, Karachi, Lahore, Rawalpindi, Peshawar, Kabul and Khandahar within the first decade of the new millenium are the tragic outcome of these untruthful and iniquitous policies.

Soon after "*9/11*" Paul Kennedy wrote "*At 8:45 a.m. Tuesday, Sept. 11, 2001, and not the first day of the year 2000, America fully entered the 21st century. The millennial celebrations in New York's Times Square were ephemeral acts. The devastation of the World Trade Center, only a mile to the south, was an epic, transforming event..... America is our modern-day Colossus, bestriding the world with aircraft-carriers, communications systems, giant corporations and cultural impress. And yet this Colossus is also extremely vulnerable to weapons that are far different from Yamamoto's aircraft carriers and Hitler's panzer divisions. It has an Achilles' heel that is, to a great extent, of its own making. Its cultural and commercial superiority and the relentless drumbeat of its free-market doctrines have been seen as a threat to many religious and class groups, especially in traditional societies. Its powerful corporations are viewed by America's critics as having an undue and powerful influence, say, in blocking international agreements on climate control, in forcing changes upon restricted markets, and in overawing weak Third World governments."*

Karen Armstrong echoed the same sentiment: "*The world changed on September 11th. We now realize that we in the privileged Western countries can no longer assume that events in the rest of the world do not concern us. What happens in Gaza, Iraq or Afghanistan today, is likely to have repercussions in New York, Washington or London tomorrow and small groups will soon have the capacity to commit acts of mass destruction previously only possible for powerful nations*".

Much terrorism in recent years has emanated from Muslim countries. Samuel Huntington provides a clue to its cause. "*The West's efforts to universalize its values and institutions, to maintain its military and economic superiority, and to intervene in conflicts in the Muslim world generate intense resentment among Muslims. During the fifteen years between 1980 and 1995,the US engaged in 17 military operations in the Middle East, all of them directed against Muslim states. No comparable pattern of US military operations occurred against the people of any other civilization.*"

Richard Clarke, Counter Terrorism Director under Presidents Clinton and George Bush until he resigned in March 2003, has written "*Instead of addressing the Al Qaeda threat with all the attention it required after 9/11, we went off on a tangent, off after Iraq, off on a path that weakened us and strengthened the next generation of Al Qaedas. For even as we have been attriting the core of Al Qaeda, it has metastatized. Like a Hydra it has grown new heads. There have been far more major terrorist attacks by Al Qaeda and its regional clones in the 30 months since 9/11 than there were in the same period prior to this momentous event.*"

In an era of terrorism, asymmetric warfare and an illicit arms trade, including in components of Weapons of Mass Distruction (WMDs), the path of truth, justice, non-violence and elimination of root causes of conflict is the safest for all political leaders and nations to follow. 7/7 in London has shown how easily people with anger and hate in their hearts can assemble and explode bombs in subways and buses even when intelligence and security services are placed on highest alert. 9/11 provides an even starker lesson for in this case the assailants were armed only with box cutters and used US flying schools to learn how to fly and US planes, US gasoline and US airports to destroy some of its most valuable assets, in broad daylight and in just one hour. Since then expert hackers, one of whom was a teenager, have managed to break into top secret computers of the US Defence Department. India's former National Security Adviser M.K. Narayanan has revealed that some of India's top Secret Computers have been invaded by Chinese hackers. Google has revealed likewise. A *"Cyber Pearl Harbour"* is now a distinct possibility. Some defence analysts have written about highly destructive ultrasonic weapons and micro unmanned aerial vehicles, *"the size of a humming bird"* networked to ground controls which could destroy shopping malls, railway stations and even planes by *"acting as aerial mines"*. Michael Brown, in *'Grave New World: Security Challenges in the 21st Century'*, enumerates other such fearsome threats. To avert all these threats, more imperative and effective than stern security measures and preemptive strikes is to remove anger and hatred from peoples minds, and replace them with hope based on Justice and compassion. As President Kennedy had stated *"Those who make peaceful change impossible will make violent revolution inevitable."* The grave problem of terrorism is as much a symptom of the hateful delirium gestated by iniquitous domestic and foreign policies, as they are of evil mind sets.

Jonathan Schell writes *"As the new century begins, no question is more important than whether the world has now embarked on a new cycle of violence, condemning the 21st century to repeat or even outdo, the bloodshed of the 20th."* He states the present dangers are not, as before, *"the massed conventional armies and systematized hatreds of rival great powers"* but *"the persistent and steady spread of nuclear weapons and other weapons of mass destruction and the unappeased demons of national, ethnic, religious and class fury"*. He argues that, notwithstanding the shock of September 11th and the need to take forceful measures to meet the threat of global terrorism, a new and promising path has opened up. *For in 20th century history another complimentary lesson, less conspicuous than the first but just as important, has been emerging. It is that forms of non-violent action can serve effectively in the place of violence at every level of political affairs. This is the promise of Mohandas K. Gandhi's resistance to the British Empire in India, of Martin Luther King's civil rights movement in the United States, of the non-violent movements in Eastern Europe and Russia that brought down Communism and the Soviet Union"*.

Gandhi as the Ideal Leadership Model

Deepak Chopra affirms "Mahatma Gandhi expressed a profound truth when he said '*There is no way to peace. Peace is the way*' ". He explains what Gandhi meant was that peace cannot be achieved through violence and war but by adopting life styles and policies that promote peace. He points out that humanity has achieved many feats - rationality, exploring the psyche, overcoming superstition and disease etc and affirms " *The next evolutionary step is for humanity to renounce war and violence. Just as Newton's formulation of the law of gravity meant human beings were finally and forever on the road to a new science, a road that led to a completely transformed world, you and I can create a new turning point.*"

Gandhi's leadership, completely self made, sprouted and grew to full stature as his '*Experiments with Truth*' and application of the "*Eternal Verities*" to his daily challenges progressed. He neither had the benefit of personality development, communication, organization, management or leadership courses nor good looks nor great oratory. His only guidance came from his "*inner voice*". Among the vital truths it taught him were that: One man can make a difference; strength comes not from physical capacity but from an indomitable will; given a just cause, capacity for self suffering, and avoidance of violence, victory is a certainty; he who fears fails and leadership by example is the most effective. Striving to reach the greatest of all Truths - God - he discovered great truths in diverse fields including leadership, politics, economics, science, ecology and management and most importantly, the fact that the fundamental law governing human existence is love. He himself acknowledges this. "*The deeper the search in the mine of truth the richer the discovery of gems buried there*". A century earlier, Emerson had asserted : "*What lies behind us and what lies before us are small matters compared to what lies within us*". Carl Jung enunciated the same truth more pithily: "*Who looks outside dreams; who looks inside awakes.*"

Extremely timid in his youth Gandhi became a fearless "*star performer*" once he took up the sword of Truth and the shield of non-violence. Dressed like a "*half naked fakir*" he ended up becoming a citizen of the world and in at least two cases an icon of the information age: Apple computers used a seated picture of his in their 1998 global advertising campaign with just two words below it : "*Think different*", A Tata Finance advertisement used

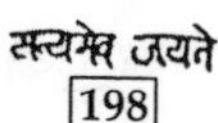

TATA FINANCE

Bezzola Complex, 6th Floor, Chembur, Mumbai 400 071
Tel: 527 6410 • Web site: tatafinancesolutions.com

Find Purpose The Means Will Follow

The march to Dandi still reverberates with inspiration for us all. In 1997, to celebrate the 50th anniversary of India's independence, we used a Dandi march photograph to launch a commemorative campaign. The campaign was heralded as among the most evocative use of Gandhiji's legacy for a public service message. The response to the campaign was so overwhelming, its theme became our corporate theme. This, we believe, also reflects the fact that the Tata brand values resonate well with Bapu's belief systems.

a photograph of his, with the words *"Find Purpose, The Means Will Follow"*.

"Each of us must be the change wish to see in the World" Gandhi urged. Many, particularly among young, mistakenly assume Gandhi was born a saint, lived like a saint and died a martyr. This is quite untrue. His autobiography clearly reveals he had the usual youthful foibles. On one occasion he purloined a piece of family jewellery to enable his brother repay a debt. On another occasion had a *"meat eating escapade"* with Muslim friend though brought up a strict vegetarian. As a young man had strong sexual appetite and a violent temper and also went through an agnostic phase. It was only after he embarked on his *'Experiments with Truth'* at about the age of 35 and took the *'bramhacharya vow'* that he firmly adopted the ascetic path, and that too in stages. His *"half naked fakir"* stage began only in 1922 when he was 53. However his thinking was always focused on finding practical solutions to problems, and on how best to inspire and lead his countrymen, none of whom were as ascetic or nonviolent as him, to freedom and social reform.

The path that Gandhi took to become and outstanding leader is open to all those willing to adopt his principles, descipline and dedication. Most people in the world, particularly in India, have deep reverence for God in all His manifestations, particularly as *'Sat'*. *'Ahimsa Paramo Dharma'* has been an integral element in India's spiritual tradition since Mahaveera and Buddha, six centuries before Christ. Truth, Justice, Love and Peace are basic elements in all religious traditions as the following excerpts from their sacred scriptures reveal :

"Truth is victorious, never untruth, Truth is the way;
Truth is the goal of life,
Reached by the sages who are free from self will"
Mundaka Upanishad (3.1.6)

"That one I love who is incapable of ill will,
Who is friendly and compassionate; living beyond the reach of I and Mine,
And of pleasure and pain, patient, contented, self controlled,
Firm in faith, with all his heart and all his mind
Given to me. With such a one I am in love".
The Gita (Chapter 12. Verse 13)

"The force of arms cannot do what peace does.
If you can gain your desired end with sugar, why use poison?
What sensible man would abandon his bale of cotton
For fear of having to pay a toll on it?"
Nitivakyamrta (344- 50)

"Therefore, O Ananda, be ye lamps unto yourselves. Be ye a refuge unto yourselves. Hold fast to the Truth as a lamp. Look not for refuge to anyone beside yourselves.... And whosoever, Ananda, either now or after I am dead, shall be a lamp unto themselves, and a refuge unto themselves, and hold fast to the Truth, it is they Ananda, among my Bhikkus, who shall reach the very topmost height. But they must be anxious to learn."
From the Buddha's last sermon

There are ten strong things. Iron is strong but fire melts it;
Fire is strong but water quenches it;
Water is strong but the clouds evaporate it;
Clouds are strong but the wind drives them away;
Man is strong, but fears cast him down;
Fear is strong but sleep overcomes it;
Sleep is strong yet death is stronger; But loving kindness survives death.
The Talmud

"May peace triumph over discord,
may generosity triumph over niggardliness.
May love triumph over contempt,

May the true spoken word triumph over the false spoken word,
May the Truth triumph over falsehood"
Zoroastrian Yasna 60.5

"Then you will know the Truth, and the Truth shall set you free
The Bible : John 8:32

"You have heard it said, "Love your neighbour and hate your enemy." But I say to you love your enemies and pray for those who persecute you, so that you may be children of your Father in heaven."
The Bible: Mathew 5:43-45

"God has given the sun a shining glory, and the moon a wondrous light,
And through their measured beauty, people have the count of time
And learn the number of years.
He has created these to advance righteousness and Truth,
And to explain His signs to people who understand"
The Koran Sura 10 : 5

"O believers, be seekers after Justice, witnesses for God, even though it be against yourselves or your parents and kinsmen."
The Koran: Surah 4 : 133

"Those who spend their wealth in the way of God will be rewarded like a grain of corn which grows seven ears and each grain sprouts a hundred grains, for he knows and gives in abundance"
The Koran: Surah 2:261

I laugh when I hear that the fish in the water is thirsty,
You do not see that the real is in your home,
and you wander from forest to forest listlessly.
Here is the Truth! Go where you will, to Benares or to Mathura;
If you do not find your soul, the world is unreal to you.
Kabir

"Those who seek Truth, and speak Truth
Their bodies and minds become truthful....
Those who have forgotten Truth, cry in agony
And weep while departing"
Adi Granth, Sri Raga

"O Son of Spirit! Know thou of a truth : He that biddeth men be just and himself committeth iniquity is not of Me, even though he bear My name".
Baha'ullah

Adhering to truth, justice, love, non-violence and charity is therefore not as difficult as it might appear to those who equate this path with Gandhi's asceticism. By adopting this path everyone can, like Gandhi, emerge from trembling timidity into fearless, inspired and trustworthy leadership, like Martin Luther King and a host of other non-violent leaders, without becoming ascetics.

In affirming that *"Each of us must be the change we wish to see in the World"* Gandhi was calling upon us to provide this leadership in our respective spheres whether we are politicians, government officials, diplomats, lawyers, corporate or business executives, scientists, knowledge workers, professors, teachers, military personnel, students, peace activists, or just ordinary men and women.

Everyday, each of us is confronted with some untruth, injustice, hatred, anger, despair or violence and have a choice of either ignoring it, participating in it or confronting and fighting it. Leadership lies in choosing the last mentioned course. Gandhi provides an excellent model and beacon for this.

Leadership potential is embedded within each of us, but has to be located through introspection and nurtured through disciplined and dedicated effort. Like the man with an artificial leg who climbed Mount Everest and the totally handicapped man in a wheel chair who has emerged as the present world's greatest astrophysicist, each of us can achieve great things if we strive wholeheartedly for them. Demosthenes, handicapped in youth by stammering, overcame it with persistent orations on a lonely beach with pebbles in his mouth, and emerged the greatest orator in Classical Greece!

Each of us not only has the potential for leadership but also the duty of providing it for improving our families, professions, societies and nations. Einstein's words " *The world is a dangerous place to live not because of the people who are evil but because of the people who don't do anything about it.*" are very pertinent to each of us.

To be the change we wish to see in the world we do not need to make dramatic changes in our lives. We only need to firmly resolve to be ever truthful in all our actions, never to cause physical, emotional or mental injury to anyone and replace all anger and hate in our hearts with love and compassion. Taking the simple resolution to always speak the Truth has a remarkable immediate effect. It becomes quite difficult thereafter to commit any sin, since every sin has to be camouflaged with very many lies !

Rotary International was founded in February 1905, by Paul Harris, a Chicago attorney . In 1932,(a few months after Time Magazine named Gandhi its "Man of the Year' and put him on the cover of its January 4,1931 issue), a Chicago Rotarian named Herbert Taylor formulated a simple ethical code called the 'Four Way Test'. In 1943, Rotary International formally adopted it as the *'4 Way Test of the things we think, say or do'*. Since then it has been translated into over 100 languages. It reads :

Is it the Truth?
Is it Fair to all concerned?
Will it build Goodwill and Better Friendships?
Will it be Beneficial to all concerned?

Over a million Rotarians all over the world have Truth as the touchstone of their lives for many years now. This simple four way test can easily be adopted by each of us.

All those who adopt the path of Truth, justice, love and non-violence become pin points of light and emitters of positive energies in the encircling darkness of untruth, injustice, hate and violence. As these pinpoints of light and positive energy emitters proliferate, the resultant effulgence reveals new paths for transformation of families, neighbourhoods, societies, nations and the world, which in energy terms, as scientists and ecologists have established, is a single, enormous, living organism.

When those in apex positions adopt the path of truth, justice, love and non-violence they become role models for others to follow. "*Yatha raja, thatha praja*" (As is the King, so are his subjects) the ancient Sanskrit maxim verily states. With inspiring, trustworthy, just and peaceful leaders, their governments, countries, corporations and other institutions, are best equipped for good governance and the security, progress and prosperity of their citizens and stakeholders.

Politicians, at every level, have the best opportunity for exercising inspiring, trustworthy, leadership. They deal with the interests of more people than any other type of leader. The respect they command today is minimal, because many of them are charged with serious criminal offences and MPs among them frequently absent themselves from parliament yet regularly raise their salaries perquisites and constituency development allotments, demand payments for asking questions in parliament, a Chief Minister accepts garlands strung with thousand rupee notes and an 85 year old politician governor is caught on camera in a sexual romp at his official residence. All these misdemeanours have shocked and revulsed the nation. For those politicians, particularly the youthful ones, who wish to cleanse the system Toynbee's words about Gandhi wading into the slough, showing how it can be purified and remaining uncontaminated despite immersion in it, are good beacons. Uncontaminated by corruption, communalism, casteism, sex and violence, politics can be transformed into what it is meant to be - selfless service of the nation and its people. Political leaders of vision, integrity and dedication like Jawaharlal Nehru and Lal Bahadur Shastri in the first three decades of India's Independence, and now Sonia and Rahul Gandhi who reject the power and pelf of high office to campaign among the masses for secularism, social justice and national unity are revered and widely admired. On the other hand those who indulge in *"politics without principles"*, pursue narrow personal, communal, caste, economic and ideological interests, mislead their *"Temples of Democracy"* and do not hesitate even to take their countries to war on blatant falsehoods become objects of contempt not only of their fellow citizens but also of the world. The same applies to government officials who work hand in glove with their political masters in corrupt practices and politically instigated communal massacres, betraying their oaths to protect the Constitution. In the 2002 Gujarat massacre and the 2009 Karnataka church attacks some senior administrative and police officers actively colluded with the rabid communal outfits and unscrupulous politicians who instigated them. For those dedicated officers determined to resist nefarious political pressures the resignation of Harsh Mandar, Gujarat cadre IAS officer in protest against the politically instigated 2002 communal massacre in that state is a good example. So are those of IPS officers, R.B.Sreekumar, Sanjeev Bhat and Rahul Sharma who have/are stoically undergoing harassment for exposing ensconced facts about political masterminding of the 2002 Gujarat massacre, The first mentioned has written a revealing and moving book titled *'The Diary of a Helpless Man'*

In recent years Police Service personnel have often been caught on camera brutally assaulting unarmed protesters with lathis and even shooting them. Such instances at Nandigram, Singur and Jaithapur have already been mentioned earlier in this book. The one on the outskirts of Pune on August 9th have again shocked the nation as TV footage has shown policemen firing on fleeing protesters and killing three of them. The contrast with the restrained handling by the British police of the recent rioting and looting in London and other British cities is stark and has been much commented upon. Our police officers and personnel must keep in mind that maintaining law and order requires safeguarding the people's rights to peaceful assembly and protest as much as ensuring order and security. They should remember that in Los Angeles 1992 and in Britain 2011 the initial spark for the widespread rioting and looting was a single case of police brutality which was broadcast on TV screens.

Gandhi's leadership is very relevant to lawyers and judges since he held a prestigious law degree and showed how a good knowledge of the Law could be effectively used to fight injustice and oppression. Those lawyers who are doing this, through pro bono legal advice and public interest litigation, have earned much respect and gratitude from their fellow citizens. So have eminent Supreme Court judges like Justices K.R. Krishna Iyer and M.N.Venkatachaliah with their seminal judgements on vital issues, and more recently Justices G.S. Singhvi and A.K. Ganguly who frankly rued that the courts, including the *"highest court in the largest democracy of the world"*, have lost sympathy for the common man. They drew attention to *"precarious consequences"* if the Supreme Court and other courts dilute constitutional imperatives to accommodate "so-called trends of globalization". Sadly, in the last two decades there have been instances not only of dilution of *"constitutional imperatives"* but also of financial and other misconduct by two Supreme court and three High Court Judges. This is indeed a serious and tragic development which needs to be urgently and effectively countered. Fortunately, the Law Ministry has initiated steps for doing so. Separately a Citizens Campaign for Judicial Accountability and Judicial Reforms with a close *"Judge and Judgment watch"* has been launched.

Gandhi's *"level five"* leadership and trusteeship concept as also Peter Drucker's assertion that good management is *"deeply involved with spiritual concerns - the nature of man, good and evil"* are very pertinent to corporate industrial, business, banking and others leaders in the economic field. *"Commerce without morality"* might bring short term gains, but ultimately leads to disaster as numerous recent examples in the Financial, Accountancy and Housing sectors of the US and Europe have shown. The same applies to those who forsake the work ethic and take to enjoying *'Wealth without work'* with no concern for their disadvantaged fellow citizens. As Alan Axelrod has emphasized in his Gandhi CEO book *"a humane & people oriented approach, transparency and equal emphasis on means & ends "* are vital requirements for corporate success.

For India's planners at national and state levels Gandhi's *Talisman* is most pertinent. What the poor really need is employment and not doles. Arun Maira, a member of India's Planning Commission has acknowledged and written about this (*'Keys to Inclusive Growth'*, Economic Times, August 9, 2011). He has averred *"Rapid creation of more productive jobs is a strategic imperative for India's planners"*, as there will be 250 million more job seekers by 2030 and neither agriculture nor manufacturing nor IT enabled services can provide these many. What is essential therefore is to nurture *"those service sectors that can create employment at many skill levels and are also more geographically dispersed"*. He has pointed out that *"Micro and small enterprises and tourism are the extensive seed beds for inclusive growth by the widespread opportunities they provide for employment and incomes"*. and that tourism, for which *'Incredible India'* has enormous potential, creates 78 jobs per million rupees of investment compared to 45 jobs for similar investment in the manufacturing sector. Its additional benefits are that it provides employment over a much wider spectrum from unskilled to specialized , specially to women, and even in remote areas.

For ardent votaries of nuclear power, the present views of T.P. Sreenivasan, former Indian Ambassador to IAEA, who previously was one of them, should induce some thought. He concluded his 2011 Nagasaki Peace Day Lecture at Institute of Defence Studies and Analysis (IDSA) New Delhi thus *"Hiroshima and Fukushima have brought to light two facets of the danger from the nuclear genie. Mankind developed nuclear weapons in his quest for security and realized the folly of Mutually Assured Destruction. The quest for energy security has driven it to develop nuclear power, the more benign manifestation of the atom. The time has come for it to pause and ensure that the second quest does not prove as dangerous as the first."*

Enstein and Gandhi *-by M.F. Husain*

The fact that much modern scientific and technological progress has magnified human and environmental destruction rather than safeguarded them establishes the validity of Gandhi's words that *"science without humanity"* is a cardinal sin. Scientists like Louis Pasteur, Thomas Edison, Alexander Fleming, Linus Pauling, Norman Borlaug, M.S. Swaminathan and others, whose scientific discoveries and work have contributed enormously to human welfare will always be gratefully remembered. All present day scientists might like to recall the great respect which the twentieth century's greatest scientist Albert Einstein had for Gandhi and how alike their views were about being Energy being Ultimate Reality and about the need to *"widen our circle of compassion to embrace all living creatures and the whole of nature"*

The inspiring words of Henry Adams *"A teacher affects eternity. He can never tell where his influence stops"* ; of Abraham Lincoln to his son's teacher:*"Teach him to listen to all men, but teach him also to filter all he hears on the screen of Truth and take only the good that comes through"* and of Gandhi *"To secure real peace in the world one has to start with the children"* are excellent leadership beacons for all those in the teaching and knowledge professions. They are best placed to mould the minds and characters of the innumerable youth who come into their class rooms and lecture halls and to fashion them into well informed, incorruptible and trustworthy leaders.

For students aspiring to be leaders, Gandhi's transformation from trembling timidity to fearless leadership through steadfast adherence to truth and extensive reading of the sacred books of all religions and those of the world's great thinkers, is the best path to follow. They should always remember that Gandhi's transformation from a timid young man to a fearless and determined leader occurred when he was just 24 years old.

Sarojini Naidu, Usha Mehta, Aruna Asaf Ali and other women Satyagrahis of the National Struggle and now Dr. Ela Bhat Medha Padker, Vandana Shiva, Arundhati Roy, Aruna Roy, Kiran Bedi and Mamata Banerjee, who though Chief Minister of West Bengal since May 2011 still lives in her own modest home, are inspiring examples of intrepid leadership for women. So is Rosa Parks, the Afro-American woman who, on December 1st, 1955, boldly refused to give up her seat on a Montgomery bus to a white man, and set in motion a non violent civil rights struggle which in 1970 secured passage of the US Civil Rights Act and in January 2009 put a black family in the White House.

Gandhi's role as husband and father has been severely criticised by many including his laudatory biographer Louis Fischer, who wrote *"From young manhood, he was sweet and kind towards everybody except his wife and sons"*. Eric Erikson, though very laudatory of Gandhi's Satyagraha strategy is quite critical of his treatment of his wife Kasturba and son Harilal. In an imaginary letter to Gandhi (Chapter 1, Part Three of his *'Gandhi's Truth'*) he writes *"Not once in all your writings do you grant that a sexual relationship could be characterized by what we call mutuality......I submit that ' sufficient detachment ' is possible only where the renunciation was chosen by both and not based on the vindictive insistence of one partner"* About Harilal he has written *"You call Prince Prahlad the first Satyagrahi and exhort your son to be truthful like him but threatened to disavow and disown him when his truth meant rebellion against you. Would it be farfetched to say that in such moments of wrath you were a facsimile of the very Demon King whom Prahlad resisted ?* " However, Uma Dhupelia Mesthrie, his grand daughter, (through his second son Manilal) has deliberately titled her biography of him *Gandhi's Prisoner?* and written *"My book aims to provide a more rounded impression of Gandhi as a father. The picture that emerges shows how wrong Fischer was in his judgement of the two brothers and their father. While one could, by selective selection of episodes, see how Fischer reached his conclusion, the sum total of the relationships was one of deep love on all sides"*. However, all husbands and fathers, particularly those in active political and professional lives, would do well to ponder over this criticism of Gandhi and its refutation of this aspect of Gandhi, so as to draw useful lessons for themselves.

Orthodox Gandhians might like to take heed of what Mark Tully has written about them. *"Instead of encouraging a nuanced understanding of the Mahatma they have canonized him, turned him into a saint.... have given the impression his words and his example enshrine absolute truths and that we should take them as Gospel truth"*. He affirms *"If Gandhi is taken too literally, it is all too easy to debunk him. How could independent India take seriously a man who said he did not believe in industrialization and who regarded cities as evil things. ..... But, what if we were to peel away the crust in which Gandhians have encased their hero, to try to understand the symbolism of Gandhi's language instead of taking him literally. What is he saying about our needs. The answer is contained in his own words"Renunciation does not mean that if one has wealth it should be thrown away and wife and children should be turned out of doors. It simply means that one must give up attachment to these things* ". Johann Galtung concurs and states. *"Gandhi is sufficiently great for us today to criticize him. We can always learn enormously much from him but not if we accept him uncritically"*.

Similarly Ralph Bultjens avers *"In hagiography, Gandhi's personality and activities risk becoming embalmed in his own fame"*. He critiques Gandhi's treatment of Subhas Chandra Bose. *"Though elected and re-elected as Congress president, Gandhi made it impossible for him to carry out his functions and eventually brought about his resignation....thus disposing of his most serious political challenger"*. He has also critiqued Gandhi's assertion that he would confront nuclear bombs *"by coming out in the open and letting the pilot see I have no trace of ill will against him"* by pointing out *"It is unlikely that earthbound people can project their compassion through space and awaken the latent goodness in pilots. This is even less possible when we consider the nature of modern warfare - computer guided missiles which sow distant destruction without prior warning".* However, he has added "*This does not negate the merit of the ethic itself.....Perhaps we need to adapt Gandhi's method from a curative to a preventive function. Instead of attempting to deter nuclear attack after it has been launched, modern strategy of non violence could focus more fully on reduction and elimination of these instruments of conflict.....As with much other wisdom, Gandhi's injunctions retain their validity but need updating and reapplication."*

For Joseph Lelyveld the real tragedy of Gandhi's life was not that he was assassinated nor that his noble qualities inflamed the hatred in his killer's heart but that *"he was ultimately forced, like King Lear, to see the limits of his ambition to remake the world".*

Vinay Lal (in The Sexuality of a Celibate life, Deccan Chronicle / Asian Age, May 1, 2011) has critiqued Gandhi for being constantly surrounded by women despite his vow of Brahmacharya and affirmed "*Though he repudiated sex, which he saw as mere physical consummation, he was a consummate player of sexuality who delighted in the infinite pleasures of touch, companionship and the eroticism of longing and withdrawal". However he has added "More than any other Indian political figure of his time Gandhi made very little distinction between men and women, fundamentally treating them as alike and endeavouring to bring out something of the feminine in men and something of the masculine in women."*

The last three decades have been tragic and shameful ones for India because of the destruction of the Babri Masjid in December 1992, the anti-Sikh and anti-Muslim massacres of 1984 and 2002 the subsequent attacks on the Akshardam Temple and Christian churches, priests and nuns in Orissa and Karnataka. India's well deserved reputation as the birthplace of religious tolerance with its age old maxim of *"Ekam Sat Viprah Bahuda Vadanti"* (the Truth is one but has many names) has been greatly tarnished. The need for enlightened leaders, both religious and secular, in all religious communities, to prevent such nefarious acts is both urgent and imperative. Gandhi's words: "I reject any religious doctrine that does not appeal to reason and is in conflict with morality" and *"Independent India as conceived by me will have all Indians belonging to different religions, living in perfect friendship"* are good leadership beacons for them.

Renowned sitarist Ustad Amjad Ali Khan has expressed these ideas beautifully in musical terms. *"For any musician 'swara' is God. I am trying to reach God through music. When different 'swaras' are brought together they create a beautiful 'raga'. In the same way, different religions, which are like different 'swaras' in a 'raga' have created an incredible India. This is my notion of God and the nation".*

Mark Tully affirms: "*Varanasi demonstrates that a marriage of East and West is possible. For me, as some one brought up as a Westerner yet much influenced by India, it also confirms that if the marriage is to take place the West must be flexible in its thinking and suspicious of its certainties. It must seek balance between the material and the spiritual, between reason and other means of perceiving reality, between tradition and change, between individuals and society, between humans and nature. It must have the humility to live respectfully with different faiths and cultures and to be prepared to learn from them too. That of course means that the East also has to have the humility to learn from the West. We should not fall into the error of assuming that the East has got it all right and the West has got it all wrong. For me, India acknowledges that we can never find absolute answers to the most important questions in life, but we must go on asking them. This is why I have titled my book 'India's Unending Journey' It is a journey we can all learn from*".

Our armed forces are the largest, most disciplined, secular body of men and women in India today. The prime requisites for leadership among them is to safeguard this precious legacy and ensure high morale among officers and troops at all levels. Even super powers have been defeated by poorly armed but well led, highly motivated and fearless Vietnamese and Afghan fighters. As some highly industrialized European countries have already incorporated 'Civilian and Social Defence' in their national defence plans all military leaders, including our own, should give due consideration to this form of defence, particularly since Naxalism has emerged as a major internal security problem with serious ramifications for external security also. Though their military training is focused on mastering skills for handling the most sophisticated weapons including WMDs, they need to note that 9/11 has radically changed the nature of war and opened a new era of asymmetric warfare, and as Clausewitz affirmed "*Each age has its own peculiar forms of war ......and a shrewd glance at its main features in each particular age*" is an imperative need. National Security Adviser Shiv Shankar Menon echoed the same thought in his keynote address at the Golden Jubilee Seminar of National Defence College, New Delhi "*The definition of force, the classic marker of power, has now expanded, thus changing the utility of force as traditionally configured, The security challenges of the twenty-first century are radically different from those of the twentieth.*"

Our diplomats should always remember the old adage *"It is when the diplomats fail that the generals are called in"* . They are essentially peace makers. India's earliest ambassadors were the Buddhist monks Emperor Ashoka sent out to Sri Lanka, Burma, Khotan, Bactria, Damascus. Athens and Alexandria over two thousand years ago. They all carried the message of peace, non violence, universal brotherhood. Diplomats are also their nation's eyes and ears in the countries they are accredited to. What they report and recommend are important inputs into foreign policy formulation. They therefore need to carefully consider what India's long term rather than short term national interests are and always remember that the neighbour is always more important that the far away friend and that collaborating with the military occupier of any country, building bases or roads for their troops to stay or travel on and facilitating their economic interests in said countries never serves India's long term interests even though short term benefits might accrue. The permanent element in history is always the nationalism of peoples, their ardent love for their countries, strong hatred of those who invade and occupy them and firm determination to valiantly fight the invaders until their occupation ends. They should also remember that India's greatest strength lies in its *"Soft Power"* of which Gandhi is now a prime component.

The Iraq war, globalization and the internet have created a well knit, global, anti-war, justice and peace *"people's movement"*. The World Social Forum (WSF) is the best and most impressive embodiment of it. All those individuals and NGOs wishing to participate in this non violent global movement to secure economic and social justice for all can now do so quite easily. His Holiness the Dalai Lama has enunciated the essential conditions for securing peace : *"Through training our minds we can become more peaceful. This will enable us to create peaceful families and human communities which are the foundation of world peace. ...... Once we have developed a peaceful society in which problems are negotiated through dialogue, we can seriously think about demilitarization, first on the national level, then on the regional level and finally on the global level."*

Finally, for every man and woman, of whatever faith, community, nationality or station in life, Gandhi's words *"Real Swaraj will come not by the acquisition of authority by a few, but by the acquisition of the capacity by all to resist authority when it is abused. In other words, Swaraj is to be obtained by educating the masses to a sense of their capacity to regulate and control authority* " are a clarion call to leadership. Whenever and wherever authority is abused and untruth becomes the basis for public policy and conduct, whether at local, state, national or international level, every citizen has the bounden duty to resist it, and motivate others to do likewise. Probity of leaders and accountability in governance can only be ensured thus. Gestating leadership at grassroots level and protecting citizens' rights and freedoms are also best achieved thus. There are many instances of abuse of authority in India and other parts of the world, Those in India have already been referred to in dealing with the functioning of its parliament and the mega 2G and CWG scams. Those in Britain are as scandalous. The extensive fraudulent claims of MPs of the '*Mother of Parliaments*' caused a nationwide uproar which constrained Speaker Michael Martin to resign on May 19, 2009 and Prime Minister Gordon Brown to apologize *"on behalf of all politicians"*.

Rajmohan Gandhi has defined his renowned grand father as "*The Good Boatman.*" Despite the euphemism, it is a good definition for in *"sailing over life's solemn main"* there is no greater comfort than a good boatman, well attuned to its eddies, sub-surface currents and storms. Life's *"solemn main"* flows not only in broad watery expanses like the Gangesand the Amazon in their lower courses, but also in narrow streams and rivulets in their upper reaches. These too need good boatmen to lead timid wayfarers across them. Each of us has the opportunity, and duty, to meet that need.

Glossary

Ahimsa : Non injury; non-violence

Ashram : A spiritual retreat; training centers for Gandhian Satyagraha and constructive programmes.

Bania : A member of the trader or merchant class.

Bhakti : Devotion, worship

Bhoodan : Voluntary gift of land for the landless;

Brahmacharya : Celibacy; one of Hinduism's four stages of life.

Brahmin : A member of the priestly caste, the highest in Hindu society.

Dharma : Duty, customary social obligation, Hindu morality.

Dhoti : A piece of ankle length cotton cloth fastened at the waist; the traditional dress of the Indian peasant.

Hartal : work stoppage ; an informal, non industrial strike

Jainism : The religion of strict non-violence preached by Mahavira (6th Cty. BC)

Jain : a follower of Jainism.

Jati : caste or subcaste

Kali Yuga : The last and worst of the four ages in the Hindu cycle; the Black Age.

Khadi : Hand spun cloth; the prime element in the first phase of Gandhi's freedom Struggle in India

Khilafat : Post First World War Muslim movement to protect the traditional rights and privileges of the Caliph (Khalifa) of Islam, who was the Imperial Sultan of Turkey.

Kshatria : Member of the warrior or kingly caste.

Lakh : 100,000; One hundred lakhs ; A crore

Lathi : A wooden stave used by Indian policemen

Lok Pal/ Lok Ayukta : Public Ombudsman at National / State level

Padayatra : A long march

Mahatma : Literally means great soul; a respectful title conferred on Gandhi by the Nobel Laureate poet Rabindranath Tagore.

Mantra : A religious or magical formula.

Maulana : A respectful title for a Muslim scholar.

Marwari : A merchant caste, originally from Rajasthan in Western India

Naxalite : One belonging to a Maotse Tung inspired rural militant movement that traces its origin to Naxalbari a small village in northern West Bengal state.

Panchayat : A village council of elders, which makes community policy by consensus and also arbitrates disputes

Panchayat Raj: Village democracy; a polity based on the village.

Pucca : Properly built; well laid out.

Ramayana : One of the two great religious epics of India, the other being the Mahabarata.

Sabha : Association, assembly.

Saivite : A worshiper of Lord Shiva, the third deity in the Hindu Trinity, the first two being Brahma and Vishnu.

Sanatanist : Orthodox Hindu.

Sanyasi : A holy man; a wandering monk.

Satya : Truth; Ultimate Reality.

Satyagraha : Literal meaning is firmly adhering to Truth; Truth Force; Gandhi's strategy for active, non-violent resistance

Sarvodaya : Literal meaning is the total uplift of all; Gandhi's social philosophy based on Ruskin's 'Unto the Last'

Shuddi : Hindu reconversion programme initiated by Swami Dayanand Saraswati, founder of the Arya Samaj movement in the late 19th century.

Sudra : Member of the lowest (fourth) caste in Hindu society; generally a peasant or labourer.

Swadeshi : Literally means produced within the country; Gandhi's programme of self reliance.

Swaraj : Self rule which Gandhi redefined as rule over self.

Taluq : Sub-division of a district.

Taluqdar : Title of a large landholder, particularly in North Eastern India.

Tapas : Ascetic practices

Ulema : Muslim clerics

Vaishnavite : Hindu sect worshipping Vishnu, second Deity in Hindu Trinity.

Varna : Literally colour; the Hindu caste system.

Vedas : the ancient sacred texts of Hinduism.

Vedantin : A vedic scholar; the philosophical tradition based on the Vedas.

Zamindar : Title of the largest landholder, particularly in North Eastern India.

Bibliography

Andrews, Charles F:*Mahatma Gandhi - His Life and Ideas* (Mumbai, Jaico Publishing House, 2005)

Arendt Hannah : *Eichman in Jerusalem - A Report on the Banality of Evil* (New York, Viking Ress, 1963); *On Violence*, Harcourt Brace, New York 1969.

Ariyaratne, A. T : *Religious Path to Peace and Building a Just World* (Sarvodaya Prakashan, Colombo 1984.)

Armstrong, Karen : *Islam - A Short History* (London, Phoenix Press, 2000) & *The Battle for God* (New York, Alfred A. Knopf, 2002)

Arne, Naess : Gandhi and Group Conflict:An Exploration of Satyagraha (Oslo, Universitets forlaget 1974)

Axelrod Alan : ,Gandhi CEO: 14 Principles to Guide & Inspire Modern Leaders (London, Sterling Publishers, 2010)

Baker Laurie : *Laurie Baker's Mud* (Center for Science and Technology for Rural Development (COSTFORD), Trivandrum).

Baldoni John : Lead by Example: 50 Ways Great Leaders Inspire Results (New York Amacom, 2008)

Bethel Dayle M : Makiguchi : The Value Creator (New York, Weatherhill, 1989

Bhatia Gautam : *Laurie Baker : Life, Works, Writing* (Viking, New Delhi : 1991)

Bode, Carl (Ed) : *The Portable Thoreau* (New York, Viking Press, 1947)

Bondurant Joan :*Conquest of Violence : Gandhian Philosophy of Conflict* (Princeton U. Press, 1988)

Bouvard Marguerite Guzman : *Revolutionizing Motherhood: The Mothers of the Plaza de Mayo* (1994).

Brown Michael : *Grave New World - Security Challenges in the 21st Century.* (Washington, Georgetown University, 2003)

Brown, Judith M. : *Gandhi : Prisoner of Hope* (New Haven : Yale University Press, 1989)

Brown, Judith M. : *Gandhi and Civil Disobedience: The Mahatma in Indian Politics 1928 -34* (Cambridge University Press 1989)

Bruni Luigino (Ed) : The Economy of Communion - Toward a Multi-Dimensional Economic Culture (New York, New City Press, 2002)

Capelli Peter (Ed) : *The India Way: How India's Top Business Leaders Are Revolutionizing Management (Boston,Harvard Business Press, 2010)* Jitendra Singh (Author)

Chakravarti Sudeep : *Red Sun : Travels in Naxalite Country (New Delhi, Penguin Books 2008)*

Chatterjee, Margaret: *Gandhi and Challenge of Religious Diversity* (New Delhi, Promila & Co, 2005)

Chattopadhyay, Kamaladevi: The Awakening of Indian Women (Madras, Everyman's Press, 1939)

Chopra, Deepak:*Peace is the Way: Bringing War and Violence to an End* (Random House, 2005)

Clarke,Richard:*Against All Enemies Inside America's War on Terror* (New York, Free Press, 2004)

Clausewitz, Carl Von : *On War* (New York, Viking, 1988)

Cohen Stephen P. : *Beyond America's Grasp: A Century of Failed Diplomacy in the Middle East" (New York, Farrar, Straus & Giroux, 2009).*

Collins Jim: *Good to Great: Why Some Companies Make the Leap... and Others Don't (* New York, Harper Business, 2001)

Copley, Antony : *Gandhi Against the Tide* (Oxford University Press, 1987)

Dalton, Dennis: Gandhi : *Non-Violent Power in Action* (New York, Columbia University Press, 1993)

David Shulman : *Dark Hope :Working for Peace in Israel and Palestine(Chicago, University of Chicago Press, 2007)*

Desai, Mahadev : *The Gita According to Gandhi* (Navjivan, Ahmedabad, 1946)

Doke, J.J. : *M.K.Gandhi : An Indian Patriot in South Africa* (London, 1909)

Drucker, Peter : *The New Realities* (New Delhi, Asian Books, 1991)

Duffy James & Robert Manners (eds): *Africa Speaks* (Van Nostrad Co. Princeton, 1961)

Durant, Will : *The Story of Civilization* (Volume 1), New York, 1957 Simon & Schuster)

Eashwaran, Eknath:*Badshah Khan-A Man to Match His Mountains*(New Delhi,Penguin Books, 2001)

Einstein, Albert : *Selected Writings* (New York, Ocean Press, 2003)

Erikson, Erik :*Gandhi's Truth:On the Origins of Militant Non Violence*(New York, Norton, 1969)

Fahmy, Ismail : *Negotiating for Peace in the Middle East* (London, Croom Helm, 1983)

Feinstein Alan : *African Revolutionary : The Life and Times of Nigeria's Aminu Kano* (Davison Publishing House, Devizes, Wiltshire, 1973)

Fischer, Louis : *The Life of Mahatma Gandhi* (Harper & Row, 1950)

French Patrick : *Liberty or Death* (New Delhi, Harper Collins,1997)

Galtung, Johann : *The Way is the Goal : Gandhi Today* (Ahmedabad, Gujarat Vidyapith, 1992)

Gandhi, Rajmohan : *The Good Boatman : Portrait of Gandhi* (New Delhi, Viking 1995); *Gandhi : The Man, His People and The Empire* (New Delhi, Viking 2007)

Godbole Madhav : Indian Democracy on trial : Roopa Publications (New Delhi, 2011)

Gandhi, M.K :*Autobiography - Story of My Experiments with Truth*(Navjivan,Ahmedabad, 1927); *Hind Swaraj or Indian Home Rule* (Navjivan, Ahmedabad, 1927); *Satyagraha in South Africa* (Navjivan, Ahmedabad, 1947); *India of my Dreams* (Navjivan, Ahmedabad, 1947); *Trusteeship* (Navjivan, Ahmedabad, 1927); *Collected Works* (New Delhi, Publications Division, GOI, 1958-84)

Gore Albert : *An Inconvenient Truth - The Planetary Emergency of Global Warming and What We Can Do About It* (New York, Bloomsbury. 2006)

Green, Martin : *Gandhi : Voice of a New Age Revolution* (New York, Harper Collins,1993)

Green, Martin : *Origins of Non-Violence : Tolstoy and Gandhi in their Historical Settings* (New Delhi, Harper Collins, 1998)

Gregg, Richard : *The Power of Non-Violence* (Navjivan, Ahmedabad, 1960)

Guha, Ramachandra : *The Unquiet Woods : Ecological Change and Peasant Resistance in the Himalayas* (New Delhi, Oxford University Press, 1987); India after Gandhi - The History of the World's Largest Democracy (New York, Harper Collins 2007)

Hardiman, David : *Gandhi in His Time and Ours* (Delhi, Permanent Black, 2003)

Hasan Mushirul (Ed) : India's Partition : Process, Strategy and Mobilization (New Delhi, Oxford, 2005)

Hayner Priscilla : *Unspeakable Truths -Confronting State Terror and Atrocity (Routledge, 2002)*

Henderson Archibald : *George Bernard Shaw: Man of the Century* (N.Y, Appleton-Century-Crofts, Inc., 1956),

Herman Arthur : *The Epic Rivalry that Destroyed an Empire and Forged Our Age* (New York, Bantam Books 2009)

Howe Russell Warren : *Black Africa : From Colonial Era to Modern Times* (New Africa Library, London 1967)

Hughes Richard : *Encountering the Dharma: Daisaku Ikeda, Soka Gakkai, and the Globalization of Buddhist Humanism(University of California Press 2006)*

Hunt, James : *Gandhi and the Non Conformists : Encounters in South Africa* (Promilla and Company, New Delhi, 1986.)

Hunter, Doris : *Non-Violence - Ethics in Action* (Gandhi Peace Foundation, New Delhi, 1971)

Huntington, Samuel : *The Clash of Civilizations and the Remaking of World Order* (New York, Simon & Schuster 1997)

Huxley, Aldous : *Ends and Means : An Inquiry into the Nature of Ideals and Methods Employed for their Realization* (Edinburgh, Chatto & Windus 1938)

Ingram, Catherine : *In the Footsteps of Gandhi* (Rupa Publication, Calcutta, 1997)

Iyer, N. Raghavan : *Moral and Political Thought of Mahatma Gandhi* (New York, Oxford University Press, 1973)

Jha, D.C:*Mahatma Gandhi,Congress & Partition of India* (NewDelhi,Sanchar Pub. House, 1995)

Jurgensmeyer, Mark : *Gandhi's Way: A Handbook of Conflict Resolution* (Berkley, University of California Press, 2003)

Keer, Dhananjay : *Dr. Ambedkar: His Life & Mission* (Bombay, Popular Prakashan, 1954)

Kelly, Petra : *Non Violence Speaks to Power* (Honolulu, Centre for Global Non Violence, 1992)

Kennedy, Paul : *Preparing for the 21st century* (New York, Random House, 1993)

Keynes, John Maynard : *Treatise on Money* (London, Palgrave McMillan 1930)

King Martin Luther Jr. : *Strength to Love* (London, Hodder & Stoughton.1964) & *Stride to FreedomThe Montgomery Story* (New York, Harper, 1958

King, Mary Elizabeth : *Mahatma Gandhi and Martin Luther King Jr. - The Power of Non Violent Action* (Paris, UNESCO, 1999)

Kissinger, Henry : *For The Record:Selected Statements 1977-80*(Boston, Little Brown, 1980)

Komisar Lucy : *Corazon Aquino - The Story of a Revolution* (George Braziller, New York, 1987)

Korten David C. : '*When Corporations Rule the World*', Kumarian Press/Berret Koehler Publishers, San Francisco 2001.

Kramer Michael : *Arab Awakening & Islamic Revival* (London, Transaction Publishers 1996)

Krolick, Sanford & Cannon, Betty (Eds) : *Gandhi in the Post Modern Age* (Golden, Colorado School of Mines Press, 1984)

Kumarappa, J.C. : *Economy of Permanence* (Varanasi, Sarva Seva Sangh Prakashan, 1997)

Kurlansky Mark : Non Violence : Twenty Five Lessons From the History of A Dangerous Idea - Modern Library, Random House, New York 2006.

Lahiri Prateep K : *Decoding Intolerance - Riots and the Emergence of Terrorism in India.* (New Delhi, Rolli Lotus Books, 2009)

Lelyveld Joseph: Great Soul : Mahatma Gandhi and His Struggle with India. -Alfred A. Knopf. (New York 2011)

Lanza del Vasto J.J. : *Warriors of Peace : Writings on the Technique of Non Violence* (New York, Alfred A. Knopf, 1974)

Lerner, Rabbi Michael : *Healing Israel Palestine* (Berkeley, Tikkun Books, 2003)

Liyanage, Gunadasa : *Revolution under the Breadfruit Tree: story of Sarvodaya Shramadana Movement and its founder Dr. A.T. Ariyaratne.* (Sinha Publishing House, Calcutta, 1988)

Lubich Chiara : Essential Writings - Spirituality, Dialogue, Culture (London, New City Press, 2007)

Lumby, E.W.R : *The Transfer of Power in India* (George Allen and Unwin Ltd., London, 1954)

Lutz, Mark : *Trusteeship - The Gandhian Alternative* (New Delhi, Gandhi Peace Foundation, 1986)

Madeleine, Slade : *The Spirit's Pilgrimage* (London, Orient Longman, 1960)

Malhotra Rajiv (Editor) : *Universal Responsibility (From The Essential Dalai Lama : His Important Teachings : (New Delhi, Penguin Books 2005)*

Mandela Nelson : *Long March to Freedom* (Little Brown & Company, Boston, 1994) & *The Sacred Warrior : The Liberator of South Africa Looks at the Seminal Work of the Liberator of India.* (Time, New York, December 31, 1999)

Manserg Nicholas & Penderel Moon : *The Transfer of Power* (London, HMSO, 1981)

Markovitz, Claude : *The Un-Gandhian Gandhi* (Delhi, Permanent Black, 2003)

Mathews, James : *The Matchless Weapon - Satyagraha* (Bombay, Bharatiya Vidya Bhavan, 1989)

McRobie, George : *Small is Possible* (London, Jonathan Cape,1981)

Mehta, Gita: *The Raj* (New York, Simon & Schuster, 1989)

Menon, V.P. : *Intergration of Indian States* (Calcutta, Orient Longmans, 1956)

Merton, Thomas : *Gandhi on Non-Violence - Selected Texts from his Non Violence in Peace and War* (New York, New Directions Publishing Corporation, 1964)

Mesthrie Uma Dhupelia : *Gandhi's Prisoner : The life of Gandhi's Son Manilal (New Delhi, Permanent Black, 2004*

Montgomery, Field Marshal : *The Path of Leadership* (London, Fontana, 1963)

Nair Kesavan *: A Higher Standard of Leadership: Lessons from the Life of Gandhi (San Francisco, Berrett-Koehler Publishers;1997)*

Nanda, B.R.: *Mahatma Gandhi - A Biography* (Oxford University Press, 1958) & *In Search of Gandhi* (New Delhi, Oxford University Press, 2002) & *Gandhi and his Critics* (New Delhi, Oxford University Press, 1985) & *Gandhi : Pan Islamism, Imperialism and Nationalism* (Oxford University Press, 1989) &*Indian Foreign Policy - The Nehru Years* (New Delhi, Vikas, 1976)

Nauriya Anil : *The African Element in Gandhi* (New Delhi, National Gandhi Museum, 2006)

Nehru, Jawaharlal : *Autobiography* (London, John Lane, 1936) & *The Discovery of India* (Calcutta, Signet Press,1946) &*Indian Foreign Policy* (New Delhi, GOI Publications Division, 1961)

Nkrumah Kwame : *Revolutionary Path* (International Publishers, New York, 1973)

Noorani A.G. : The RSS and the BJP (New Delhi, Left Word, 2000)

Ostergard, Geoffrey: *Non-Violent Revolution in India* (Gandhi Peace Foundation, New Delhi,1985)

Paige, Glenn : *Global Non Killing Political Science* (New Delhi: Gandhi Media Center, 2002; Xlibris 2002; Honolulu: Center for Global Nonkilling, 3rd ed. 2009).

Paige, Glenn and Satha Anand, Chaiwat : *Islam and Non Violence* (Honolulu, Centre for Global Non Violence, 1992)

Pande Malabika : Gandhi's Vision of Social Transformation; Rawat Publications, New Delhi 2011.

Pani, Narendar: *Inclusive Economics :Gandhian Method and Contemporary Policy*(New Delhi, Sage Publications, 2001)

Panter-Brick Simone : *Gandhi Against Machiavellism: Non-Violence in Politics* (Bombay, Asia Publishing House,1967) & *Gandhi and the Middle East - Jews*

Arabs and Imperial Interests (New York, I.B.Tauris, 2008)

Pappe Ilan : *Ethnic Cleansing of Palestine* (London, One World Publishing, 2006)

Parel, Antony (Ed) : *Gandhi - Hind Swaraj and other Writings* (Cambridge University Press 1997)

Pinto, Vivek : *Gandhi's Vision and Values* (New Delhi, Sage Publications, 1998)

Prahalad C.K : *'The Fortune At The Bottom Of The Pyramid : Eradicating Poverty Through Profits' (Philadelphia, Wharton School of Publishing, 2005*)

Prakash Virendra : *Hindutva Demystified* (New Delhi, Virgo Publications, 2002)

Rashid Ahmed : *Descent into Chaos: The U.S. and the Disaster in Pakistan, Afghanistan, and Central Asia (London, Penguin 2009)*

Ray Allen Billington : *Westward Expansion* (New York, Macmillan, 1967)

Ray Rabindra : *The Naxalites and their Ideology (New Delhi,Oxford University Press, 2002)*

Ring Kenneth & Abdullah Ghassam : *Letters from Palestine: Palestinians speak out about their lives, their country and the Power of Non Violence. (Tucson ,Wheatmark, 2010)*

Roberts, Adam :*Strategy of Civilian Defence : Non Violent Resistance to Aggression*(London, Faber, 1967)

Romain Rolland and Gandhi Correspondence (New Delhi, Publcn. Div. GOI, 1976)

Rubinstein, Amnon: From Herzl to Rabin: The changing Face of Zionism; Holmes & Meir Publishers, New York 2000

Rudolph, Lloyd & Suzanne : *Gandhi - The Traditional Roots of Charisma* (Hyderabad, Orient Longman, 1987) & *Post Modern Gandhi* (Chicago, Chicago Univ. Press, 2006)

Ruskin, John : *Unto This Last* (London, George Allen, 1905)

Sadat, Anwar: *In Search of Identity* (New York, Harper & Row, 1977)

Schell, Jonathan : *The Unconquerable World* (New York, Metropolitan Books, 2003)

Schumacher, E.F. : *Small is Beautiful*(New Delhi, Radha Krishna, 1970)

Segev, Tom : *One Palestine Complete* (New York, Henry Holt, 1999)

Sen Amartya : *Identity & Violence: The Illusion of Destiny (London, Penguin, 2006)*

Senge, P.M. : *The Fifth Discipline : The Art and Practice of the Learning Organization* (New York, Doubleday 1994)

Sharma, Asha; Nandini Sharma (2008). *An American In Khadi: The Definitive Biography of Satyananda Stokes.* Indiana University Press

Sharp, Gene : *The Politics of Non-Violent Action* (Boston, Porter Sargent, 1973) & *Waging Non Violent Struggl : 20th Century Practice and 21st Century Potential* (Boston, Porter Sargent, 2005)

Shean, Vincent : *Lead Kindly Light* (New York, Random House 1949)

Shlaim, Avi : *The Iron Wall : Israel and the Arab World* (New York, W.W. Norton)

Shridharani, K. : *War Without Violence* (Bombay, Bharatiya Vidya Bhavan, 1962)

Singh Jaswant : *Jinnah: India Partition Independence (New Delhi, Rupa, 2009)*

Sonnlietner, Michael W. : *Gandhian Non-Violence - Levels of Satyagraha* (New Delhi, Abhinav Publications, 1985)

Sorokin A. Pitrim : *The Ways and Power of Love* (Boston, The Beacon Press, 1954)

Soros George : *The Crisis of Global Capitalism (New York, Perseus Books, 1998)*

Srimati Kamala : *Mahatma Gandhi - An American Profile* (Washington, Mahatma Gandhi Memorial Centre, 1987)

Stiglitz Joseph : Free Fall (New York, Allen Lane, Penguin, 2010)

Tathinen, Unto : *Ahimsa - Non-Violence in Indian Tradition* (Navjivan, 1983)

Thomas T. K : *A Christian Response to Gandhian Satyagraha* (Christava Sahithya Samithi/ Ecumenical Christian Academy, Kottayam, 1970)

Thomson, Mark : *Gandhi and His Ashrams* (Mumbai, Popular Prakashan, 1993)

Tolstoy, Leo : *The Kingdom of God is Within You : Or Christianity not as a Mystical Teaching but as a New Concept of Life* (New York, Noonday, 1961)

Tully Mark : India's Unending Journey (London, Random House 2008)

Tutu Desmond : *God has a dream - A Vision of Hope for Our Times* (New York, Doubleday, 2003): *The Rainbow People of God.* New York: Doubleday, 1994.

Washington, James M : *A Testament of Hope : The Essential Writings and Speeches of Martin Luther King Jr.* (San Francisco, Harper 1991)

Weaver Mary Ann : *Pakistan: Deep Inside the World's Most Frightening State (New York,Farrar, Straus and Giroux; 2010*

Webb, Thomas: *On the Salt March* (New Delhi, Harper Collins Publishers, 1997)

Weber, Thomas : *Conflict Resolution & Gandhian Ethics* (New Delhi, Gandhi Peace Fndn, 1991)

About The Author

Holding a Masters Degree in Economics from Madras University, Pascal Alan Nazareth was selected for the Indian Foreign Service in May 1959. He has served in India's diplomatic and consular missions in Tokyo, Rangoon, Lima, London, Chicago and New York and as India's High Commissioner to Ghana and Ambassador to Liberia, Upper Volta, Togo, Egypt, Mexico, Guatemala, El Salvador & Belize.

During the 1982-85 period, when Mr. Nazareth was ICCR Director General, multifaceted Indian cultural festivals were held in Britain, USA and France, and international conferences on 'Buddhism and National Cultures' and 'India and World Literature', and a World Poetry Festival at New Delhi. An India-Greece Symposium organized during this period at Delphi resulted in the scholarly publication 'India and Greece'. Subsequently when Mr. Nazareth was Ambassador to Egypt and Mexico 'India and Egypt' and 'India and Mexico' were published, following similar symposia held in Cairo and Mexico City.

Mr. Nazareth retired in May 1994 and since then has been guest lecturer at National Institute of Advanced Studies & Indian Institute of Management, Bangalore and National Defence College, New Delhi. Among the foreign institutions he has lectured at or participated in seminars are Gandhi Memorial Centre at Washington DC, American, Yale, Columbia, Stonybrook, UC Berkeley & Stanford Universities, MIT, San Francisco World Affairs Council, East West Centre and University of Hawaii, and Aspen Institute in the USA, Asian Institute of Management & Ateneo and Phillipine Universities in the Phillipines, Udayana and Shiyarif Hidayatullah Islamic Universities in Indonesia, Universities of Trinidad & Tobago and the West Indies in Port of Spain and Mahatma Gandhi Institute at Moka, Mauritius. His lectures have been published in electronic form as two CDRs titled 'Historical Perspectives - Asia' and 'Historical Perspectives - Europe'.

Mr. Nazareth is a founder and Managing Trustee of Sarvodaya International Trust which is dedicated to promoting the Gandhian ideals of Truth, nonviolence, communal harmony, humanitarian service and peace. It was established in March 1995. Its website URL is www.sarvodayatrust.org. His widely acclaimed book 'Gandhi's Outstanding Leadership' was released in New Delhi by the former Prime Minister of India Dr. I.K.Gujral and at the UN in New York by Under Secretary General Shashi Taroor.

On October 9, 2007 he was presented the U Thant Peace Award by the Sri Chinmoy Peace Meditation Group at the United Nations, for his 'Life Time of Dedication and World Service by promoting of the Gandhian Values of Truth, Non Violence, Communal Harmony and Humanitarian Service'. Among previous recipients of this Award were Pope John Paul II, The Dalai Lama, Mother Theresa, Mikhail Gorbachev, Nelson Mandela and Desmond Tutu.